FACTORY-ORIGINAL
SPORTING MK1 ESCORTS

The originality guide to the sporting variants of the Ford Escort Mk1

By Dan Williamson

Photography by Simon Clay

Herridge & Sons

Acknowledgements

This book wouldn't exist without the help of all the Escort enthusiasts who've kept these special cars alive.

Biggest thanks go to friend and Escort expert Richard Farrell, whose encyclopedic knowledge of Mk1 Escorts is unparalleled. He's also the owner of some stunning machines, in particular the Modena Green 1300E photographed for this book. What's more, Richard's talent with a spray gun is well worth the decade-long wait for the author's own Mexico.

Huge thanks go to the custodians of each Escort made available for photography – every picture of these cars truly is worth a thousand words. In particular, we'd like to express gratitude to Brian Gosling, Mark Harper, Mark K, Jonathan Evans, Geraldine Ridgewell, Brent Mould, Clive Shaw, Darren Peacock, Stuart James and Kevin Curtis.

Credit, too, to all the members and committee of the AVO Owners' Club, without whom the upkeep and usability of Mk1 Escorts may not be quite so enjoyable (or possible) in the 21st century. Likewise, the Sporting Escort Owners' Club and the RS Owners' Club.

Personally, I'd like to thank Dave Hill at Ford, Dan White at Fast Ford, Ed Herridge, Phil Wyllie, Jeremy Walton and Graham Robson (for writing books that held my fascination with Fords 20-odd years ago), plus my parents – not only for supplying my first Mk1 Escort but also owning the Marine Blue Mk1 that started the obsession. Finally, special thanks to Sarah for the chassis plate illustrations and putting up with all those absent hours lost to the humble Ford Escort.

Photography credits

Simon Clay, Ford Motor Company, Dan Williamson, Jonathan Evans

Published in 2011 by
Herridge & Sons Ltd
Lower Forda, Shebbear
Devon EX21 5SY

Reprinted 2014, 2020

© Copyright Dan Williamson 2011

All rights reserved. No part of this publication may be reproduced in any form or by any means without the prior written permission of the publisher and the copyright holder.

ISBN 978-1-906133-22-1
Printed in China

CONTENTS

INTRODUCTION 4
ESCORT GT 6
ESCORT TWIN CAM 26
ESCORT RS1600 52
ESCORT MEXICO 76
ESCORT SPORT 106
ESCORT 1300E 124
ESCORT RS2000 146
ACCESSORIES AND SPECIAL BUILDS 172
BODY SHELLS 182
BUILD PLATES 194

INTRODUCTION

Rows of AVO Escorts awaiting delivery to eager owners. A left-hand-drive Daytona Yellow RS2000 sits in front of a Monza Blue Mexico equipped with Rally Lighting Pack. Were the low-slung, plain white machines destined for a short, hard life in motorsport?

Passion. It's the strong, deep-routed human emotion. The intense feeling of adoration. The sheer heart-fluttering thrill of being innately and inseparably connected. It's not exactly the word a sane person could associate with a four-wheeled machine. Even less so a mass-production motor car.

A Jaguar D-type, maybe. A Ferrari 250GTO, perhaps. But a humble Ford Escort? It's hardly what you could call exotic. Attempt an explanation to even your closest loved ones about why a little old family car can stir up such unbridled passion and at best you'll be met with a vacant stare.

The truth is, the sporting Ford Escort was, is, and always will be much more than the sum of its Cortina engine, Capri brakes and Merseyside-made bodyshell.

Sporting Escorts were cars for the common man. Cars created by enthusiasts for enthusiasts. Cars made for going quickly, built to win all kinds of rallies and races – internationally, at clubman level and yes, even on the roads.

Whether mainstream go-faster models or hand-assembled AVO specials, sporting Escorts were built to be used, abused and at any opportunity improved.

And that's where there's a snag. Ford changed its Escorts without a second thought. Did Uncle Henry keep records? Of course not – if you're pen-pushing you're clearly not nudging the limits of development, speed and motorsport success. No one made notes – they were just glad the

INTRODUCTION

machines were better (or cheaper, in true Ford tradition) and beating the competition.

Many components were modified at the factory, some parts were altered seemingly without reason, changes were implemented gradually and supply difficulties meant several bits simply weren't available at the time. But that couldn't hold up the production line; no, let the dealer or customer worry about it later.

Today, our rose-tinted spectacles picture Ford factories crammed with Escort enthusiasts lovingly crafting hand-built machines with Rolls Royce levels of mastery. In fact, Escorts were small, cheap goods from a firm with legendary bean-counting ability. Ford didn't seem to care whether each car's specification exactly matched the brochure (or even the order sheet), never mind the fit and finish

Panel gaps were far from perfect. Stickers were slapped on at jaunty angles (you wonder if the staff ran post-pub contests to see who could get theirs wonkiest), and many were missed off altogether. Paint was primer-thin in places and dripping with runs in others. Seam sealer was messy and splashed around. And as for AVO hand-made modifications and welding, the less said the better.

Were no two cars ever the same? Of course they were. But could two machines from beside each other on the production line have wildly differing specs, even unintentionally? Hmm, maybe so...

Reams of accessory catalogues were crammed with options, Rallye Sport dealers actively encouraged modifications, and even Ford literature contradicted itself. To pin down the exact specification of every Escort would be a lifetime's work.

And that's where we are right now. No one at Ford expected Escorts to last beyond the first few seasons of motorsport or many miles of being thrashed around ring roads. The cars weren't really meant to be long-term things.

So this book is not perfect (admittedly, there may be errors – and we'd welcome reader comments or corrections). It's more a guide to what a lot of Escorts had, and what we're likely to see on Escorts today. It's not a restoration manual. It doesn't list the sizes of every nut and bolt, nor does it describe methods of reproducing zinc-passivated coatings. Instead it's a reference to all those little parts that made the sporting Mk1 Escort so much more than the sum of them all.

A transporter-load of Type 49 body shells transferred from Halewood to Aveley for fitting of the special AVO mechanicals. Windows, wiring and trim were already fitted. From there, anything could happen...

FACTORY ORIGINAL SPORTING MK1 ESCORTS

ESCORT GT

It might be a bit too brown and over-endowed in the door department for many Escort enthusiasts, but this October 1971 model has its own unique charm. A 39,000-mile car, it was recently treated to a minor makeover by owner Rich Farrell. Although it's had structural repairs and an off-shade respray, much of what's seen in these photos is what Ford fitted to GTs at Halewood. The car was registered in November '71 but many of its components are date-stamped July or August – so there's a fair bit of specification crossover. A thorough restoration is impending, including return to the original (darker) Tawny Brown.

For a so-called sporting Escort, the GT looked decidedly tame. On face value – with its tiny 12in wheels, 71bhp and even the option of an estate bodystyle – it had the apparent athleticism of a retired librarian.

But at the time of its 17 January 1968 launch, the GT was a serious sports saloon. "The Escort GT is no pussycat," said Ford's original publicity material for its new grand tourer. "Our Escort GT may be small-sized, but one thing it's not is small-minded."

Taking cues from its Cortina GT stablemates, the first fast Escort boasted an uprated engine, gearbox, suspension and brakes. That was enough to hit 60mph from standstill in around 13 seconds and hint at the lively handling a nation of budding rally drivers would grow to love. As Ford was quick to point out, "With a car like this you need good suspension."

The Escort GT was an integral element of the Mk1 range from the outset, planned alongside its De Luxe and Super counterparts. It was as essential to Ford's marketing men as it was for the junior executives whose purchasing power helped to boost the model's image on the UK's motorways and back lanes.

ESCORT GT

Very under-wheeled by modern standards, the GT's 4.5Cx12in pressed steel rims tucked well under the standard Escort arches. Their tiny diameter meant remarkably brisk acceleration, especially with an early (or optional) 4.125:1 axle ratio. This car's coachline is a non-standard period addition.

A satin black back panel was painted onto GTs after August 1970, nipped neatly around the edges by a pair of aluminium trims that continued along the boot lid. Note this car's straight rear bumper, lacking the cutout introduced in December 1972.

GT production took place in Great Britain and Germany, starting at the end of September 1967; most cars destined for the UK came from Halewood in Merseyside. Initially built only in two-door form, the GT used a Type 48 bodyshell, which related mainly to various pressings and drillings. A strengthened heavy-duty version was available for export markets in right- or left-hand drive.

"With a car like this you need comfort," claimed Ford. The GT was aimed at the upper reaches of Escort buyers, so its luxury trim level was closely related to the Super. Externally the models were almost identical, wearing rectangular lamps (which remained throughout production) and chrome beading around the wheelarches; discreet GT badges were the biggest giveaway. Inside, the Super's padded vinyl seats and carpeted floor were joined by the sporting Mk1's most instantly recognisable feature – the six-dial dashboard. As Ford agreed, "With a car like this, you need full instrumentation."

Under the skin, the GT's uprated suspension, wide steel wheels (4.5in rather than the normal 3.5in), radial-ply tyres, front disc brakes and close-ratio gearbox were a perfect match for the breathed-on 1297cc Kent powerplant. Special pistons and a big-valve cylinder head increased the compression ratio, a high-lift camshaft helped the engine to rev, fuelling was fed by a twin-choke Weber carburettor and a four-branch exhaust manifold got rid of the gases.

FACTORY ORIGINAL SPORTING MK1 ESCORTS

Aimed at a luxury market, the GT received Ford's idea of high-class styling, with rectangular headlamps and bumper overriders (made standard during the 1970 facelift). This car's wing mirrors were a dealer-fitted accessory.

This family-friendly saloon was immediately available in GT form, starting from chassis number BB5GJ_11071. At the same time, the car's external bonnet release was replaced by a lever under the dashboard.

April 1970 brought the short-lived Escort GT estate (it was deleted by mid-1972), while September that year saw big changes across the Escort range (two-door chassis number BBATK_35842, four-door BBAFK_35835). Engines swapped from imperial to metric dimensions, and most of the GT's unique internals disappeared; gone were the fancy pistons in favour of a regular 1300HC motor fitted with revvy cam, new Weber carb and revised free-flowing exhaust manifold. Meanwhile, the Escort's interior was updated with reworked dashboard layout and so-called harmonious two-tone trim.

By 1973 the GT was becoming barely distinguishable from the XL, while the identically-powered Sport and 1300E were stealing sales at both ends of the target market. The four-door GT was discontinued in April 1973, with the two-door dropped from price lists by November. Subsequently, it's reported that a batch of about 200 Halewood-built 1300XL four-doors were converted to GT specification in early 1974 and exported to New Zealand in order to aid a shortage of locally-assembled cars.

Revisions began within months. The early GT's twin rear radius arms soon disappeared, as did the compression strut front suspension; by September 1968 (from chassis number BB48H_28034), the GT was running regular Macpherson struts with anti-roll bar. The bare alloy grille received matt black treatment, while the GT's cabin gained colour-keyed interior plastics and mock-wood trim.

September 1969 witnessed the introduction of the four-door Escort bodyshell, demanded by the German market.

Because the GT was a mainstream model produced in Halewood, Saarlouis and Australia it's impossible to speculate how many were built. Sadly, very few GTs survive in their original guise, and today most remaining two-doors have been converted into RS replicas. In a way, though, that's fair enough; after all, the very first Twin Cams were little more than GTs fitted with Lotus Cortina engines.

In the great scheme of sporting Escorts, the GT was the great grandfather – and it laid the groundwork for many legendary machines.

Arguably a less pleasing profile than the two-door bodyshell, the four-door Escort nonetheless had its advantages, including better crosswind stability and reduced tendency for the door frames to rot. Not that they don't rust, of course – they're still Mk1 Escorts, after all.

When GT powerplants became metric, they lost the fancy pistons and cylinder head of imperial engines but retained a high-lift cam, twin-choke Weber carburettor and four-branch exhaust manifold. Note the blue airbox, which appeared on GTs during 1970.

Engine – Block, Head and Sump

Early GTs were home to a significantly uprated 1297cc four-cylinder OHV engine, internally quite different from a mainstream Escort's Kent Crossflow. As the model evolved, imperial gave way to metric, costs were cut and the unit became increasingly similar to the regular 1300HC – despite which, Ford's power and performance claims for the 1300GT increased. Make of that what you will…

The very first GTs were fitted with an imperial 2733E or 2735E pre-Crossflow cylinder block with 1297cc Crossflow internals. It was swapped in February 1968 for a 681F block, identifiable by circular shaping around the core plugs and 681F-6015-T-A or 681F-6015-C-A casting in raised characters on the side of the crankcase.

In November 1968 the 691M cylinder block appeared, featuring reinforcements around the core plug jackets, a revised crank and square-section main bearing caps. Still an imperial engine, the 691M looked visually identical to the later (metric) 711M block but had the inferior casting and small cam followers of previous units. What's more, the 691M said 691M-6015-A-A in raised characters on the crankcase. A GT-spec 691M would often have T7 or T9 cast between the core plugs, whereas a normal Crossflow would usually say T3 or T4.

To find a Kent's casting number, check the back of the

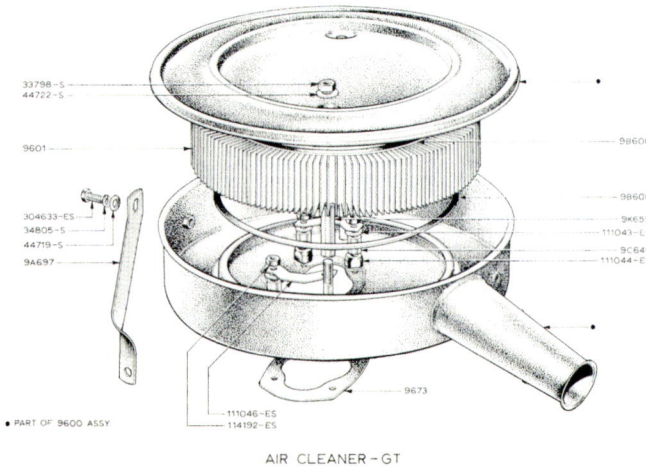

Exploded diagram of GT airbox shows support bracket, introduced in July 1968.

block near the starter motor. Its unique engine number was stamped by hand into a rectangular flat on the top of the block below the cylinder head between exhaust manifold ports one and two. It was a series of two letters (representing year and month of manufacture), followed by five numbers that matched the car's chassis number.

By September 1970 imperial engines had given way to stronger metric motors, featuring wider main bearing shell housings, larger cam followers and a stiffer cylinder block. From then onwards (until the end of Escort Mk2 production), the 1300GT had a 711M block, complete with 711M-6015-A-A cast onto the crankcase. Again, its individual engine number was stamped into the top of the block; again a series of seven unique digits to match the car's chassis number.

There were few outward differences between 691M and 711M blocks but virtually no parts were interchangeable; the imperial engine had circular recesses around the core plugs on the exhaust side, whereas the later engine had stiffer core plug jackets and a square reinforcer around the plugs.

A 1300GT block usually said T12 between its core plugs. Urban myth suggested cylinder blocks with higher T-numbers (they went up to 20) benefited from thicker walls, but there's no evidence to back this up. Likewise, you'll hear folk suggesting the M in 711M stands for Mexico, which is complete nonsense – not only was the 711M block introduced long before the Mexico, it was made in all kinds of sizes and specifications.

Whether imperial or metric, a 1300GT's cylinder block was semi-gloss black; a white paint splash could have been seen on a lug near the starter motor.

All 1300GTs housed a mildly balanced crankshaft, drilled through the crank webs. Connecting rods were the same throughout 1300cc Crossflows but imperial-engined 1300GTs had unique pistons. Pre-711M pistons were flat-topped cast alloy, with valve cutouts to match a chambered cylinder head. All were standard bore sizes, but had micro-gradings, numbered one to eight in stamps atop the cylinder block or pistons.

Metric 1300GT engines used regular cast alloy 1300HC pistons with valve cutouts in their crowns. Ford continued to quote a compression ratio of 9.2:1 but it's almost certain the metric 1300GT ran a normal 9:1 ratio. Strangely enough, Ford brochures by this point quoted a power output of 72bhp, 99mph top speed and 0 to 60mph in 12.6 seconds – quite a contrast from the apparently superior early GT's 71bhp, 93mph top end and 13.7-second 0 to 60mph crawl.

Maybe Ford's camshaft choice had something to do with it. The very earliest 1300GTs contained a Cortina 1500GT-type 116E cam, soon replaced by a 112E or 117E depending on availability – technically for a 1600GT but virtually identical. The 1300GT cam's colour code was always red.

Metric engines had a BA or CA camshaft with 272-degree duration, along with wider lobes and larger followers than imperial units. Apparently, supply problems meant many GT engines left the factory with standard 1300HC-type CC cams.

Imperial 1300GT powerplants were topped with a chambered cylinder head from the Cortina 1600GT. Like all Kent engines, it was cast iron, with four individual inlet ports on the right and four exhaust ports on the left.

From September 1970 the GT was fitted with a normal metric Crossflow flat cylinder head, valves and springs. Each head had a number cast into the top, visible under the rocker shaft – on a metric 1300cc (or 1600cc) head it read 37, whereas an 1100cc Kent or non-GT imperial head was marked 33.

Fitted to an engine, metric 1300cc and 1600cc heads all looked the same, although the 1100cc part lacked the second lug on its thermostat housing and twin casting lugs adjacent to its middle exhaust ports. No British GT should have a casting number on the outside; after October 1973 an engine code was stamped into Crossflow heads near the top rear-

Early imperial-engined GTs had this FoMoCo oil filler cap, which swapped to a Ford oval logo when metric motors were introduced. For true authenticity, the car in these photos should be fitted with the later type.

ESCORT GT

most exhaust manifold stud but this came after GT production ceased.

The normal metric 1300HC head's big valves no doubt helped the post-September 1970 GT's performance; inlet valves increased to 38.02-38.28mm from the imperial's 35.69-35.94mm. All featured 31.5-31.75mm exhaust valves.

A semi-gloss black rocker cover sat above every GT engine, with a red-on-blue 1300GT sticker. A lengthened and angled oil filler neck replaced the previous vertical spout from September 1970, bunged with a black plastic oil filler cap featuring a Ford oval, rather than the previous FoMoCo lettering. Imperial covers also had an inbuilt throttle cable bracket.

Beneath the GT engine was a normal Kent sump, while imperial 1300GTs were fitted with a vibration damper running from the rear of the sump to the bellhousing. All Escort Crossflow engines had the same unpainted dipstick in a black tube, but 1300GTs had an extended tube to clear the Weber carburettor's airbox. The exception was the very early GT, which had an oval-shaped dipstick handle plus extension tube.

Like all Kent engines, the GT had an externally-mounted Ford 35-40psi oil pump under the distributor, painted black or left bare. Imperial GTs came with a bolt-on oil filter, replaced by a spin-on cartridge filter for metric models. A larger oil pressure adaptor was fitted from September 1970.

Cooling System

The Escort GT's cooling system was similar to that of a regular 1300HC Kent, with the only exception of a beige fan rather than the 1100's red and the 1300's yellow. Before September 1970 there were 12 short blades but metric models featured seven big blades.

Everything else was identical: there was a bare aluminium water pump, 88 degree wax thermostat, black rubber hoses (with no specific numbers or stamps, because they were sourced from various suppliers) and wire clips rather than Jubilee types; that said, breather and servo pipes occasionally had stainless screw clips.

All 1300 Crossflows were theoretically accompanied by a small, 12-fins-per-inch radiator (or 15 fins after August 1970), with an angular copper top painted black. But it wasn't unusual for the factory to fit the radiator from an Escort 1100, with only nine fins per inch. All had a 13psi, standard-reach cap.

Fuel System

Imperial 1300GT engines (pre-September 1970) were equipped with a Weber 32DFE downdraught dual-choke carburettor, including a clip-on throttle linkage built into the rocker cover. Metric GTs (from September 1970) wore a Weber 32DGV-HA, with a unique throttle cable bolted onto the linkage.

From January 1972, some GTs were fitted with Spanish Bressel carburettors, which looked the same as Weber

Early brochure shot of engine bay, showing silver airbox and four-branch exhaust manifold. The brake servo was standard GT kit, accompanied by front disc brakes.

32DGV-HAs and functioned identically.

A Ford alloy manifold was made specifically for the GT, which changed from September 1970 to incorporate a casting for the two-bolt throttle linkage, then again in June 1972 (from part number 711F 9424 HB to 711F 9424 HC). Early engines had a normal AC glass-top fuel pump and black braided fuel lines, positioned on the cylinder block under the inlet manifold. After August 1970 it was replaced by a sealed AC mechanical fuel pump with bare metal top and bigger-bore fuel lines.

The GT's choke cable was revised in August 1969, gaining an additional plastic anti-chafing sleeve.

The GT featured a round metal airbox, which on imperial engines had a silver hammered finish and fixed forward-facing intake. A rear support bracket was added in July 1968, while the cleanable wire-mesh filter was swapped for paper in October that year.

Metric GT motors had a large round metal airbox, complete with AC lettering on top and provision for changing the angle for hot or cold running. Early versions were painted silver, swapped for blue in autumn 1971. The shade of blue was always the same solid colour found on mainstream Ford cars at the time – such as Marine Blue, Royal Blue or Electric Blue.

Exhaust System

The Escort GT's exhaust system received several minor changes, with major upgrades coming alongside the September 1970 switch from imperial to metric.

Early cars had a four-into-one manifold in steel tubing, clamped around the starter motor. Later GTs instead received a four-into-two-into-one version, clamped adjacent to the gearbox.

The regular Escort's exhaust system was replicated for the GT in slightly bigger bore, with rounded back box and oval centre silencer. From new it had a steel finish but genuine Ford replacements were silver-grey or blue-grey.

Until autumn 1969 a double-loop rear silencer hanger was used (similar to, but not the same as, the Twin Cam's). It then swapped to an L-shaped bracket.

Ignition & Electrical Sytem

Like every other mainstream Escort, the GT's battery lived under the bonnet. At first it was a 12-volt Autolite 38AH in black rubber, then swapped for a Motorcraft 38Ah or 57Ah for cold climate applications; either type could be black rubber or white plastic. Batteries always had flat bolt-on terminals.

The GT was fitted with a Lucas M35J 12-volt starter motor, date-stamped some time before the age of the car; there was also the option of a pre-engaged starter (often standard on export models) from August 1969. Until late 1972 there was a flat, square solenoid, which changed to the Lucas round bobbin type for the 1973 model year.

Imperial-engined cars had a CIU nine-volt ballasted ignition coil, while later models were equipped with an Autolite/Motorcraft version in a revised regular Escort bracket, with blue label and round terminals. At first it was mounted high at the back of the offside inner wing, then near the offside engine mount, before being moved down to the front (underneath the brake servo) during September 1970. Flat terminals were seen until October 1971, with round used thereafter. All coils had an aluminum finish and blue label.

Until September 1970 the GT used a C7AHC (1967) or C8AHC (1968) distributor, fitted with a splashguard from September 1968. With the change to metric parts came a distributor swap. Now running less ignition advance, the part used was either a 71-EB-12100-JA or 71AB-12100-JA; each had a blue colour splash on the vacuum advance module (incidentally, a low-compression Crossflow had a green splash, and a high-compression's was red). Up to late 1972 the vacuum advance mechanism had a removable nut, after which it was sealed.

Distributor part numbers changed several times from September 1968 until September 1973 but the unit remained otherwise identical.

A handful of early cars were fitted with brown/terracotta Lucas distributor caps, but it was more common to find a standard black plastic FoMoCo or Motorcraft cap.

Plug leads were made by Rist/Lucas, printed on in white, along with the Ford oval logo. The leads were the same as other Crossflows, despite bearing different part numbers. They were black siliconised rubber with black rubber caps, connected onto Motocraft AG22 spark plugs.

A Lucas C40 22-amp dynamo was fitted to the early GT, swapped for a 25-amp Lucas C40/L in cold climates, then as standard from August 1970. A Lucas 16ACR 34-amp alternator was optional in conjunction with a heated rear window

Lucas C40/L 25-amp dynamo was standard on the GT, complete with regulator affixed to the nearside bulkhead.

GT's standard post-August 1969 fuse box had no extra spade terminal for accessories.

after September 1970, then standard-fit from October 1972. It was bare aluminium with a black plastic back. Plain rubber drive belts were never ribbed or notched but were usually marked as Motorcraft or Ford.

The normal Escort wiring loom was wrapped in grey tape, usually with a Ford or Motorcraft tag tied on in a random position, plus a green tag near the fuse box. From launch, GTs had six fuses and external fuse box wiring, visible within the engine bay. From August 1969 there were seven plastic continental fuses, screwed onto the passenger-side bulkhead, with internal connectors and wiring. The fuse box always had a clear plastic cover.

Transmission

A good portion of the GT's increased performance came from its close-ratio gearbox and well-selected differential ratios. The latter was offered with a variety of options and revisions, so it's easy to understand why one GT could drive quite differently from another.

The gearbox was a fairly standard Type 2 four-speed manual with the following ratios: first 3.337:1, second 1.995:1, third 1.418:1, fourth 1.000:1, reverse 3.867:1. From November 1967 until the end of Mk2 Escort production, these GT ratios remained the same. Pre-September 1970 units, though, had a smaller gearstick ball and different thread.

The GT gearbox casing was black (Ford reconditioned units were often dark green), with a blue or red paint splash on the starter motor casting (the standard Escort 'box had a yellow splash). It had a metal tag on the tail housing, which said E/F or sometimes F/F. In theory, E/F was for a GT with 12in wheels and 25-tooth speedometer drive gear, while F/F meant 13in wheels and 23-tooth speedo drive. But this wasn't always the case...

Inside the bellhousing was a thin – almost flat-looking – 16lb lightweight flywheel (although the imperial engine's was slightly heavier) and regular Escort Borg & Beck cable-operated 7.5in diaphragm-spring single dry plate clutch.

Like other 1300cc Escorts the GT's transmission tunnel contained a two-piece propshaft with rubber-mounted centre bearing. Like everything underneath the car it was thinly coated in black paint.

A Timken one-piece axle housed a removable differential. The tag on a differential bolt described the ratio, which changed depending on year, what was specified and what the factory had available. An imperial-engined GT usually had a 4.125:1 differential, with optional 3.777:1 or 3.89:1 (available from July 1968); up to '73 it had 3.777:1 as standard with the option of a 4.125; the last GTs were equipped with 3.89:1 or optional 3.777:1.

Identification colour codes were 3.777:1 – orange/yellow/orange; 3.777 (after July 1968) – orange/yellow/green; 3.89:1 – orange/green/red; 4.125:1 – orange.

GT suspension was a mildly uprated version of standard Escort kit, rather than the beefy Capri-type units on RS models. Early models featured chunky strut top mounts, swapped for waisted versions in autumn 1971.

Steering and suspension

Underneath, the GT looked pretty much like any other Escort, with black rubber bushes and most components painted satin black.

There was a normal 3.5-turn lock-to-lock steering rack, and the crossmember was identical throughout the regular range, with square rubber engine mounts. The crossmember was updated in August 1968 when the front suspension setup was revised.

Originally the GT featured compression struts, running from the outer end of each track control arm at the base of each suspension damper to strengthened mounting brackets on the side rails. From September 1968 a 20mm anti-roll bar was used instead, fitted on mounting brackets with a yellow colour splash (meaning standard brackets, rather than AVO parts). It's worth noting that earlier cars had no provision for the brackets.

All had black, Ford-branded, Sachs-built Macpherson struts, with red and blue splashes denoting GT spec. A heavy-duty option was available, with orange splash. The damper insert diameter changed in autumn 1971, along with smaller top mounts with waisted middles; all top mounts were gloss black with paint splashes (in no specific colour or neatness) to confirm they'd been torqued to factory settings. The cranked retainers had only one lug until late 1969, after which there were two.

Compression strut-equipped GTs had 135lb front springs with a red and blue paint splash but after September 1968 there were 100lb front springs with a blue blob of colour. From September 1970 a heavy-duty option offered 135lb front springs with a red and blue code.

An early GT's rear suspension looked similar to a Twin Cam's, having body-to-upper axle twin radius arms until August 1968; after this date they were discontinued. The rear axle was clamped to a pair of 2in wide, 47in long semi-elliptical three-leaf springs with twin inverted U-bolts and rubbers at either side. In black with a battleship grey paint splash they were rated at 97lb, although 116lb versions were optional. After September 1968, four-leaf rear springs with grey paint splash were used instead; they were still 97lb.

Hydraulic shock absorbers were mounted ahead of the axle on U-bolt plates, inclined by 60.5 degrees. At their tops they had a bracket on either side of the car, but from September 1968 this changed to the more familiar single bracket spanning across under the boot floor.

Dampers were made by Armstrong (metallic blue paint) or Ford (black), with a brown code until September 1968, then brown and white thereafter. In October 1973 Escort floorpans were redesigned to take upright rear shock absorbers and a thin rear anti-roll bar. Although the GT's official end came in November 1973, it's doubtful any cars left the factory with the revised rear suspension layout.

Brakes

Unlike lesser Escorts, the GT always came equipped with front disc brakes as standard. Girling twin-piston calipers in satin black or burnished gold and Ferodo or Mintex pads clamped onto 8.6in solid discs.

To aid pedal pressure, a Girling Hydrovac direct vacuum servo was fitted on a long bracket attached to the driver's side inner wing. The servo had no sticker but there was a yellow stamp on its round, black drum. Attached was a Girling 75 aluminium master cylinder, with a clear FoMoCo cap.

A dual-circuit system was specified for some export markets, but the British GT got single lines with bare steel pipework, UNF fittings and ribbed flexible rubber hoses.

The GT's rear brakes were black-painted 8x1.75in drums. Standard or heavy-duty assemblies (basically, uprated shoe compounds) were available from new.

Wheels & Tyres

Tiny by today's standards, the GT's 4.5Cx12in pressed steel wheels were an inch wider than standard Escort rims. They were painted silver and until August 1972 wore stainless steel hubcaps – the same plain chrome domes as every other Escort or Cortina. Super-style wheel trim rings weren't included on the GT but were available as a FoMoCo accessory from September 1968. In September 1972 the hubcaps were changed for chrome-plated items with circular blue FORD stickers in their centres. Eleven-slot rim embellishers were added too. Sports-style hubcaps were an official Ford accessory.

GTs used 7/16 UNF open-ended wheel nuts on hub studs with dished ends. Very early GTs had Dunlop SP Aquajet 155R12 radial tyres, while later cars wore Michelin ZXs or Dunlop SP41s.

Body

The original GT's bodyshell was designated Type 48 but differed very little from other Escorts. It was sold in two-door form from launch, a four-door from September 1969 and estate after April 1970. Various markets received export (heavy-duty) shells, which occasionally cropped up as British GTs.

The GT's front wings were standard Escort parts, never having flared arches. It always wore a rectangular-headlamp front panel – usually with a starting handle hole but some later cars came without. Very early GTs featured a bare bright metal alloy grille with a black outline painted around the headlamp

This Ford studio shot from 1967 shows a GT in its original guise, complete with chrome wheelarch trims and bare grille with black highlights. This left-hand-drive example also featured optional-fit bumper overriders

ESCORT GT

Another 1967 GT, this time showing the Escort's smooth, clean lines. The Ford oval badge fitted to the nearside front wing was a feature of all early Mk1s, including the GT. Note this car's optional opening front quarter windows, red-painted chassis rails and lack of passenger door lock.

recesses. From September 1968 the grille became satin black with a bright metal surround. Black GT grilles never had silver horizontal bars, but after September 1968 always benefited from black-painted metal on the bodywork behind.

Until August 1969 the grille had a centre cutout for the car's bonnet release button; a Wilmot Breeden lock was an optional accessory. After that, the bonnet was released by a remote lever under the dashboard; the lever moved from the passenger's to the driver's side in September 1970.

Cars with a grille-button release also had an early-type bonnet including a central hole for the windscreen washer nozzle; later cars from around April 1970 featured twin nozzles in the scuttle panel, but there was a gradual changeover during production. Beginning in September 1970 and only for a very limited time, the GT was offered with a matt black bonnet. All bonnets wore chrome FORD badging along the leading edge, which came with softer edges from September 1968.

A regular Escort front bumper stretched across the GT's nose. Super-type overriders in chrome with rubber inserts were available as dealer-fitted accessories from launch, then standard from around September 1970. The back bumper was completely straight until December 1972, when the

For the 1969 model year GTs gained chrome beading around the windows and black-painted grille. The September 1968 updates also included the option of these Super-style wheel trim rings, which did little to flatter the GT's stance.

FACTORY ORIGINAL SPORTING MK1 ESCORTS

Early GT wing badge, with red-on-silver chequered flag design.

1300 GT was what it said, although Ford literature generally referred to the car as Escort GT. This silver-on-red design first appeared in August 1970.

entire Escort range received a central bumper cutout for better spread from the single-bulb number plate light.

Before September 1969, GTs had early-type doors with slimline chrome-plated door handles (the driver's side handle had a lock and the passenger side was plain), and single-slam lock mechanisms on the frames, along with rubber buffers at the top of each B-pillar and in the far corners of each inner door skin. Chunkier chrome handles with separate locks beneath each side were introduced in August 1969; with them came two-position latches and B-pillar strikers in a revised location. Doors and boot lid shared the same all-metal key, with a separate ignition key.

The GT's door window division channels were painted body-colour, or chrome on four-doors made before autumn 1970. Early two-door GTs featured a stainless steel drip rail trim, but it was left body-coloured from September 1968 onwards; bright chrome side window surrounds were added instead.

GT window rubbers were ridged around the rear three-quarters (two-door models), and fitted with chrome inserts around the front and rear screens. A Triplex Zebrazone toughened glass front windscreen was standard-fit, with small green or blue Zebrazone sticker in the lower centre, placed inside facing out. A heated rear window was optional from September 1970 and standard from autumn 1972; it had black wiring fed from the boot harness, and an earth cable usually on the driver's side.

Opening front quarter vents were made for export markets, or optional from launch. Two-door GTs could be specified with opening rear quarter windows after August 1970, and featured them as standard-fit from September 1972. Their forward-facing hinges were stainless steel, stuck on with Cyanoacrylate adhesive. The glass sat directly onto the window rubber, with no chrome edging.

The GT struggled with a single-speed windscreen wiper motor until August 1969, with two speeds thereafter. Normal Escort stainless steel wiper arms were always used.

Until August 1970, the GT wore chrome beading along its sills and around its wheelarch edges. The beading was deleted in favour of a chunkier aluminium sill trim, complete with black pinstripe and attached with pop rivets through the stripe, hand-fitted in no set places. Underneath the trim, the sills were body-coloured.

At the same time, the GT was equipped with a satin black back panel, surrounded by aluminium boot edge trim and

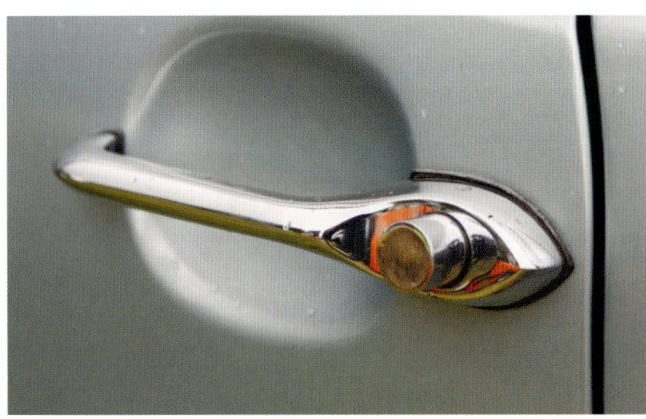

Until September 1969 the passenger door had no external lock; the driver's side had a key slot in the push button.

Protruding petrol filler was found on all Escorts prior to August 1969. Locking cap was a non-standard accessory.

hockey sticks. The boot lid was identical no matter which Escort you bought, but its lock changed in 1971, from recessed slot to flat. It sat in the middle of individual chrome FORD letters, with an Escort script always on the boot lid's offside. After September 1968, the FORD badges had softer edges.

GT badging changed frequently, with the first design (chequered flag and GT lettering in silver and black) seen in 1967 but probably never fitted to production cars. Most early models featured a silver badge with red GT lettering, which by 1968 switched to a red motif with silver GT lettering and black chequering. From August 1970 the badge was red, saying 1300GT in silver.

A Ford oval badge was fitted to the bottom of the nearside front wing from October 1967 until September 1968; from then it was dropped in favour of a small metal Ford oval in blue and silver inside the passenger door step. During late 1971 the badge was swapped from a raised to flat Ford logo.

A dealer-fitted coachline was fairly common from 1971 onwards (generally silver or white) but it became an official factory option in August 1973, in black, red, gold or white. A vinyl roof was also offered on late GTs.

In typical Ford tradition, a catalogue of upgrades and accessories was available for buyers of the Escort GT. Exterior rear-view mirrors were never standard, although a variety of wing mirrors or an "overtaking door mirror" were widely specified, always in chrome finish (only Escort vans received the painted parts). Wing mirrors were factory

Pre-August 1969 external bonnet release button, fitted with period locking mechanism.

The familiar Ford oval was fitted onto the passenger's sill step. This raised metal badge was swapped for a flat version during late 1971.

Some say it didn't exist, but here's proof of the Escort GT estate. Launched in April 1970, it had the same specification as its saloon counterparts. Sadly, few were built and, barring a few prototypes, Ford fell out with the idea of sporting station wagons for many years to come.

FACTORY ORIGINAL SPORTING MK1 ESCORTS

Matt black bonnet was a short-lived GT option from September 1970. Do any examples still survive? And was the car in this photograph really so-equipped? Typical of Ford's brochure shots, dubious airbrushing added items to suit the current spec, including this car's bumper overriders and stainless sill covers. A GT of this age should have had a dipping rear-view mirror; the Ford oval behind the front wheel suggests the car is a 1968 model.

A shot taken at Aveley of a 1969 GT's engine bay displays the silver air pan, "cheese wedge" washer bottle, early fuse box arrangement and suspension top mounts with single-lug retainers.

optional on four-door models from August 1969 and two-doors after December 1969.

Telescopic radio aerials were also common, generally hand-fitted in the offside front wing. Authentic items had a Ford logo stamped in the base and a rubber water seal underneath.

Underbonnet

Unless a GT was built around a heavy-duty export shell, it had standard Escort inner wings without suspension top reinforcing plates.

The very first cars had shorter bonnet hinge platforms than later models, which were changed due to bulkhead-flexing issues. Hinges and retaining bolts were factory-sprayed in situ, so were always body-coloured. Sometimes a bonnet prop would also be painted but generally they were left with a galvanised metal finish. Until September 1969 the bonnet prop was located on the left-hand-side slam panel, after which it was attached to the underside of the bonnet, with clear/white plastic retaining clip affixed to a welded-on loop.

August 1969 also saw a bonnet release cable running down the nearside inner wing to a release handle under the dashboard. The entire mechanism was moved to the offside in September 1970, and the previously uncoated cable gained a black plastic coating around autumn 1972. The slam panel was also altered to accept the bonnet release mechanism.

The GT's bulkhead was a normal Escort part, with the usual black plastic, twisted-shape bulkhead drain. The only alteration was an oil pressure pipe poking through a hole on the driver's side. In September 1969 the bulkhead was swapped for a later style with revised heater dome.

There remains some confusion about the position and type of Escort windscreen washer bottles, and GTs certainly don't help to find any answers – because they were built with multiple variations. Early cars had a white "cheese wedge" reservoir positioned on three body-coloured studs, usually in front of the driver but sometimes on the passenger side as production progressed. Fluid ran inside clear or green plastic tubing with a white barrel-shaped T-connector.

Later GTs had two types of similar-looking but incompatible washer bottles. The first (with British part number beginning 70AB in moulded raised letters) was an opaque plastic tank with rounded corners and water outlet on the top left-hand side; it slid onto a body-colour bracket screwed onto the nearside bulkhead. The other (German 70AG part number) was the same shape but instead had a central water outlet; it slid over a mounting bracket spot-welded to the nearside bulkhead. According to parts lists, the 70AB bottle was fitted from January 1970, with the 70AG item probably introduced around late 1971.

The Trico barrel-shaped pipe fitting was swapped for a Wingard T-piece with ball bearing in late 1971 but both types were used for quite some time. Foot pedal-operated washers were the norm, but an electric motor was available from

August 1969, revised in August 1973.

The apparently random fitting of washer bottles is nothing compared to the haphazard nature of where stickers were slapped onto the inner wings. A white/black negative earth sign was usually found on the bulkhead heater dome or nearside inner wing beside the battery. A coolant decal in white/black was commonly placed on the nearside slam panel and an engine tuning information sticker (in yellow until September 1970, silver thereafter) was positioned around either of the strut tops.

Looking down through the engine bay you'd probably also notice a GT's black cardboard undertray. Held on with six screws (three each side) to the front chassis legs and clipped to the engine crossmember and lower valance, these underbody shields were found on all high-spec mainstream Escorts after August 1968.

Lighting

Most of the GT's lighting setup was the same as any other Mk1 Escort's, and very little changed during production.

True to Ford's temporary fascination with fitting rectangular headlamps to its executive models, the GT was equipped with 9in wide Lucas 45/40-watt semi-sealed beams with replaceable tungsten bulbs. A headlamp wiper kit was offered in the UK from August 1973.

Beneath the headlamps were indicators with amber plastic lenses and chrome-effect rims; GTs never had plain orange parts. White lenses were specified for some export markets and available in the UK if required. Likewise, 1300E-type side repeaters were standard on several foreign Escorts from launch, and could be ordered on a British GT.

Rear lights were the same throughout the range – with chrome surrounds and black plastic seals – although one or two export countries received red flasher lenses. Their chrome surrounds had harder swage lines before September 1970. British GTs always had a single number plate lamp but overseas cars were equipped with a twin-bulb unit.

Reversing lights were offered as a dealer-fitted accessory from launch, dangling on a bracket from the rear bumper, as one or a pair; their lenses were white plastic (or amber in France). Styled-in reversing lights (Ford branded, with white plastic lenses, stainless lens surrounds and black plastic backs) were optional from August 1969 and standard one year later.

A single rear foglamp was never stock but often dealer-fitted to the offside rear bumper bracket, with a toggle switch and warning lamp on the dashboard. Similarly, rectangular under-bumper "standard" or Iodine Quartz front fog and spot lamps were commonly seen in brochures – they too were Ford dealer accessories.

Finally, the interior light: the GT had a standard Escort courtesy lamp with operating buttons in both A-pillars. Officially, the switches were updated in March 1972 from protruding pins to smaller, round, rubber-encased types.

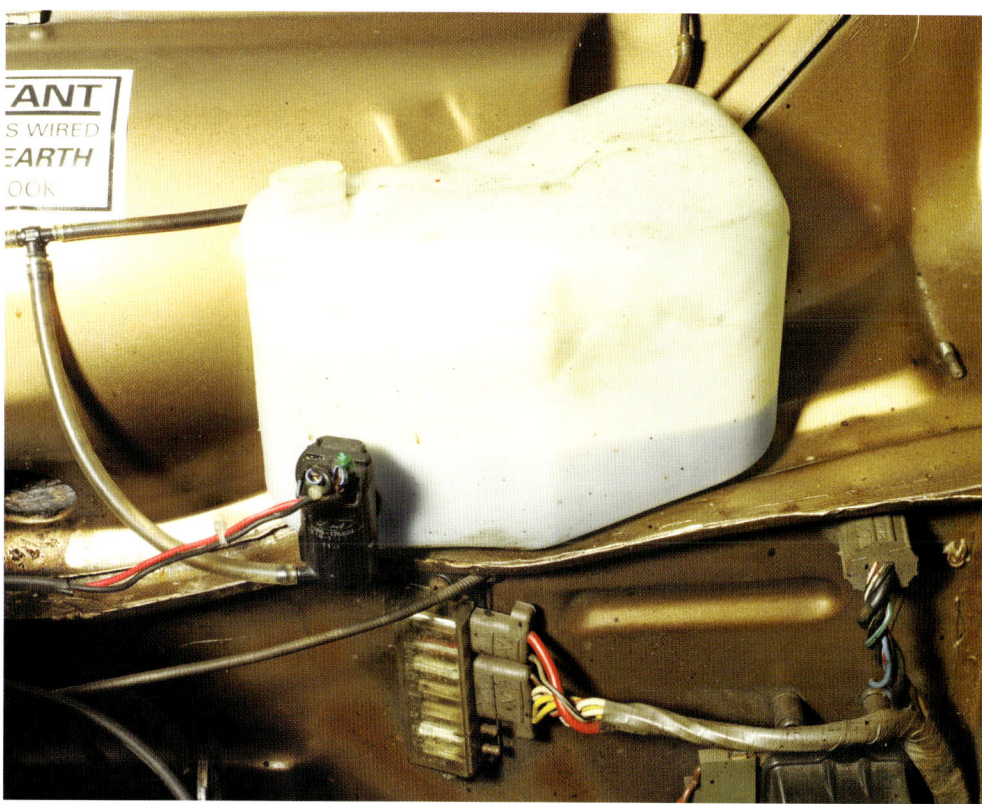

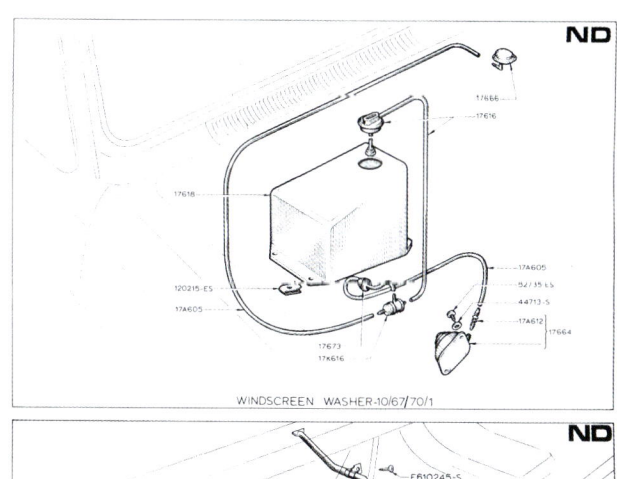

Depending on build date, a GT could have one of three different windscreen washer reservoirs. This slide-on 70AB bottle first saw service during January 1970 and was superseded in late 1971 by the German-sourced 70AG tank. Both looked similar but had their water outlets in different places. This car's aftermarket electric pump is a later addition.

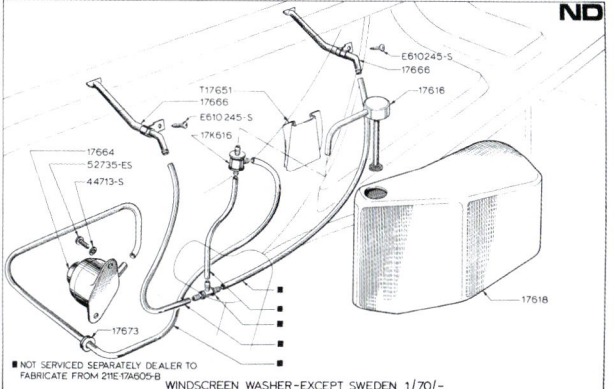

The first two types of washer fluid reservoir, as fitted to the Escort GT. Upper "cheese wedge" bottle was replaced by lower version in 1970, with a similar version introduced fairly soon afterwards. Does anyone really know why?

Interior

Unlike the other cars in this book, GTs could have cheerful, colourful cockpits. Or they could have been completely black – including the headlining. It all depended on build date and customer requirements.

On the earliest GTs, black was the only option. But with the September 1968 facelift came a range of interiors matched to the bodywork, including dashboard, heater vents, A-pillars, parcel shelves, carpet, seats, steering wheel, shroud and so on. White cars were the exception, offered only with tan or black trim.

From August 1970 until autumn 1972 came a two-tone "harmonious" interior – for example, tan vinyl seats with brown hard plastics; pale blue seats alongside dark blue; red seats with maroon, and so on. Finally, the last GTs reverted to black dashboard and plastics plus coloured seats and door cards.

The GT's cockpit was marketed as luxurious, which meant it came packed with Ford's idea of high-end kit. Super (or, later, XL) padded PVC seats were standard – recognisable by their perforated inner panels, smooth moulded-in bolsters at the side of each squab and matching two-bucket-effect rear seat. Until 1970, two-door front seats tipped forward using a button on the base of the cushion, after which they had a lever poking through the side of the backrest. The fully-tilting seat frames were swapped for fixed bases in October 1973 but it's unlikely any GTs were built in this spec.

Cloth upholstery was an optional extra from September 1970, again in a variety of colours. The bri-nylon material was replaced by Beta cloth in early 1973.

GT door cards were always padded, matching the seats. The block-type stitching effect was superseded in September 1970 by a plainer design. Two-door rear cards changed from plastic to fibreboard in September 1970; they featured push-round plastic ashtrays and plastic armrest extensions. In August 1969 the armrests swapped from nut-and-washer fixings to screw clips.

Spindly chrome Cortina-type door release and window winder handles were used until autumn 1968, when they were replaced with the later flat, textured type. For a brief period around winter 1969 they had soft rubber knobs rather than the usual hard plastic. Door lock internal release buttons were found on both front doors after August 1969; initially narrow plastic pins, they were swapped for a fatter mushroom-headed design in August 1973.

GTs were fitted with looped-pile carpets, colour-keyed from September 1968 until autumn 1972. Originally the carpets were joined before the front seat crossmember, but January 1970 saw a new single-piece carpet with improved contours. On GTs the rear seat crossmember was covered in black vinyl, over body-coloured metalwork. Rubber over-mats were an official Ford accessory, in black or grey nap pattern, black box pattern or a shaped, reversible nap/honeycomb design.

In September 1968, mock wood-grained cappings were added to the GT's doors, rear quarter panels and dashboard; the dash pressing changed slightly in September 1970 to accompany alterations for switch and cigar lighter positions.

The GT cockpit's centerpiece was its six-dial instrument cluster. Made by AC, it comprised a large speedometer (incorporating main beam warning light) and rev counter plus small fuel gauge, battery charge indicator, oil pressure gauge and water temperature gauge. Round warning lights for alternator and direction indicators were mounted between the two main instruments. The dials all featured black faces and white needles, with chrome bosses within the speedometer and rev counter.

A silver surround with chrome-effect dial rings was fitted until September 1968, when it was replaced by a mock wood finish, again housing chrome-style rings.

The earlier type contained dished dials with tall, thin lettering (gauges read MPH, RPM, TEMP, BATT, FUEL and OIL), 7,000rpm tachometer and 110mph speedo. From September 1968, instruments featured flatter-faced dials with easier-to-read font. In late 1972 the TEMP, BATT, FUEL and OIL lettering was dropped in favour of symbols.

Until September 1971 the rev counter had a 6,500rpm red line, from September 1971 a 6,300rpm red line and after late 1972 none at all. From October 1971, the milometer tenths indicator changed from black-on-white to yellow-on-black.

To mount the sports six-dial cluster, the GT's metal dash-

The GT's interior was based very closely on the Escort Super/XL, with plush vinyl seats and colour-keyed plastics. This complementary mix of tan and dark tan shows how broadly Ford's "harmonious" design extended – there's very little of the usual Escort expanse of blackness.

board pressing was unique to its Type 48 bodyshell (which later became part of the Twin Cam's Type 49). It was revised in September 1970 – the heater rocker switch was moved from the dashboard to the fascia panel and the main light switch repositioned under the instrument binnacle – but the padded vinyl top remained the same. Until September 1968 a GT badge (identical to those found on the car's front wings) was attached to the passenger-side dashboard.

Twin swivelling air vents were fitted: early types had bevelled edges, from September 1968 they were flat, and from September 1970 they gained adjustable flaps.

Controls for the GT's two-speed heater fan were under the vents, with a convex plastic-chrome surround ditched during August 1969 in favour of a flat aluminium surround with black Mazak diagram.

A plastic facia panel sat beneath the dashboard, covering the heater box. Three types were fitted to GTs. Early models had a two-tier layout incorporating an ashtray with horizontally ribbed lines, choke knob (in black plastic, with a silver and black insert), rocker switches (for headlights and wipers) and AC cigar lighter (standard-fit on all GTs, it gained a deep-set holder and moved up to the passenger-side metal dashboard in September 1970).

An updated fascia design came in September 1970, identifiable from its grained-finish swivel ashtray flanked by narrow rocker switches. Until around August 1971 the GT had a fascia with slots for only two switches (plus ashtray and choke knob, of course) unless the car was equipped with four-way hazard flashers – when a five-slot panel was fitted instead, complete with blanking plugs in redundant holes. The five-slot fascia was made standard in summer 1971 but old stocks were used up gradually over the following months, especially coloured plastics. Hazard warning lights became part of every GT's specification in September 1972.

With the dashboard revisions came a change in rocker switches. Always in black plastic with chromed plastic surrounds, they were slimmed down in September 1970; meanwhile the main light switch moved to a position beneath the instrument cluster.

Besides the switches for headlamps, heater and wipers, various accessories brought their own rocker controls – including those for auxiliary lighting, hazard flashers and low brake pressure warning. When specified, early models had separate panels mounted beneath the dashboard, sometimes containing lamps and toggle switches, with words swapped for diagrams in September 1968.

Black cardboard parcel trays were found under both sides of a GT's dashboard, with reinforced lips on their leading edges and attached to black metal brackets with plastic-headed brass clips. Black cardboard kick panels were in each front footwell, with a vinyl map pocket stitched onto the driver's side from August 1969.

Despite its sporting pretensions, the GT had a mainstream

Escort steering wheel. On early cars it was deep-dished, with a hard plastic rim (never leather), three spokes and a GT centre boss badge featuring a pair of crossed flags and GT emblem.

A so-called sports steering wheel was optional from 1969, which was actually just the export-spec padded wheel with

A sea of brown plastics added an earthy appeal to this colour-keyed cockpit. Central to the experience was this dished steering wheel bearing a suitably bold GT badge. On UK cars it was replaced by a Euro-spec padded wheel from September 1971 onwards. Note the optional centre console. Post-September 1970 GTs were fitted with a revised fascia panel and narrow rocker switches, naturally in whatever shade of plastic Ford thought suited the car's bodywork. At first, there were slots for two switches (seen here) unless hazard warning flashers were specified. After around August 1971, five-slot panels were standard, with blanking plugs in redundant holes.

Brochure shot of the late 1968 GT interior showing the so-called "harmonious" colour-keyed effect. Vivid, bold and red are all words that spring to mind. Is that a Ford oval on the driver's door step too?

FACTORY ORIGINAL SPORTING MK1 ESCORTS

Escort GTs received this style of dials long before AVO machines, with flat faces and chunky numbers. With their September 1968 introduction came the wood-grain effect surround, here encased in dark tan plastic. Note the 110mph speedometer, 6,500rpm tachometer red line and detailed supplementary gauges.

A properly sporting environment, reminiscent of the contemporary Cortina GT. This studio shot of a 1967 Escort GT displays its silver-finish instrument surround, padded vinyl seats, early-type door handles, pedal rubbers and chrome heater control bezel. The opening quarter lights weren't standard.

black leather rim and three silver brushed metal spokes. This wheel became standard in September 1971, when the GT badge was dropped in favour of a plain grey/black Escort logo. Depending on interior specification, the spoke pad could be colour-coded but the leather was always black.

A steering lock was optional from launch (and standard in Germany) but became part of the UK spec in August 1970. A single stalk protruded from the plastic column shroud, used for indicators, headlamp dipping/flashing and sounding the horn; there was a chrome horn button, although aftermarket Lucas replacements were black (the single-tone horn itself sat behind the car's front grille; a dual horn was optional).

GTs featured a regular cable-clutch Escort pedal box with black levers, along with black floor button for screen washers. Until September 1970 the brake and clutch rubbers were black with a grid pattern, the accelerator pedal was bare metal. Later cars had black pedal rubbers with moulded horizontal ridges, including the throttle.

A GT's gearstick was always chrome, with normal Escort black knob and black gaiter, regardless of interior trim colour. There was a black metal handbrake lever with bare steel push button. Behind it sat a pair of buckles for the seat belts, which were listed as a compulsory extra. Early models had Wingard static seat belts with two-handed fasteners, textured metal clasps painted satin black and a silver push release button. After September 1970, static three-point belts were fitted, featuring fixed stalks with black plastic coating and silver push buttons.

Inertia reel seat belts were optional from the outset, using static belt fastener arrangements. A child's rear seat safety harness was a dealer accessory, rear belt anchors were optional from June 1973 and the belts from that October.

Several different types of rear-view mirror were found on the GT. Early cars had a non-dipping mirror, with a dipping version available as a dealer accessory – white/ivory in colour, followed by grey from February 1969. A dipping mirror became standard in September 1970 – generally a shaped grey Wingard. A black dipping mirror, with black stalk, followed in October 1973.

Above the mirror, the GT's headlining started out as Cortina-style white Lodestar pattern. A putty-coloured headlining replaced it by September 1970. Colour-keyed GTs with a black interior were listed as including a black headlining, but this was very rare and probably deleted before the 1970 facelift. A pair of sun visors matched the headlining material, with a vanity mirror added to the passenger side from September 1970.

Early cars (until August 1970) had a pair of ivory-coloured coat hooks at the tops of their B-pillars, which were replaced by grab handles – one on the passenger side plus a pair in the back. Early grab handles were dark grey, but in 1971 they changed to black with chrome end caps; the rears featured black sliding hooks.

A plastic centre console was optional for a GT after August 1968. The same type as found on the 1300E and early RS1600/Mexico Custom Pack, it ran from underneath the heater panel to the back of the handbrake lever. On colour-keyed GTs the whole console and gearstick gaiter were matched to the hard plastic trim.

From 1970, a factory-optional Kienzle round electric clock with white hands (as seen in the Cortina 1600E Series Two) could be mounted in a pod screwed to the centre console.

On the subject of extras, the GT could be purchased with a variety of sound systems. On early cars it was a factory-optional Phillips manual radio or dealer-fitted Plessey push-button radio, sometimes bearing a Ford oval. Plesseys were generally used from August 1970 until September 1973, while a tape player was offered from August 1970. Early models had their radios underslung from the driver's or passenger's side of the dashboard in a vinyl surround, colour-keyed after September 1968. A single speaker was mounted in the passenger-side panel under the dashboard, later swapped for a square speaker with chrome finish in the rear parcel shelf. From August 1970 the radio housing was mounted centrally under the fascia panel and the rear shelf speaker replaced by a round item.

With a GT's XL-specification interior came this padded bucket-style back seat, rounded at the corners for better access into four-door cars. Vinyl was standard but cloth was an optional extra

Talking of the rear parcel shelf, it came in black or colour-keyed cardboard, depending on year. In 1969 the fixings changed from three plastic studs to two self-tapping screws covered by plastic buttons; after autumn 1971 the domed screw caps became larger.

Inside Boot

It was unremarkable in appearance, but a GT's boot compartment showed several trim and bodyshell changes. Most obvious was the bulkhead dividing boot from back seat, which was a solid panel up to September 1970, with cutouts thereafter.

On the offside was the GT's nine-gallon petrol tank. Until August 1969 it was painted black, with a protruding filler neck sticking through the back wing and smooth cap outside. Later cars switched to a zinc primer-grey fuel tank with smaller neck and flush-fitting cap, which was also the colour of the last long-neck tanks. Locking caps were a popular dealer accessory, all chrome or with a black plastic centre.

In the nearside well sat the GT's upright 12in spare wheel, with no hubcap. A strap held it in place, which also kept the

GT door cards were the same as other high-spec Escorts of the period, here taken directly from the Escort XL, along with fake wood trims. Four-door models featured different window winder and door release handles from two-door cars, with rear-mounted clips rather than simple screws.

fawn muslin tool bag from rolling around the boot. Early versions contained a jack with separate ratchet handle (replaced by mid-blue vertical jack in September 1970), and two-piece wheel nut wrench, which was superseded by a single cranked satin black wheelbrace.

The GT had a full black Hardura rubberised boot mat, while a luggage compartment light was added in September 1970. The boot lid latch had no rubber cover. The GT's plastic lamp protectors were always black; at first there was one only on the left-hand side, but there was a pair from September 1968.

GT colour schemes

Body colour	Colour code	Introduced	Discontinued	Interior colour
Beige 67	BVP	Launch	April 1970	Black
Medium Grey	C	Launch	April 1970	Black
Light Blue	CGP	Launch	April 1970	Blue
Light Green	CRP	Launch	April 1970	Aqua
Maroon	C	Launch	September 1970	Red or black
Blue Mink	CR/A3P	Launch	September 1970	Black
Saluki Bonze	CS/A6P	Launch	September 1970	Black or Beechnut
Pacific Blue	9	Launch	January 1972	Tan
Glacier	4 or BY	Launch	January 1972	Red, tan, black
Ermine White	AB or B or BA or ABP	Launch	January 1972	Black, Beechnut, tan or red
Light Grey	D	Launch	January 1972	Olive or black
Garnet	P	Launch	January 1972	Ruby or black
Silver Fox	3 or CV/A2P	Launch	November 1973	Black, Ruby or tan
Black or Ebony	A or Y	Launch	November 1973	Black, tan, red or special oeder
Non-standard	Y	Launch	November 1973	–
Monaco Red	BS	November 1967	January 1968	Black
Red	BNP	September 1968	April 1970	Red or black
Aquatic Jade	A5P	September 1968	September 1970	Black
Lagoon Blue	CJ	November 1967	September 1970	Aqua
Dragoon Red	CU	November 1967	September 1970	Black until '68, then black or red
Purbeck Grey	CH	November 1967	September 1971	Black or tan
Anchor Blue	G or CW/BJP	November 1967	January 1972	Black, Marquis, tan, blue or navy
Spruce Green	BZ	November 1967	Autumn 69	Black or pale green
Alpine Green	CM	November 1967	Autumn 69	Black or tan
Fern Green	5	July 1970	September 1970	Tan
Maize Yellow	T	September 1970	January 1972	Tan or black
Black Cherry	CL or P	September 1970	September 1972	Red or black
Diamond Blue	E	September 1970	September 1972	Black or Marquis
Sapphire	1	September 1970	October 1973	Black or Marquis
Evergreen	6	September 1970	October 1973	Tan or olive
Tawny	S	September 1970	October 1973	Tan or black
Marine Blue	G	September 1970	November 1973	Blue
Sunset	J	September 1970	November 1973	Black or Ruby
Pearl Grey/Gunmetal	2	Autumn 1971	April 1973	Black
Lime Green/Le Mans Green	M	January 1972	November 1973	Black
Daytona Yellow	T	January 1972	November 1973	Tan or black
Electric/Monza Blue	U	January 1972	November 1973	Black
Diamond White	B	May 1972	November 1973	Black, red or tan
Sebring Red	N	May 1972	November 1973	Black or saddle brown
Copper Brown	7	August 1972	November 1973	Tan or black or saddle brown
Burgundy Red	CL or P	September 1972	November 1973	Red
Purple velvet	F	December 1972	November 1973	Black or tan

Interior trim (early models)

Trim code	Seat colour	Carpets	Introduced	Discontinued
B884	Ravenna Red (vinyl)	Dark red	October 1967	September 1968
B885	Aqua, medium (vinyl)	Dark aqua	October 1967	September 1968
B886	Saddle (vinyl)	Saddle	October 1967	September 1968
B887	Black (vinyl)	Black	October 1967	September 1968
B888	Ravenna Red (cloth)	Dark red	October 1967	September 1968
B889	Aqua, medium (cloth)	Dark aqua	October 1967	September 1968
B890	Saddle (cloth)	Saddle	October 1967	September 1968
B891	Black (cloth)	Black	October 1967	September 1968
D401	Black (vinyl)	Black	September 1968	August 1970
D402	Parchment (vinyl)	Black	September 1968	August 1970
D403	Cherry (vinyl)	Cherry, dark	September 1968	August 1970
D404	Beechnut (vinyl)	Beechnut, dark	September 1968	August 1970
D405	Aqua, (vinyl)	Aqua, deep	September 1968	August 1970
D406	Blue (vinyl)	Blue, deep	September 1968	August 1970
D407	Black (cloth)	Black	September 1968	August 1970
D408	Cherry (cloth)	Cherry, dark	September 1968	August 1970
D409	Beechnut (cloth)	Beechnut, dark	September 1968	August 1970
D410	Aqua (cloth)	Aqua, deep	September 1968	August 1970
D411	Blue (cloth)	Blue, deep	September 1968	August 1970

Interior plastics

Colour	Introduced	Discontinued
Black	Launch	December 1974
Deep Aqua 69	August 1968	August 1970
Deep Blue 69	August 1968	August 1970
Dark Beechnut 69	August 1968	August 1970
Dark Cherry 69	August 1968	August 1970
Dark Olive 70	August 1970	August 1972
Dark Tan 70	August 1970	August 1972
Marquis Blue 71	August 1970	August 1972
Dark Ruby 71	August 1970	August 1972
Aubergine	August 1970	August 1972
Deep Blue	August 1970	August 1972
Jade 71	August 1970	August 1972
Mid Blue	August 1970	August 1972
Ruby	August 1972	December 1974
Tan	August 1972	December 1974
Marquis	August 1972	December 1974

FACTORY ORIGINAL SPORTING MK1 ESCORTS

ESCORT TWIN CAM

Stunning October 1968 Twin Cam owned by Brent Mould was fully restored around ten years ago. The car spent its former life in the hands of an elderly chap who'd used it for club rallying since the early '70s. When found it was in a pretty poor state, sporting a humble Pinto powerplant under the bonnet. Its front chassis rails had been strengthened to take the strain. Now an Ermine White masterpiece, a sympathetic rebuild introduced desirable period modifications including Contour front seats, Springalex steering wheel, Bilstein suspension and roller bearing top mounts. Meanwhile, a stainless steel exhaust helps to keep the car useable.

It was 25 January 1967. Something special was about to happen. Ford competitions manager Henry Taylor was holding a low-key meeting to make plans for a reinvigorated attack on the world of motorsport. A legend was being born.

Towards the end of 1966, Taylor and team foreman Bill Meade had managed to sneak a peek at the firm's top-secret new Anglia replacement, yet to be named Escort. Seeing the small, agile saloon being tested on track, its potential was immediately obvious. "One of those things would go like hell with a Twin Cam engine!" Meade reportedly enthused.

So while development work continued on the Lotus Cortina, proposals were prepared to raid its important parts for a stronger, lighter replacement. All Taylor needed was a car to work on…

Eventually, bosses agreed to lend the team a plastic-bodied Escort prototype. It arrived at their Boreham workshop one Friday afternoon in March 1967, where Ford's motorsport crew had only a weekend to take measurements and draw sketches. And so the J25 project (named after that January 25 proposal) was put into action.

The Lotus Cortina's engine was slotted between the Escort's inner wings, twisted to make room for the Weber carburettors. Its battery was relocated to the boot, its gearbox was persuaded to fit into the little tunnel, while the front struts and rear axle were offered into place. And those

ESCORT TWIN CAM

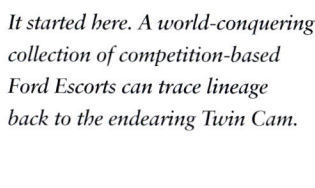

It started here. A world-conquering collection of competition-based Ford Escorts can trace lineage back to the endearing Twin Cam.

oversized 165x13in tyres definitely needed more clearance.

By November 1967 the J25 was gradually gaining approval from Ford bosses. An early Escort 1300GT was plucked off the Halewood production line and sent to Boreham for turning into a fully-functioning prototype. The Escort Twin Cam was suddenly taking shape.

Between then and February 1968, the first 25 Escort Twin Cams were hand-built by the competitions department. All were based on GT shells (with a chassis code beginning in BB48, and an R instead of a Z on the identity plate) using Cortina mechanicals and a few specially-created components, including stitch-welded strut top reinforcing plates and bodged-together front wheelarch flares. The cars were cleverly distributed among press and motorsport teams, well in advance of the 1,000 units required for rallying homologation.

On 17 January 1968 the Twin Cam was revealed to the public, when the regular Escort was launched in Morocco. Some of the details would change before proper production but all the important bits remained.

For full-scale manufacturing, the Twin Cam was constructed at Ford's Halewood factory, with a special workshop set aside from the Escort assembly line for adding its running gear. There, a dedicated team took partly-completed cars and fitted the suspension, brakes, gearbox and Lotus-built engine, shipped up complete from Hethel in Norfolk.

Halewood production of the Escort Twin Cam began in February 1968. The very first examples were probably white Type 48 GT shells (still with BB48 chassis numbers), but by March the full Type 49 strengthened body had been phased in, complete with BB49 chassis number; officially, the first Escort Twin Cam was BB49G_01304. The Type 49 was essentially an export-specification GT with stiffened floorpan and chassis mounts, along with modified transmission tunnel, radius rod locating points, flared front wheelarches and battery tray bunged in the boot.

Despite low production figures, the Twin Cam achieved Group 3 homologation on 1 March 1968 (500 units required), and Group 2 (1,000 cars) by May the same year. It was instantly a motorsport success, taking the Cortina's place to score innumerable rallying, rallycross and circuit-racing victories.

As for the Twin Cam road car, its on-paper figures (of 106bhp, 113mph and 0-to-60mph sprint in 9.9 seconds) told only half the story – because the Twin Cam was widely praised for its performance, amazing handling and tuning potential.

Externally, though, it looked much like the GT on which it was based. Yes, the Lotus Cortina's suspension gave the Escort a low ride height and extreme negative front camber. Yes, the Cortina's 13in steel wheels were bigger than what Ford intended for under the (now reworked) arches. Yes, there were front quarter bumpers and discreet Twin Cam

FACTORY ORIGINAL SPORTING MK1 ESCORTS

Escort's Coke-bottle styling can be seen in its originally-intended purity. Twin Cam's front wheels sat further forward in the arches thanks to uprated anti-roll bar and mounts.

badges. But nothing really gave the game away.

Even the GT's inadequate oblong headlamps were retained, thanks to Ford's insistence on associating rectangles with refinement (or some such marketing nonsense). Likewise, the GT's well-appointed cabin was used in the Twin Cam – always with black trim and a mildly revised version of the early silver-finished instrument cluster.

According to legend, Ermine White was the only colour offered to the Twin Cam-purchasing public. While that's true of the initial batch, a few were resprayed in alternative Escort shades before registration. More to the point, from January 1970 other Escort paint schemes were readily available.

Minor revisions were made to the Twin Cam's bodywork and suspension in September 1968 (from chassis number BB49H_10994) but it wasn't until December 1968 (officially chassis number BB49J_20645 in July 1969) that the most notable change took place – the swap from rectangular to round headlamps. At last, rally drivers could see where the next night stage would lead (to victory, of course).

September 1970 brought an alteration to all Escorts' identities. Twin Cams now had their BB49 chassis numbers switched to a BBAT code, along with new-style underbonnet VIN tags. The following month (from chassis number BBATK_07452) saw further revisions in line with the entire Escort range, including an improved dashboard.

By this time, of course, the RS1600's career was already under way, and for most Ford fans the Twin Cam was fast becoming a happy memory. Even so, both models were built alongside one another at Halewood (very early RS1600s were simply re-engined Twin Cams) until the Advanced Vehicle Operations (AVO) plant was opened at Aveley. Twin Cam manufacturing was never transferred to AVO, and official production ceased on 9 June 1971, with final vehicle number BBATLC40214.

Almost all Twin Cams were right-hand drive and sold in the UK. No four-door versions were built, but there were 50 left-hand-drive German examples constructed at Genk in 1969; apparently all were silver and had a chassis code starting GBAT.

Educated guesses put total Twin Cam production at 1,263, with 883 built before the switch to BBAT chassis numbers in September 1970. The figures also don't include cars shipped overseas (most notably to Australia), where they were supplied as knock-down kits of parts. Such models had their own country's chassis plates.

Production continued abroad until late 1972. And that was the end of arguably the most charming, exceptionally appealing of all Escorts.

Quarter bumpers, rectangular headlamps and negative suspension camber gave aggressive stance. An imposing sight in any 1968 rear-view mirror.

Nothing gave the game away until the Twin Cam was a tiny spec in the distance. Even the wider wheels looked pretty innocuous from this angle.

Engine – Block, Head and Sump

The Escort Twin Cam took its engine from the Lotus Cortina Mk2, as fitted from March 1967. The chain-driven, DOHC, 1558cc powerplant was fully assembled by Lotus, and was therefore the same unit found in the contemporary Elan and some Europas (that said, many were higher spec than Escort versions, with bigger valves, raised compression and sportier cams).

The setup included a purpose-built cast iron Lotus cylinder block, with a large letter L cast onto the crankcase between the right-hand engine mounting bolt holes (and obscured by the mount).

Early Twin Cams had a 681F-6015-G-A block, while later cars used a 701M-6015-B-A part. The codes referred to the year of the part's introduction – so the 68 in 681F was for the 1968 model year (first introduced in late 1967); the 70 was for the 1970 model year (introduced during late 1969).

The Twin Cam 681F block was a modified version of the Mk1 Lotus Cortina pre-Crossflow 116E bottom end with thin-wall cast iron block, although the 681F benefited from a 3020E-type six-bolt flywheel fixing to the crank (early Lotus engines built until mid-1967/engine number 7800 were four-bolt). There was a Ford cast iron, five-bearing crank, Vandervell lead-indium bearings and no crankshaft damper. Most 681F engines had round mains caps, although some say the last few had square caps like a 691M block. The 701M was a stronger cylinder block, with square mains caps.

All Lotus blocks were graded on the top left front face with L, LB or LLB to indicate maximum possible bore. There was also a T number (from 1 to 20) on the side of the block, which simply related to the casting batch. The block colour was Lotus Grey – a glossy battleship grey similar to Massey Ferguson Stoneleigh Grey enamel but with an extra hint of blue.

A Lotus-specific engine number (prefixed LP or LF followed by a series of numbers) was hand-stamped on a pad above the offside engine mount, below the cylinder head and inlet manifold; because the engine and car were constructed at separate factories (by different companies) the engine and

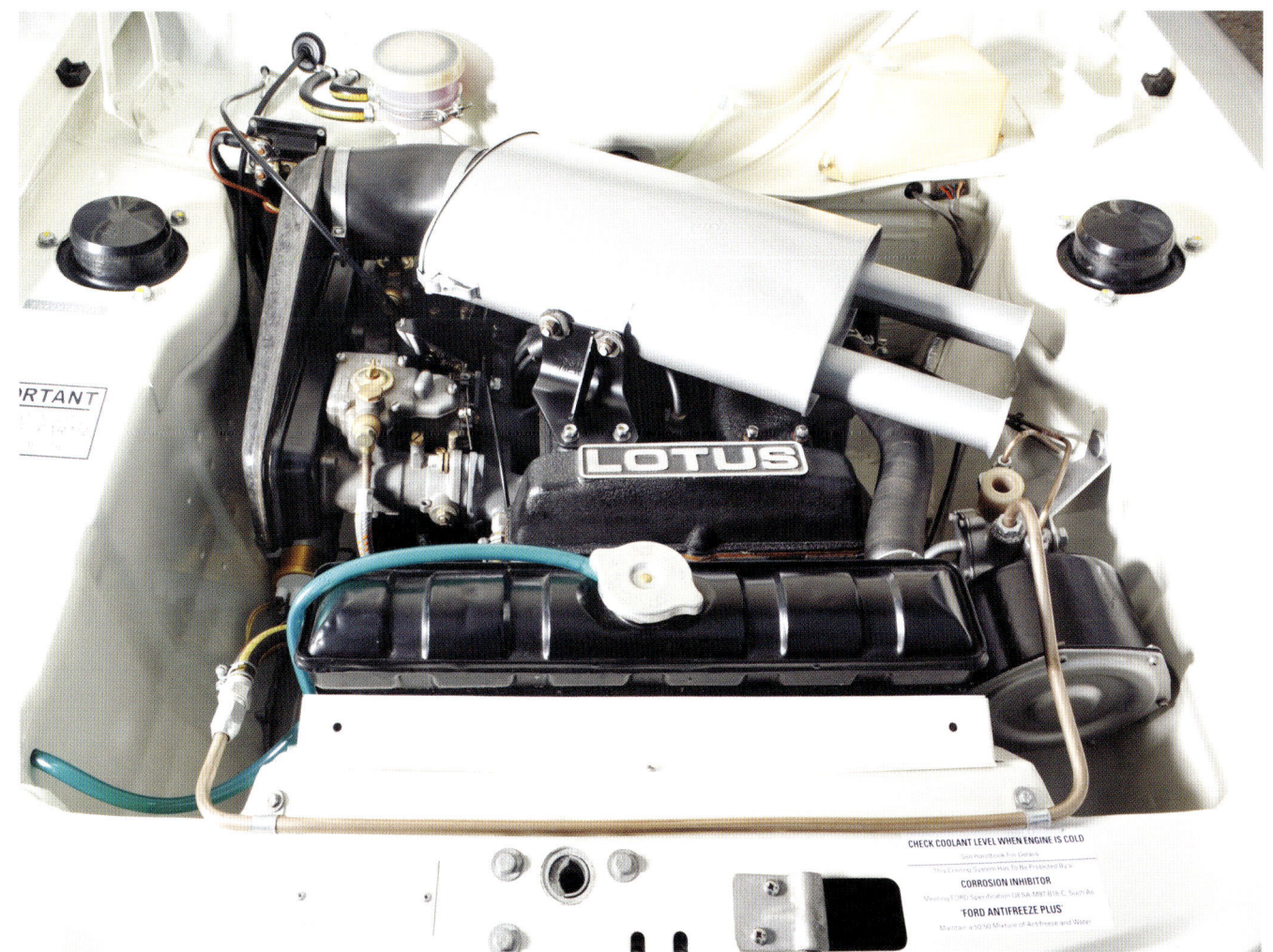

This was where an unsuspecting Escort GT was turned into something very special. The Lotus Cortina Mk2's entire engine was squeezed under the little car's bonnet, giving rise to an unbeatable rally machine.

FACTORY ORIGINAL SPORTING MK1 ESCORTS

Jokingly referred to as a Range Rover exhaust back box, the Twin Cam's air filter housing came straight from the Lotus Cortina engine donor. Colloquially-named "cheese wedge" washer bottle sat on body-coloured pins on the nearside bulkhead. Pipework fed a white Trico barrel-shaped T-connector.

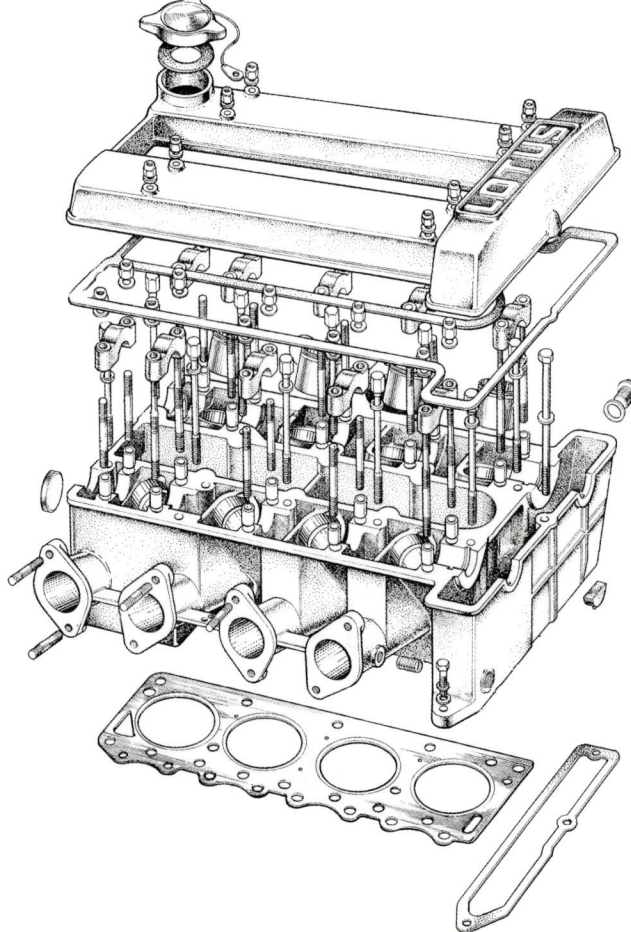

Exploded diagram of the Twin Cam's Lotus cylinder head.

chassis numbers never matched. Besides, they were rarely legible because they were always painted over.

The Twin Cam featured a 9.5:1 compression ratio, with AE light alloy C-type pistons (with small cut-outs and three rings – two compression and one oil control). Its connecting rods were strong forged steel 125E Lotus Cortina parts.

Like the block, the Twin Cam's cylinder head was painted Lotus Grey. Made from aluminium alloy, it featured part-spherical combustion chambers, individual inlet and exhaust ports and a Weber DCOE-type inlet manifold cast into the head. From 1969/engine number 18,820 it gained stronger, non-shouldered head bolts. Some cylinder heads had their own serial numbers stamped in, but this wasn't necessarily done at the Lotus factory.

Inside the head was a pair of C-type camshafts (with one groove at the front), driven by roller chain. There were eight valves, with face diameters of 38.8mm (inlet) and 33.5mm (exhaust); the valve springs were single.

Above the head sat the usual dual-bank cam cover, in bare alloy with the word Lotus cast along each side until October 1968. Afterwards, there was a satin black Trimite enamel crinkle-finish cover, with polished alloy Lotus lettering across the front in block capitals. The Escort Twin Cam never received Lotus's big-valve ribbed rocker cover.

At the rear of the cam cover (against the bulkhead) was the Twin Cam's oil filler cap, which changed from a circular shape to a three-eared type in October 1968, probably to counter problems with the earlier type working loose.

The oil pump was bolted to the right-hand side of the cylinder block, and was revised in September 1970 (engine number 23,607) to accept a spin-on canister filter rather than the previous bolt-on type with replaceable element.

The Escort Twin Cam also had an oil cooler adaptor sandwiched between oil pump and filter, with a cooling radiator mounted upright in front of the water radiator, towards the nearside headlamp; it attached on one side through the radiator fittings and the other on a bracket to the centre support; its pipework was fed under the offside headlamp and across inside the front panel, through hand-drilled holes.

Whereas the Lotus Cortina's dipstick went through the front of the water pump, the twin-cam Escort's ran through the back of the engine block, in a flexible tube behind the airbox. The dipstick itself was different from the normal Escort type but identical to its successor, the RS1600; it had a bare alloy handle.

At the other end, the dipstick was dunked into a semi-gloss black big-wing sump (just like the part found on the later RS1600 and Mexico), fitted the opposite way around from the Lotus Cortina's for crossmember clearance. The sump's extensions were crudely welded from new.

Talking of the crossmember, the Twin Cam used the same mildly modified Escort part as subsequent AVO machines. The round rubber engine mounts were in the usual positions but with special brackets on the crossmember, skewing the block diagonally over to the left by a couple of inches to give clearance for the Twin Cam's carbs against the offside inner wing. Very early Twin Cams had solid rubber block engine mounts.

Most Escort Twin Cams also had a black engine stabiliser bar, securing the gearbox bellhousing to the bulkhead through a large rubber bush. It was bolted to a reinforcing plate on the passenger-side bulkhead, which was roughly welded into place and brushed with seam sealer. Very late (after June 1970) Twin Cams lost this setup in favour of an RS1600-type heavy-duty gearbox support.

Cooling System

A satin black big-header radiator sat behind the Twin Cam's slam panel in the usual Escort position. It had five square dimples across the faces of the header tank, with three along the bottom and angled metal brackets straight down each side, pressed in one piece. Its colour code was canary yellow.

The radiator had a standard 13psi cap and overflow outlet pointing towards the driver's side, running out through a drilled hole in the offside inner wing.

A distinctive radiator top hose in black rubber with horizontal red stripe ran alongside the cam cover and beneath the air filter. Wire clips secured all the hoses. An 88-degree wax thermostat was contained within a bare alloy housing above the exhaust ports, which was obscured from view by the airbox.

The Twin Cam engine featured a Lotus-designed impellor, housing and O-rings with Ford bearing, seal and hub. It was bare aluminium, and looked very similar to the usual Crossflow water pump. On the front was an eight-blade 12in plastic fan in cream/off-white with rubber V-belt; it's unlikely the Lotus Cortina two-blade metal fan found its way onto any Escorts.

Fuel System

Taken straight from the Lotus Cortina, the Escort Twin Cam's carburettors were dual Weber twin-choke side-draught 40DCOE 48s, mounted directly to manifolds cast integrally with the cylinder head.

Original Ford-fitted carbs had a metal tag attached to one of the float chamber screws plus a code on the flange where they met the inlet manifold. It described the carburettor type (40 DCOE 48) followed by a calibration code. Carbs also had their model type stamped into the jet covers, along with "Made in Italy" plus green and blue paint spots on the float chamber covers.

The throttle and choke cables weren't shared with other Escorts, but the latter was revised in August 1969, with part number 69AB-9700-CA. The Crossflow, though, did give its mechanical fuel pump (with glass bowl) to the Twin Cam.

Squeezed between the carbs and inner wings was a black airbox, secured by a pair of bright metal clips and with trunking to a metal air filter housing. The AC twin-barrel airbox came from the Lotus Cortina, in a hammered silver finish, mounted diagonally across the cam cover. It was attached to the cover at the front with a black bracket on three bolts.

Exhaust System

The Lotus Cortina gave its tubular steel four-branch exhaust manifold to the Escort Twin Cam, although the mild steel system was obviously altered for the smaller car. Here, it followed a similar pattern to the normal Escort's but now in bigger bore and featuring a cylindrical centre silencer and oval rear box (a reversal of the standard car's layout). It was finished in silver/grey.

It's probable that the first Twin Cams used an Escort GT rear hanger setup, but most production models received the double-loop rear silencer hanger welded onto the chassis rail and supported by two O-shape rubbers, as found on subsequent AVO machines.

Twin Cam plenum drain was this unusual shape. This shot also shows the three-eared oil cap, fitted from October 1968.

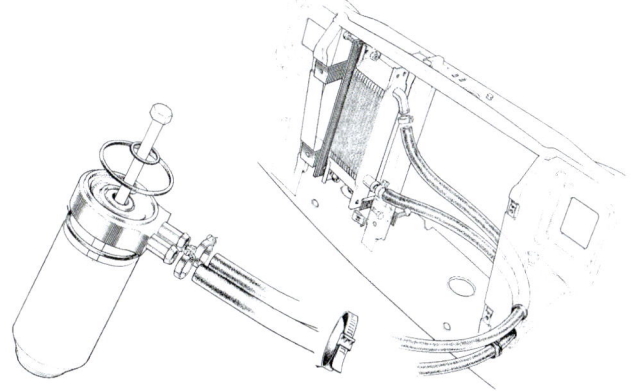

Twin Cam oil cooler setup was carried over to RS1600. Front panel holes were drilled at the factory.

Tubular four-branch exhaust manifold was plucked from the Lotus Cortina. The angled engine stabiliser bar tied the Twin Cam's bellhousing to its bulkhead.

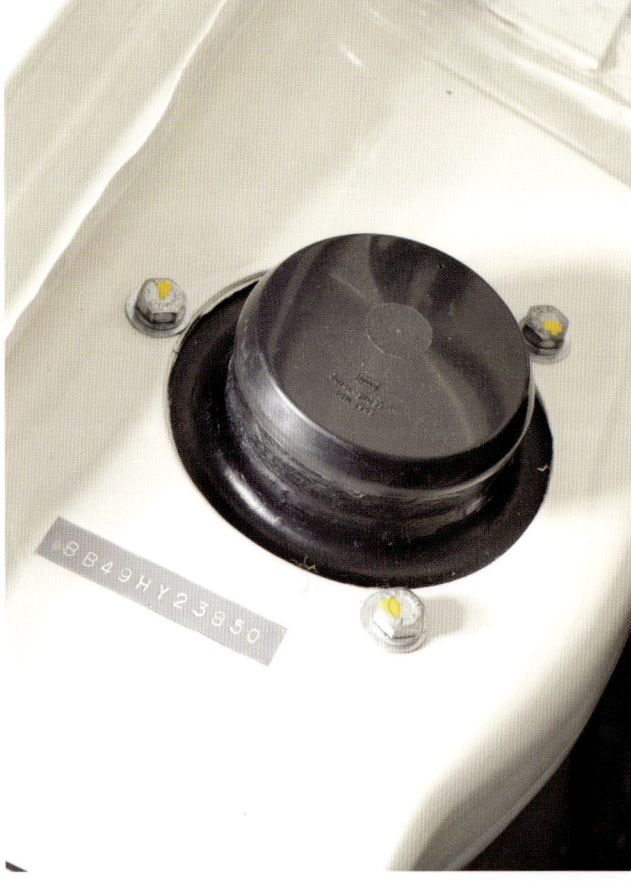

Roller bearing suspension mounts were found atop optional beefy Bilstein dampers. Type 49 reinforcing plate was stamped with the car's chassis number, but not usually this neatly.

There were no other alterations, but May 1969 saw minor changes to the Twin Cam's centre exhaust clamp assembly.

Ignition and Electrical System

Most of the Twin Cam's engine ancillaries came straight from the Lotus Cortina, including the ignition system.

The Escort Twin Cam ran a Lucas 23D4 distributor mounted under the inlet manifold, numbered 41189A, with rotor arm spring rev limiter cutout at 6,500rpm and no vacuum advance. It had a screwed-on black cap, with sockets facing downhill towards the engine mount.

Ford leads from the Lotus Cortina connected to Champion N4/Autolite AG22 14mm long-reach spark plugs. Meanwhile, there was a standard Escort coil and bracket (mildly revised for the 1968 model year) and unique clip holding the ignition coil wire to the Twin Cam's front apron.

Until July 1969 the Twin Cam used a Lucas C40L 25amp dynamo, which was then swapped for a Lucas 15ACR 28amp alternator; from 1971 there was a Lucas 17ACR 35amp alternator, which was obviously found on very few cars.

The Twin Cam's starter motor was a Lucas M35G inertia type, with Autolite solenoid mounted high on the offside bulkhead and updated in August 1969.

The Twin Cam's unique stabiliser bar was attached to the bulkhead where you'd normally find an Escort's fuse box. Instead, the Twin Cam's six fuses sat under a clear plastic cover beneath the passenger-side dashboard, above its parcel shelf and attached internally to the bulkhead, along with voltage regulator and relays. From late 1969 the fuse box had internal connectors with wiring behind the bulkhead, along with seven plastic continental fuses; it screwed onto the passenger-side bulkhead with internal connectors.

The GT-based wiring loom was also changed in August 1969 and August 1970 to accompany the alterations but looked essentially similar, wrapped in grey loom tape. From the later date it included an extension to a Lucas 6RA relay mounted in the engine bay.

Of course, the biggest electrical difference on a Twin Cam from its GT starting point was its battery position – always mounted on a tray in the boot, in the spare wheel well. It was a Motorcraft 38Ah 12-volt battery (or 57Ah in cold climates), with grey fibreboard cover in either size (with FoMoCo embossed on the underside); it's likely that some Twin Cams came without one.

Transmission

When the Lotus Cortina's engine was stuffed into the little Escort body, it also meant making room for the oversized gearbox – the Ford Type 3 four-speed with three-rail shift mechanism and remote change, colloquially known as the 2000E.

The big cast iron 'box (finished in black or a very dark shade of green for factory Ford reconditioned units) was put together at Halewood, then squeezed into place with hammer work in the transmission tunnel, a hole for the stick cut further back, a regular Escort rear gearbox mount (modified for fitting the speedometer cable) and Lotus Cortina linkage.

Like the 'box fitted to subsequent RS1600s and Mexicos, the Twin Cam's 2000E had a separate bolt-on bellhousing, cast alloy top cover and iron tail, whereas a normal Cortina single-rail gearbox tail casing was alloy.

Second gear had 28 teeth, third gear (the next one forward, after the synchro hub and selector fork) had 23 teeth – whereas the standard Cortina wide-ratio 'box featured 21 teeth and an early Lotus Cortina gearbox (which used the alloy bellhousing and tail casing) had 24 teeth.

The Twin Cam's gear ratios were first: 2.972:1, second: 2.010:1, third: 1.397:1, fourth: 1.000:1 and reverse: 3.324:1.

A hydraulic Lotus Cortina Borg and Beck 8.09in plate clutch found its way into the Twin Cam, complete with remote master cylinder (a combined brake/clutch unit mounted in the engine bay). There was a cast iron flywheel, with six-bolt fixing.

A single-piece propshaft was used, with no centre bearing support. It linked to a satin black Timken hypoid bevel rear axle, identical to the part found on RS1600s and Mexicos, including brackets for twin radius arms. It contained a 3.777:1 differential (colour code orange/yellow/green; pinion/crown wheel number of teeth 9/34) as standard, but various ratios were optional, including 3.900:1 (10/39), 4.125:1 (8/33) or 4.444:1 (9/40).

Ford's competitions department also offered an Atlas axle and ZF five-speed gearbox, although such upgrades weren't fitted on the production line, and few original road cars received them.

Suspension and Steering

It was pretty clear from outside that the Twin Cam rode on lowered suspension, and the negative camber on the front wheels was very noticeable. Much of the setup was based on Lotus Cortina components, but gradually evolved for the Escort.

Until September 1970 there was a Cam Gears steering rack, with 16.4:1 or 16.6:1 ratio; afterwards it was swapped for a 17.5:1.

The earliest Twin Cams had chassis mounts for compression strut suspension but with the struts removed. A 20mm front anti-roll bar was fitted instead on fabricated mounts, brazed to the insides of the chassis rails; the anti-roll bar was bolted up from below. From September 1968, new brackets were used – similar to those of mainstream Escorts but wider. The front anti-roll bar bushes were improved in February 1970.

Macpherson struts and integral shock absorbers were always used, with oil-filled dampers and a green colour code. They were fitted with 100lb one-inch lowered front coil springs, again bearing a green colour code. The strut tops

Fuse box was moved from the engine bay to this under-dashboard position, complete with voltage regulator attached to the bulkhead.

were satin black with black collars; their butterfly cranked retainers had only one lug until the late 1969 facelift, from when there were two. Uprated dampers and roller bearing mounts were optional from Ford's competitions deptartment.

On the back of a Twin Cam was a reworked version of the standard Escort setup, featuring semi-elliptic 97lb three-leaf springs with 51mm wide leaves (blue and red colour code) held on U-bolts over the back axle. A pair of anti-tramp bars ran from mountings above the axle to the chassis rails.

All Twin Cams had inclined telescopic oil filled dampers in black with yellow and white identification codes (canary

Crossmember was basically the standard Escort part; steering rack came with 16.4:1 or 16.6:1 ratio.

FACTORY ORIGINAL SPORTING MK1 ESCORTS

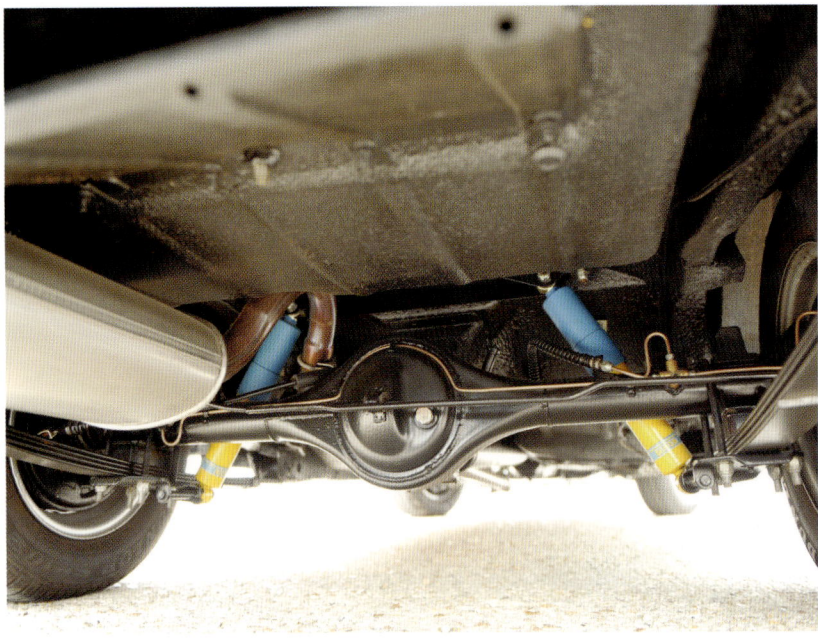

Inclined rear dampers were found on all factory standard Twin Cams. Timken rear axle was carried over to RS1600 and Mexico.

Stone deflector was mounted under the Twin Cam's boot floor. The same shield found its way onto subsequent AVO Escorts.

Combined brake and clutch fluid reservoir sat on bulkhead, alongside starter solenoid, speedo drive cable and throttle cable, which clipped into a body-coloured bracket.

Girling Powerstop Mk2A remote servo was fitted to make room for the Twin Cam's Weber carbs. It attached to the inner wing on this angled bracket.

yellow on early cars). Until September 1968 the rear shock absorber upper mounting was a bracket at either side of the damper tops, but from then on there was a single black mounting beam spanning across the car under the boot floor.

Brakes

Stopping a Twin Cam was never a problem, thanks to a big brake setup. At the front that meant a pair of Girling 9.625in discs and pads, clamped by Girling 16P calipers; the calipers had a pale gold finish, 54mm pistons, imperial fittings and large dust seals. The discs were backed by satin black metal guards.

On the back was a pair of Girling HL3A 9x1.75in drums, as fitted to the Capri 3.0 and later AVO Escorts. Rear brake pipe stone guards were fitted to Twin Cams until mid-1968; early heavy-duty shells (until this date) had similar stone guards.

A Girling Powerstop AHV 550 Mk2A remote servo sat at the nearside front of the engine bay alongside the radiator, in place of the standard Escort battery tray. The servo had a semi-gloss black body and flat silver front cover. It was attached to the inner wing on a triangular silver bracket. A steel connection pipe ran across the bonnet slam panel's rear edge, clipped into place.

Rear brakes were Girling HL3A 9x1.75in drums. On some cars the pipes were protected by these stone guards.

Lotus Cortina wide steel wheels filled the arches nicely, measuring 5.5x13in and topped with traditional chrome hubcaps.

FACTORY ORIGINAL SPORTING MK1 ESCORTS

Early Escort boot lock had a recessed key slot. FORD badges had crisper edges before the 1969 model year.

A CV combined brake/clutch reservoir was mounted on the bulkhead in the engine bay, sat on a crudely-welded, body-coloured bracket and affixed with a screw clamp. There were twin feeds (in black rubber with thick yellow horizontal stripes) taken through the bulkhead to a pair of master cylinders mounted above the pedal box.

Wheels and Tyres

It probably goes without saying, but the Escort Twin Cam's wheels were taken straight from the Mk2 Lotus Cortina – 5.5x13in pressed steels, painted silver. They came with stainless steel hubcaps, which were the usual plain chrome domes found on every other Escort and Cortina of the period (in fact, they dated back to the Anglia 105E). Underneath the caps were 7/16 UNF open-ended wheel nuts on studs with dished ends.

Standard tyres on the Twin Cam were 165SR13 radials, but the brands varied enormously, including India Super Autoband, Goodyear G800, Michelin XVS or Pirelli. Later cars wore Dunlop SP68s.

Several different wheels were optional on the Twin Cam, starting with 1600E Rostyles (chrome and black or silver-painted), which were available from Ford dealers (and later included with the Super Plush Pack). The Rostyles were

Satin black grille was a permanent feature on all but the very earliest Twin Cams. Starting handle hole gained this rubber grommet in January 1970.

phased out in 1969.

Tech Del Minilite magnesium wheels were also a Ford competitions department option from the outset, in almost any size. Genuine Minilites had centre caps fitted from the rear and Minilite stamped on; very early versions featured cooling slots cast between the spokes and strengthening vanes on the inside.

Theoretically, it was possible to buy a Twin Cam with 5.5x13in RS four-spoke alloys, which were available through Rallye Sport dealers after January 1971 and optional on new cars from March 1971. At the time, they wore chrome-and-black RS centre caps (pushed through from behind), polished rims and spokes, spoke centres and rears in dark grey, chrome nuts and chrome valves. The spokes weren't cast with any part numbers.

Body

By and large, Twin Cams had Type 49 bodyshells. Only very, very early cars (with front chassis rails built for compression struts) were built around Escort GT Type 48 shells.

All Twin Cams came with flared front wheelarches, although early pre-production cars were modified by hand – a job rumoured to involve fibreglass extensions or even welded-on Transit wheelarches. Later cars, of course, used the same pressed panels found on AVO Escorts and the Sport. It's sometimes also claimed that Twin Cams had flared rear wheelarches; this wasn't the case, but all production cars' rear arches were rolled to accept the wide wheels and tyres.

Up front, a rectangular-headlamp panel was fitted until December 1968. It always had a starting handle hole, plus from January 1970 a black rubber grommet. The radiator grille was bright metal alloy with a polished surround and satin/matt black middle, although pre-production cars had bare alloy grilles or black paint ending abruptly at the ends of the slats, with polished sections around the headlamps.

Until around August 1969 all grilles had a central cutout for a bonnet release button, with a Wilmot Breeden lock offered as an accessory. The Twin Cam included a special safety catch with securing plate. Later cars (after September 1969) had a remote bonnet release under the passenger-side dashboard, which was swapped to the driver's side during September 1970. Behind the grille, the car's bodywork was painted satin black after September 1968.

Cars with a grille-mounted release generally had one windscreen washer nozzle mounted in the bonnet, but this was gradually changed to a pair of washers in the scuttle panel during spring 1970.

The Twin Cam was always equipped with two-speed, self-parking windscreen wipers – often seen as twin-wire Trico Speedblades, but which according to Ford parts catalogues were simply standard Escort stainless wipers.

Cars were usually supplied with a Triplex Zebrazone zone-

Flared front wheelarches were added to clear the Twin Cam's bulky 165x13 radial tyres (the 185/70x13s on this car are non-standard).

A protruding petrol cap was found on all pre-September 1969 Escorts and the Twin Cam was no exception. It just needed filling more often.

Wingard door mirror was a stylish period accessory.

The stern-faced Twin Cam was forced to contend with rectangular Lucas headlights until July 1969, when they were ousted in favour of circular 7in lamps. Quarter-bumpers were a Lotus Cortina tradition.

Stainless steel roof gutter trim was common to many Mk1s, and clipped over the paintwork.

ESCORT TWIN CAM

toughened glass front windscreen (complete with small green or blue Zebrazone sticker inside), although a Triplex laminated screen was listed for the Twin Cam.

The back window was plain glass, but a heated rear window was optional from September 1970. Opening front quarter lights were available from launch, with the option of opening rear side windows from around October 1970. Window rubbers had chrome beadings and a finishing insert across the joint. A stainless steel trim was clipped onto the roof's rain gutters. A vinyl roof wasn't available.

Until September 1969, Twin Cams had early-style doors with a lock in the driver's handle, a regulator mechanism instead of rod, and rubber buffers at the top of each B-pillar and far corner of each inner door skin. From September 1969 there were later-style doors with separate locks on each side, rod mechanisms and locks with two-position latches. The

All early Mk1 Escorts had an external bonnet release in the middle of the radiator grille. The Wilmot Breeden lock was a useful aftermarket accessory.

Ford parts lists quoted standard Escort stainless wipers for the Twin Cam, but Trico Speedblades were often found on contemporary press cars. Were all customer cars similarly equipped?

Like other Escorts of the generation, most Twin Cam had just one twin-jet windscreen washer nozzle mounted centrally on the bonnet.

FACTORY ORIGINAL SPORTING MK1 ESCORTS

Early Escort rear lamp surrounds gained softer edges during production; this car's are the later type. Reversing lights weren't initially fitted.

B-pillar and striker position was altered for the new design.

The door window pillars were painted body colour. Handles were the same chrome-plated parts found on lesser Escorts. Door locks shared the same key as the boot lock (which had a recessed slot until 1971), but the ignition key never corresponded; incidentally, a steering lock was optional from launch and standard from August 1970.

Twin Cams had plain bumpers – on the front was a pair of chrome quarter bumpers taken from the back of an Escort van, while at the back was a straight chrome bumper without number plate light cutout. All were fitted with chrome-finished dome-headed bolts. There were no bumper overriders, except on the back of some pre-production press cars.

The Twin Cam had a normal Escort boot lid, never including aluminium edge trim or matt black back panel. There was a protruding petrol cap, swapped for a flush-mounted part in September 1969. Both filler caps were body-coloured unless swapped for a chrome locking Ford accessory.

Twin Cam badging was very discreet. There were the usual Escort badges (individual chrome FORD lettering on the bonnet and boot lid plus an Escort script on the boot lid's offside; the FORD letters had softer edges after September 1968), along with a small Ford oval badge fitted to the bottom of the nearside front wing from October 1967 until September 1968; after this date, a small metal Ford oval was fitted to the inner passenger-side doorstep instead. Of course, there was also a Twin Cam badge on each front wing; this was the same part found on late-spec Lotus Cortinas, in

Pre-September 1969 Escort doors featured these chrome handles with lock only in the driver's side.

Twin Cam badge on the Escort's front wings was lifted from the late-spec Lotus Cortina Mk2.

green and white with chequered flag design.

The Twin Cam never had factory-fitted mirrors, but they were available as official Ford accessories.

Lighting

Rectangular headlamps were found on the front of early Twin Cams, thanks to an absurd Ford marketing ploy. The Lucas 9in wide units were 45/40 watt semi-sealed beams with replaceable tungsten bulbs, and had very much outstayed their welcome by the time round headlamps were homologated in November 1968. Standard Twin Cam kit thereafter was a pair of basic Escort 7in Lucas 60/45-watt sealed-beams, although 75/50W circular headlights with quartz iodine bulbs were available (always accompanied by an alternator), as were twin-bulb Cibie biodes.

Beneath them were amber plastic indicators with chrome-effect rims; Twin Cams never had plain orange plastic lenses.

At the back were regular Escort rear lights with chrome surrounds and black plastic seals. The surrounds had softer swage lines after September 1970.

Beneath the number plate was a single-bulb lamp with glass lens, mounted on the rear panel. Reversing lights were an optional extra from August 1969, made standard in September 1970. Like mainstream Escorts, they had clear plastic lenses, stainless lens surrounds and black plastic backs.

Underbonnet

If the outside of a Twin Cam looked like any other Escort, the opposite was true once the bonnet was lifted. It was immediately clear the engine between the inner wings had been crammed into place at a wonky angle. Not only that, but a host of modifications had been made to get everything into place.

At the nearside front corner the battery tray had disappeared – indeed, the very earliest cars built from Type 48 GT shells had their trays literally hacked out, and not very neatly.

In front of the oversized radiator was a raised metal deflector panel, painted body colour. In the offside inner wing was an exit hole for the radiator outlet pipe.

Early Twin Cams (until September 1969) had different bulkheads from later models, featuring no flat spot on the heater dome or washer pipe cutouts, plus bonnet hinges on small platforms. All bonnet hinges and their fittings were body-coloured, because they were factory-sprayed on the car.

In the middle, the Twin Cam's bulkhead heater dome was equipped with a wide, flared-out black plastic plenum drain, bearing FoMoCo lettering. The car's speedometer cable ran from the upper bulkhead beside the brake/clutch reservoir within a black grommet; occasionally it was held on a bracket attached to the upper bulkhead's flat panel. Further towards the offside, the throttle cable was clipped to a body-colour bracket welded to the flat of the bulkhead; on some cars this was a separate bracket fastened to the rearmost strut top bolt.

Twin Cams had no clutch cable, so the tube on the bulkhead brake reinforcement plate was sealed – as was the brake pedal-to-servo hole.

Most Twin Cams (certainly up to January 1970) had an off-white squared "cheese wedge" washer bottle attached to the nearside bulkhead on three body-coloured pins. It's possible that some later Twin Cams (towards the end of production) gained a rounded opaque plastic slide-on 70AB bottle with water outlet on the top left-hand side. The washer pipes were clear plastic tubing, with a white Trico barrel-shaped pipe fitting.

The majority of Twin Cams featured an engine stabiliser bar, which secured the gearbox to the bulkhead. It was bolted through a large rubber bush to a welded-on reinforcing plate on the passenger-side bulkhead. The very last (post-October 1970) Twin Cams lacked the stabiliser bar, switching to the RS1600's gearbox mounts instead.

Of course, all Twin Cams had reinforced suspension strut top plates welded onto the inner wings.

The Twin Cam had no bonnet release cable until September 1969, after which an uncoated cable ran down the nearside inner wing; it moved to the driver's side in September 1970.

Until September 1969 there was a bonnet stay attached to the left-hand side slam panel. Later cars had the prop located on the bonnet's underside, with a clear/white plastic retaining clip attached to a welded-on loop.

Stickers under a Twin Cam's bonnet were attached somewhat randomly. There was usually a negative earth warning on an inner wing (although it may also have been in the boot near the battery), along with a white/black coolant sticker on the slam panel, commonly the nearside.

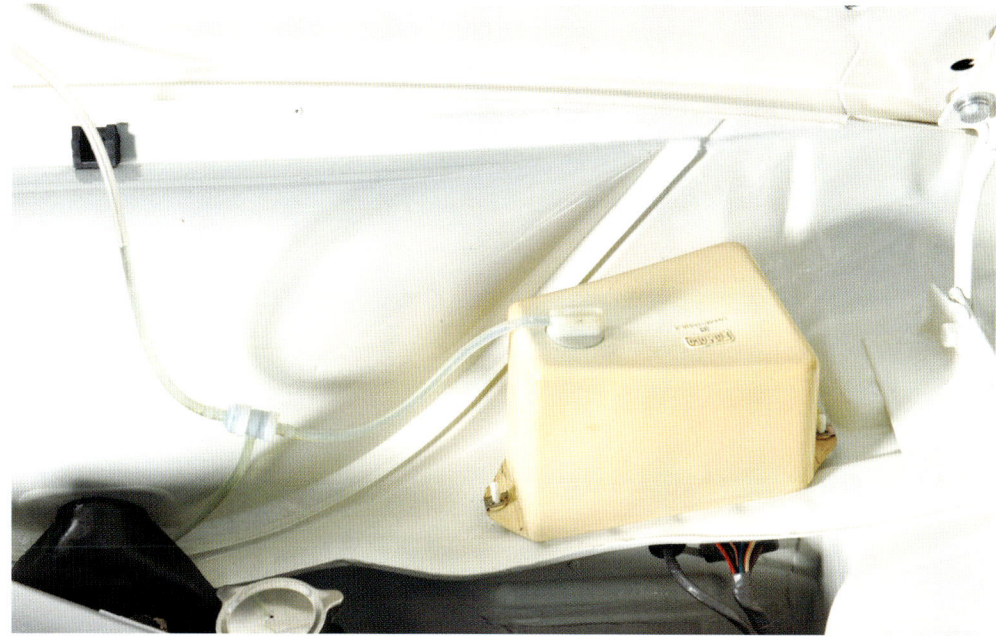

Colloquially-named "cheese wedge" washer bottle sat on body-coloured pins on the nearside bulkhead. Pipework fed a white Trico barrel-shaped T-connector.

The Twin Cam's monochrome cabin was a true case of function over form – yet it was inviting and immediately homely, especially with these optional bucket seats.

Interior

Based on the early Escort GT, the Twin Cam retained its high-spec black interior throughout production. Thankfully, none of the later GT's mock wood trim made it into place (well, not in the UK anyway).

The front seats were the fully-tilting Super/GT-type with fixed-backs and black PVC covers with perforated inner panels and smooth moulded-in bolsters. The tipping mechanism was controlled by a button on the base at the rear of the cushion, but from August 1970 it was replaced by a lever on the backrest. There was a matching contoured two-bucket-effect rear bench, trimmed in the same black PVC.

Seat options included vinyl trim with cloth centre sections (after September 1970) and Clubman Pack front seats from Boreham's competitions centre (black vinyl Contour buckets with high side bolsters). The Twin Cam was never offered with a Custom Pack.

Door cards were the padded Super-type in black vinyl, swapped in September 1970 for a plainer design than the original block-type stitched effect. At the same time, the rear quarter cards changed from plastic to fibreboard but retained the plastic armrest extensions and push-round plastic ashtrays.

Until September 1968 Twin Cams featured spindly chrome Cortina-type door release and window winder handles, after which they were replaced by the later Escort flat, textured parts. From August 1969, narrow black plastic internal lock pins were found on both doors.

Based on the early GT's cockpit, the Twin Cam boasted the same dashboard, seats and carpet. Springalex was a major improvement over the standard Twin Cam's bus-sized steering wheel.

Judging by surviving examples, most Twin Cams seemed to come with a dished Springalex steering wheel, featuring black or polished spokes, black leather rim and a variety of logos in the centre boss. In fact, standard fitment was a normal Escort black plastic three-spoke deep-dished steering wheel with spindly spokes and silver Escort badge in the centre. A single column stalk protruded from the shroud, complete with chrome horn button.

Twin Cams used the GT's satin black metal six-dial dashboard with padded black vinyl top. Cars built before September 1970 (which accounted for the vast majority of Twin Cams) contained the early Escort dash layout, with wide switch slot. Incidentally, the very first GT-based cars also featured a Twin Cam badge (sourced from the Lotus Cortina and identical to those found on the front wings) in front of the passenger.

The switch slot in the dashboard housed a rocker for the two-speed heater fan. Beside it was the centrally-mounted heater control panel, with black plastic levers inside a convex plastic-chrome surround. From August 1969 the surround was swapped for aluminium with a black Mazak stuck-on diagram. It blew air through a pair of swivelling vents set into the dashboard top. Until September 1968 the vents were round with bevelled edges, then swapped for flat rims; both types rotated but neither could be closed off. In September 1970 the flat-rimmed vents gained adjustable flaps.

A plastic fascia panel beneath the dashboard comprised a raised upper section incorporating ashtray (with horizontally

FACTORY ORIGINAL SPORTING MK1 ESCORTS

Early Escorts were fitted with Wingard three-point static seat belts. The clasp end was bolted to the transmission tunnel...

... while the buckle end was bolted to the B-pillar. Inertia reels were an extra-cost option.

ribbed lines) and choke knob (black plastic, with silver and black insert), plus single rocker switch for headlamp control. The lower section contained a cigar lighter and two-speed wiper rocker switch to its left.

The switches were wide, black plastic with chromed plastic surrounds, replaced by thinner rocker switches in September 1970. Cars built after this date also gained a later-type fascia panel with holes for two switches, grained-finish ashtray and choke control. The cigar lighter was moved up to the dashboard (in front of the passenger) and the headlamp switch to beneath the instruments. Until September 1970 the lighter was long-necked with a silver insert matching the choke knob but afterwards swapped for the later AC Escort lighter in a deep-set socket.

Like the first GTs, the Twin Cam's instruments featured six dished dials within a silver binnacle. The black-faced AC gauges had white needles and chrome bosses, comprising large speedometer (incorporating main beam warning light) and rev counter plus small gauges for fuel, battery charge, oil pressure and water temperature. Round alternator and direction indicator warning lights were mounted between the two big dials.

Lettering on the gauges was in a tall, thin, white font reading MPH, RPM, TEMP, BATT, FUEL and OIL. The speedometer went up to 140mph, while the 8,000rpm rev counter had a 6,500rpm red line on all but the earliest few cars. The speedo cable was taken from the Escort automatic; it had a blue colour code and was clipped to the dashboard from July 1969.

Black cardboard trays were found under the dashboard on both sides, including reinforced lips on their leading edges. They were attached with plastic-headed brass clips and black metal brackets. Each front footwell was kitted with black cardboard kick panels, complete with a vinyl map pocket stitched onto the driver's side after August 1969.

The Twin Cam had a special pedal box (as found on the subsequent RS1600 and early Mexico) using a standard Escort casing but with brake and clutch cylinders mounted above. The pedal levers were black, with a bare metal accelerator plus black brake and clutch rubbers with grid pattern. To the left was a floor-mounted windscreen washer button with black surround.

A black, shallow loop-pile carpet was standard on the Twin Cam. Most cars had a two-piece item, joined ahead of the front seat crossmember. From September 1970 it was swapped for a single-piece carpet. For some reason, the Twin Cam had less sound-deadening insulation under the front carpets than the GT on which it was based.

No centre console was usually fitted, but from October 1970 there was an optional coin tray available, running from underneath the heater panel to the back of the handbrake lever.

A chrome gearstick was wrapped in a rubber gear lever gaiter, similar to (but different from) the standard Escort part. The gearknob was black; again it looked like the usual Escort knob but had reverse marked back towards the driver's seat.

The Twin Cam's handbrake lever was the same as a regular Escort's, in black with a bare steel push button. Behind it was a pair of seat belt clasps. Prior to September 1970 the Twin Cam was equipped with Wingard static seat belts, which featured two-handed fasteners, seat belt webbing on both ends, textured metal clasps painted satin black and a silver push release button. Later cars had static three-point belts and fixed stalks bolted to the transmission tunnel, with black plastic coating and silver push buttons. Inertia reel seat belts were optional, with Teleflex reels, labeled "wear at all times".

Also optional was a push-button Plessey radio or manual Phillips, which would be found under the fascia panel or attached underneath the driver's or passenger's side of the dashboard in a vinyl surround. Radios were accompanied by a square speaker with chrome finish grille in the rear parcel shelf.

All Twin Cams had a black cardboard rear shelf, for which the fixings changed in 1969 – from three plastic studs to two

Lodestar headlining was a throw-back to Cortina trim, and found in all Escorts of the period. Very late Twin Cams were trimmed in black instead. Sun visors were fitted to both sides, in Lodestar pattern to match the roof lining. Back then, the passenger received no vanity mirror.

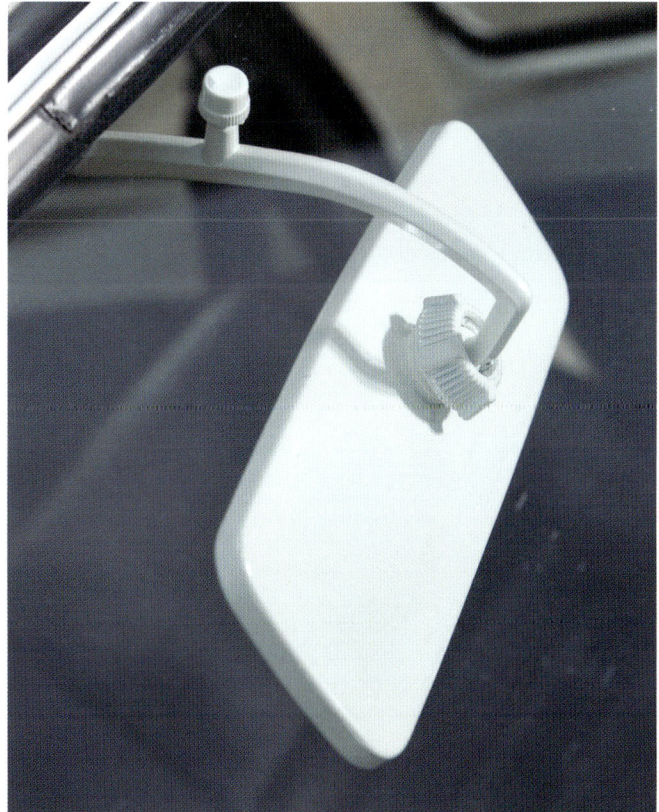

White interior mirror gave way to dipping version in 1970 but a variety of grey, white or ivory rear-view mirrors were offered as options and accessories.

Chrome gearstick, gaiter and black gearknob looked like standard Escort kit, but all were subtly different – especially the reverse position marked on top.

FACTORY ORIGINAL SPORTING MK1 ESCORTS

The Twin Cam's pedal box was developed from the standard part, adding brake and clutch master cylinders for the hydraulic setup. These pedal rubbers are a later addition.

self-tapping screws covered by plastic buttons.

The headlining found in most Twin Cams was the white Cortina-style Lodestar pattern. It was replaced by a black headlining at an unknown point – some records show a September 1970 swap to the black AVO headlining but black was certainly seen in Twin Cams before this time. Sun visors matched the headlining, incorporating a vanity mirror in the passenger's visor after September 1970.

Early cars had a non-dipping rear view mirror (rectangular with flat sides), although a dipping version was available as a dealer accessory; mirrors were white/ivory until February 1969, after which they were usually grey. A shaped grey Wingard dipping mirror (with tapered sides and rounded corners) was used as standard from September 1970.

Like regular Escorts, the Twin Cam had a roof-mounted courtesy lamp above the mirror, operated by pins in each door A-pillar.

Grab handles weren't fitted to the Twin Cam until August 1969 – when it gained three black handles with chrome end caps (one on the passenger-side front plus a pair in the rear, each with a black sliding hook). Instead, earlier cars had a white coat hook at the top of each B-pillar.

A mildly modified version of the early GT instruments, the Twin Cam's instead rose to 140mph and 8,000rpm.

Inside Boot

Thanks to its oversized engine, the Twin Cam was the first Escort to have its battery mounted in the boot. A Motorcraft 38Ah (or 57Ah in cold climates) 12-volt battery was positioned on a tray in the spare wheel well, with negative nearest the rear lights. The positive battery cable ran through a drilled hole in the boot floor, down the floorpan and across the transmission tunnel; clips were riveted to hold it in place.

A grey fibreboard protective cover (with FoMoCo embossed on the underside) was usually fitted on top; sometimes it was topped with a white-and-black negative earth decal, although that was often stuck on the nearby inner wheelarch or inner wing instead.

The Twin Cam's GT/Super-sourced door cards had this pattern until autumn 1970. Note the lack of lock pin in this pre-September 1969 door.

Back seat came straight from the GT base car, always trimmed to match the fronts in black vinyl.

Curvaceous Contour bucket seats were a sought-after competitions department extra. Standard seats were the padded black vinyl GT/Super type with tipping backrests.

FACTORY ORIGINAL SPORTING MK1 ESCORTS

Storage space wasn't a Twin Cam selling point – the boot-mounted battery meant most of the luggage compartment was taken up with a spare wheel.

Spare wheel was a full-sized 13in Lotus Cortina rim, lacking hubcap. It was bolted to the boot floor, through a hole in the boot mat.

To make room for the battery, the Twin Cam's spare 13in steel wheel was mounted to the boot floor with one large nut and bolt passing though the floor and wheel nut hole (in the three o'clock position, looking into the boot). It had no hubcap. The standard Escort's spare wheel bracket was omitted from the boot floor.

Beneath the spare wheel was a normal black Hardura boot mat, although it was listed with a different part number – possibly to account for the spare wheel bolt hole. Like regular Escorts, the Twin Cam's tool kit (stuffed between battery and inner arch or strapped to the boot mat between spare wheel and tank) comprised a fawn muslin bag containing screw jack with separate ratchet handle and two-piece wheel nut wrench – replaced in September 1970 by a mid-blue vertical jack and single cranked satin black wheelbrace.

Under the boot floor was a satin black stone deflector, with eight bolts protruding through the floor. The Twin Cam's rear bulkhead (between boot compartment and back seat) was a solid panel, but added cutouts in September 1970.

Early cars had a satin black nine-gallon fuel tank with long-neck filler and protruding cap. From September 1969 a revised fuel tank was used, with flush-fitting filler cap.

ESCORT TWIN CAM

A boot light was fitted as standard from September 1970. The Twin Cam's plastic rear lamp protectors were black; at first there was one only on the left-hand side, but a pair was fitted after September 1968.

Colour Schemes

Although it's commonly thought Twin Cams were always white with black trim, that's just a fallacy. Yes, the vast majority of UK Twin Cams were painted Ermine White, featured black interiors and the AB code on their chassis plates. But not all.

Until January 1970, the white-and-black theme was pretty much compulsory. One or two Twin Cams were non-white from new, but it's generally believed that if owners ordered a special colour the car would leave Halewood in Ermine White prior to being stripped and resprayed by the dealer (who'd usually paint everywhere except the engine bay) before delivery to the customer. The build plates still stated Ermine White.

From January 1970, Ermine White, Maize and Sunset were all 'mainstream' Twin Cam colours – although just a handful were built in such shades, and apparently only from September 1970. Twin Cams were also available in special order colours – Evergreen and Marine Blue were believed to exist.

Fifty left-hand-drive Twin Cams were built at Genk, Germany in 1969; all were believed to be silver and had a chassis code starting GBAT. Australian Twin Cams were available in almost any shade.

Early Escorts' petrol tanks were satin black, complete with long-neck external filler until September 1969.

Battery was placed on a tray in the normal Escort's spare wheel well. Negative terminal bolted to the boot floor, while positive ran underneath the car towards the engine bay.

Ford competitions department Twin Cam options, 1968

From the Twin Cam's launch a potential owner could specify competitions-developed items at extra cost:
- Ventilated cast electron high-performance wheels
- Long-distance touring seats
- Close-ratio gearbox
- Sump shield
- Extra-long-range fuel tank
- Alternative axle ratios – 3.9:1, 4.1:1, 4.4:1, 4.7:1
- LSD
- Lightweight differential casing
- Lightweight clutch housing
- Lightweight gearbox extensions
- High-ratio steering rack
- Heavy-duty front suspension
- Adjustable rear shock absorbers
- High-performance brake pads and linings
- Oil cooler unit
- High-performance exhaust system
- Fuel injection
- High-performance connecting rods, pistons, camshafts, valves and oil pump
- Lightweight glassfibre body panels for bonnet and boot lid
- Low-back bucket seats with high side bolsters
- Britax harnesses
- Minilite magnesium alloy wheels in 5.5x13in to 9.25x13in sizes. Wider than 6in require Works arches.

FACTORY ORIGINAL SPORTING MK1 ESCORTS

An Australian 1970 Twin Cam in its native environment. Jon Evans bought his 94,000-mile Escort in 2004 and spent five years rebuilding it to this stunning standard, repainted in its original shade of Vermillion Fire. Jon also added a few personal upgrades. Compomotive 6x14in alloy wheels maintain a retro theme, while '72 Twin Cam high-back bucket seats and inertia real seat belts aid modern-day safety. Under the skin, Koni adjustable shock absorbers and limited-slip differential mean it can still surprise some V8 Aussie muscle cars.

Australian Twin Cam

While Halewood was winding down Twin Cam production in favour of the all-conquering RS1600, assembly of the Lotus-engined machine began to take place overseas.

Why the delay? Well, the Australian Escort – in common-or-garden varieties – was only released during March 1970. The Twin Cam followed suit on 1 June, although manufacturing started during April that year. Why the Twin Cam, rather than RS1600? Most likely because the lack of local technicians trained to work on the advanced 16-valve BDA powerplant meant the costs and practicalities were prohibitive.

The very first Australian Twin Cams were built using parts shipped over from Halewood in England. Known as knock-down kits, they arrived as unpainted body shells, crated trim, wiring, glass and mechanical components, plus fully-assembled Lotus engines and 2000E gearboxes. Put together at Sydney's Homebush plant on a separate production line from normal Escorts, they received chassis codes starting in CK49 (C for British origin, K for Sydney and 49 relating to their extra-heavy-duty shells).

The first 1970 Australian Twin Cams were to full UK specification – including circular headlamps and front quarter bumpers – but as production continued more locally-sourced parts were introduced.

Pretty soon they were based on Australian Escorts with what the British called heavy-duty "export" bodies, including strengthening plates around the front suspension top mounts, fillets on the towers and skid plates on the foremost rear spring hangers. To make a Type 49-style Twin Cam, the Sydney factory started with a 1300GT shell (with six-dial dashboard panel) and added a variety of upgrades.

Under the bonnet, a reinforcing plate for the engine stabiliser was spot-welded to the passenger-side bulkhead, a platform was brazed to the bulkhead for the combined brake/clutch reservoir, holes were drilled for the pipework, there was a mounting bracket and hole in the upper bulkhead for the throttle cable, the brake servo reinforcer was plated over and the clutch cable hole had a cap brazed on. The battery tray was removed from the inner wing, while the radiator support panel was roughly trimmed to take a big Cortina radiator, with a Twin Cam deflector sitting ahead.

Like British shells, the transmission tunnel was mildly dressed back with a hammer to take the beefy gearbox, but in Australia a removable plate was used to accept the gearstick.

Underneath, rear trailing arms (not a tubular shape like UK radius rods) were added and their brackets spot-welded on. A stone deflector was fitted under the boot floor, along with a large nut brazed on underneath for the spare wheel retaining bolt. The rear exhaust mount was MIG-welded to the chassis rail.

Inside the boot, a battery tray was added in the spare wheel well and two hooks were brazed onto the floor for holding down the Ford tool roll.

Externally, the most noticeable change was the addition of flared front wheelarches – similar to British versions but with more rounded edges. All Aussie Twin Cams had a rubber plug in the front panel's starting handle hole.

Sydney-built cars also retained the 1300GT's rectangular headlamps, adding alloy spot light mounts, drilled through the front panel. Many also wore the GT's chrome beading around the side window recesses.

Unlike British cars, Aussie Twin Cams could be ordered in a huge variety of body colours and were offered with a host of options. They included laminated windscreen, quartz iodine driving lamps, slotted Capri wheel trims (over the usual 5.5x13in steel rims with Dunlop SP41 tyres), sports steering wheel, round door mirror, push-button radio, rear seat lap belts and heavy-duty battery. Customers could also choose a full GS (Grand Sport) pack, which boasted the driving lamps, wheel trim rings, steering wheel and mirrors, plus "tuned muffler", wooden gearknob, stripes and Super-roo stickers.

By 1971, the Twin Cam was using locally-produced glass from ACI/Pilkington. Meanwhile, the GT-spec seats gained levers on their backrests (just like UK cars) and the heater controls were replaced by the flat, Mazak-labelled type.

ESCORT TWIN CAM

Around this time a centre console/coin tray was added, along with GT-type mock wood trim on the dashboard but not around the instruments (which kept the silver surround, 140mph speedo, 8,000rpm rev counter and wording on the supplementary dials). A raised chrome Ford oval badge on the passenger-side door step was moved to the driver's side. Under the bonnet, the cheese-wedge washer bottle gave way to the later Escort rounded design. The engine stabiliser bar and flared bulkhead drain remained.

The problem was, Twin Cams were very badly put together, with thin paintwork, continuous oil leaks and lousy panel gaps. They were unreliable, unrefined and slower than cheaper homegrown Holdens.

So for 1972 the Twin Cam was renamed GT1600. It came with new front seats, when ADR (Australian Design Rules) instigated tipping high-backed buckets; they were trimmed in Robuck vinyl with Basket Weave vinyl centres, and fitted on fresh floor mountings. A range of colours was offered for the cabin, which extended to the carpets, door cards and kick panels.

The seats were accompanied by locally-produced door cards in the current British GT design (a plainer pattern than the earlier Super style), while the rear quarter panels and front kick panels changed from cardboard to plastic. At the same time, the window winders and release handles were slightly altered – the winders became chunkier and the door handles gained a three-legged bracing on the back. Seat belts switched from having metal clasps with a Ford-logoed release button to a plastic "press to release" control.

By then, the GT1600's dashboard had the later Escort lower fascia/switch panel, which was now supplied in a colour to match the interior trim, as were the padded dashboard top and newly-adjustable air vents (all were previously only in black). The rocker switches were now the Australian-produced narrower, chrome type and the headlamp switch was repositioned on the right-hand side under the instruments. Meanwhile, the cigar lighter moved from the heater cover to the dashboard. If a radio was fitted from new, it became mounted inside a pod attached to the fascia panel, rather than a shroud on the driver's side.

Behind the fascia, the heater box was switched from steel to plastic in 1972. Under the dash, all Twin Cams and GT1600s had a parcel shelf on the passenger side, but nothing for the driver. The rear parcel shelf went from smooth black cardboard on early cars to a grained finish in 1972; it remained black.

The Twin Cam/GT1600's steering wheel was leather-covered with three silver spokes (like the British Escort Sport) and full shroud. From 1972 the ignition switch was mounted on the column and included a lock.

An early car's rear view mirror was screwed to the roof, but now it became a locally-sourced part, bonded to the windscreen. Meanwhile, the sun visors were swapped for pivoting Australian components; like the headlining they were trimmed in a white "moon crater" pattern.

The wiper motor was changed for an Aussie-made component, as were the plastic front Hella indicators. Reversing lamps became part of the package now too.

Under the skin, much of the car remained the same as the original. But the engine steady bar was dropped and Ford Australia had started resealing the Lotus cam covers in an attempt to curtail the Twin Cam engine's infamous propensity for dripping oil.

Assembly of the GT1600 ceased in August 1972, by which time a few irregularities were cropping up in manufacture. Most of the GS Rally Pack was supplied as standard. The under-floor stone deflector stopped being fitted, and some cars lacked the clutch cable bung – body filler was used instead.

Indeed, it's worth pointing out that few Twin Cams or GT1600s left the factory with the same spec (much like British AVO machines). Many were built and used for motorsport, so survival rates of original cars are pretty low. It's reported that 793 Twin Cams and GT1600s were built in Australia; it's not known how many remain.

Under the bonnet of an Australian Twin Cam its heritage is obvious. Jon Evans's restored 1970 example houses its original L block, rebuilt and overbored, complete with mildly uprated cams, free-flowing air filters and uprated exhaust system. An aftermarket brake servo sits in place of the rare Girling part, but this machine's bulkhead retains the proper Twin Cam bulkhead drain.

FACTORY-ORIGINAL SPORTING MK1 ESCORTS

ESCORT RS1600

Reckoned to be one of the earliest surviving alloy-blocked cars to leave Aveley, this rare non-Custom RS1600 was built in February 1973. It sat around for six months before delivery to its first owner, who in June 1973 ordered a Monza Blue RS1600 with optional Cibie Biode headlamps and inertia reel seat belts. When it finally arrived, the extras were correct but the Sebring Red paintwork was something of a surprise… Since then, the car has covered 73,500 miles and retains its original engine. Although it's never been completely restored, a respray and some sympathetic conservation work has kept the car looking fresh. AVO Owners' Club member Darren Peacock is the car's current custodian, regularly scooping prizes in concours competitions.

The ultimate MkI Escort? That has to be the RS1600, designed and built with only one ambition – motorsport victory.

And, of course, the RS1600 was an immense success. It dominated the world of rallying and changed the face of national competition – so much that even today, no British historic motorsport event is complete without at least one RS1600.

Code-named J26 to mark its direct descendancy from the J25 Escort Twin Cam, the RS1600 took on its predecessor's mantle of mainstream four-seater saloon with a very naughty engine under the bonnet. But while the Twin Cam's Lotus-built powerplant was on its development limits, the RS1600 featured an amazing new Cosworth-designed unit known as the BDA (Belt Drive type A). Based on the Cortina 1600's Kent crossflow bottom end, the 120bhp BDA boasted an alloy 16-valve cylinder head with twin belt-driven cams. Rather than the Cortina's 1599cc dimensions, the BDA was officially quoted as 1601cc, allowing homologation into a motorsport class of 1600 to 2000cc – which meant competitors were immediately able to enlarge the unit to a healthy 1.8-litres.

Ford's initial intention was to drop the BDA into its then-new 1969 Capri but the smaller, more agile Escort was soon deemed a more suitable recipient. So the RS1600 was born.

ESCORT RS1600

Sitting slightly lower than a standard Escort, there was little else to distinguish the RS1600 from a common-or-garden Sport. Well, not until you heard the howling BDA engine anyway...

Production began alongside the Twin Cam at Halewood in January 1970, progressing next to everyday Escorts before being whisked off for fitting up with special accessories. Ford's official earliest RS1600 chassis number was BB49K_22435, although this is open to debate. In fact, the initial batch of RS1600s were little more than Twin Cams with their engines ripped out in favour of the new BDA powerplant; the very first cars even retained Twin Cam badging.

As you'd expect, most of the RS1600's spec sheet remained unchanged from its predecessor's. It used a Type 3 four-speed gearbox with 2000E ratios, mated to the Twin Cam's rear axle. The suspension, brakes and 13in wheels were all the same beefed-up, Lotus Cortina-derived items. The bodyshell was always Type 49, compete with hand-welded strengthening, flared front wheelarches and circular headlamps.

Inside the RS1600 were the plush Escort GT seats, carpets and six-dial instruments – with the Twin Cam's silver surround and 140mph speedo, naturally. Likewise, a host of options and accessories were offered, allowing purchasers to produce an off-the-shelf rally winner.

The RS1600 went on sale during April 1970, by which time over 100 had been built. Production continued until August 1970, and Group 2 motorsport homologation was achieved the following month. It's estimated that 295 RS1600s were built at Halewood; each car was finished in white, and wore a chassis number beginning with BB49.

From October 1970, RS1600 assembly was transferred to the new AVO (Advanced Vehicle Operations) facility in Essex, with the first car officially rolling off the lines on 2 November 1970. Technically, the RS1600's chassis number now began with BFAT, but in the early days a small number were stamped with the Halewood letters BBAT; the engine code was always L5.

AVO RS1600s were supplied from Halewood as painted bodies with fully-furnished interiors before being treated to

The RS badge and wide rear wheels give the game away, but everything else looks like a lesser model. The reversing lights became standard in 1971 and the back bumper gained the centre cutout during December 1972.

FACTORY-ORIGINAL SPORTING MK1 ESCORTS

Negative camber? Just a bit! The RS1600's tyre-scrubbing stance certainly sharpened its steering and cornering precision.

their uprated underpinnings. Although the RS was now available in a variety of colours – namely Ermine White, Sunset Red and Maize Yellow – its trim had been downgraded to L level with inferior seats and rubber floor mats.

Still, a series of upgrades and extras saved the day, including the Clubman Pack (ready to rally), Custom Pack (ready for everyday comfort) and Race Pack (er, ready to race). From 1972 there was even the option to have your RS1600 kitted out to your exact specifications, thanks to the Special Build Programme.

As a production car, the RS1600 lived in the glory of its competition counterpart. And, while Ford's rally drivers were wiping the floor with their opposition, the quest for power brought bigger and better components. Most notable was the Brian Hart alloy cylinder block of February 1972, which allowed an increase in cylinder capacity to two litres. By October 1972, the changes filtered down to the production RS1600; from chassis number BFATM_00112, every RS1600's common-or-garden Kent cast iron cylinder block was replaced by a light alloy unit.

Alongside the enhanced engine came a comprehensive trim upgrade, returning the RS1600 to its earlier levels of padded seats and carpets. Sports steel wheels and hazard warning flashers were also added to the spec list.

The RS1600 continued in production until November 1974, with sales gradually slipping thanks to the introduction of the more user-friendly and reliable RS2000. A total of over 1,100 RS1600s were built by Ford (the most accurate guess is 1,154), including around 100 knock-down kits supplied to South Africa in 1972 and a number of left-hand-drive examples. No RS1600 was built for the German market but several were created at Boreham for competiton use, bearing non-BFAT numbers. Ford's official final RS1600 chassis number was BFATP_00043.

But that wasn't the end of the RS1600. With fuel injection and fancy internals, circuit racing BDA-engined Escorts were already producing 280bhp. Their rally-winning RS1600 counterparts remained active until replaced by the Mk2 RS1800 in 1975. Underneath the skin it was all but identical to the RS1600, securing the Escort's status as one of rallying's most successful cars of all time.

Plain and simple, the basic RS1600 had no fancy decals or accoutrements. The front wheels sat well forward in the arches thanks to the AVO anti-roll bar.

ESCORT RS1600

Engine – Block, Head and Sump

This is where the magic happened. The centrepiece of Ford's RS1600 rally weapon was its revolutionary Cosworth-designed BDA engine, based on a run-of-the-mill mass-production bottom end.

The cylinder block was changed a couple of times during production, beginning with a slightly modified thin-wall cast iron 691M from the humble Cortina 1600GT, complete with flywheel lightweight (26lb as opposed to 18lb of the non-GT engine). Developed from the 681F Crossflow, it was recognisable from the 691M-6015-J-A cast in raised lettering on the left-hand side of the crankcase.

From March 1970 until September 1970, a 691M cast iron block was used instead, recognisable from the 691M-6015-J-A cast into the left-hand side. From September 1970, the imperial 691M was replaced by the metric 1600cc Crossflow as the BDA's base – now a 711M cast iron block with T5 cast under the exhaust manifold; it was also identifiable by 711M-6015-B-A cast onto the left-hand side.

Finally, from October 1972 (RS1600 chassis number ATM.00112) onwards, all BDAs featured an H721F Brian Hart alloy block with steel cylinder liners and identical dimensions to previous models. The casting number read H721F-6010-A-A; a Ford oval was found on the block below the inlet manifold and between the core plugs under the exhaust manifold.

Despite using regular 1599cc Crossflow con rods (along with special alloy pistons with valve cutouts), the BDA's capacity was quoted as 1601cc for motorsport classification.

A Tuftrided five-bearing cast iron crankshaft was used,

From October 1972 the RS1600 featured a Brian Hart alloy block, with H721F-6010-A-A cast onto the crankcase.

with Vandervell heavy-duty lead-indium bearings and no crankshaft damper. The compression ratio was 10.0:1.

What made the BDA special was its aluminium 16-valve DOHC cylinder head, with two siamesed inlet ports and a pair of siamesed exhaust ports per cylinder. The casting housed valves in hardened seats, above which the camshaft carrier contained two cams. The head was revised slightly in September 1973 alongside a more efficient breather system (which also introduced a new front cover, an additional oil hose and deleted the brass restrictor in the cylinder block face).

The BDA featured four valves per cylinder, with inlet faces measuring 30.9mm and exhaust 27.4mm. Its unique twin overhead cams were driven by a reinforced nylon single-row internally-toothed belt with 146 teeth.

The RS1600's 1.6-litre BDA powerplant nestled within the mildly modified Escort engine bay. Like the Twin Cam, the RS1600's engine mounts angled it off-centre.

A BDA being fettled at Aveley around 1972. Look closely and you'll make out the thin red horizontal stripe on the lower radiator hose.

Atop the BDA sat a rectangular cam cover in a hammered pale-blue finish, with bare alloy FORD lettering embossed above each cam bank. Genuine covers had the letters BDA cast inside, which was lacking on inferior aftermarket replicas. A three-eared stainless steel filler cap was fitted at the front of the cam cover; early production engines had the Twin Cam's cap retaining wire connected to the right-hand front rocker cover bolt but this was omitted on later BDAs.

The cam belt cover was made from a black/dark grey bakelite-type material; it had two upper fixings and one at the bottom.

Like the Twin Cam, the RS1600 had round rubber engine mounts to angle it askew in the engine bay; identical to parts used on the Mexico, the offside mount was longer. Some early RS1600s (notably those converted from unsold Twin Cams) used the Twin Cam's engine stabiliser bar bolted to a reinforcing plate on the passenger-side bulkhead.

The RS1600 also used the same steel 3.96-litre big-wing sump, crudely welded and painted semi-gloss black. Its dipstick was taken from the Twin Cam – similar to the 1600cc Crossflow but with the minimum mark further up.

The BDA's oil pump flowed 5.72 litres per minute, and was updated in autumn 1970 to accept a screw-on filter rather than the previous replaceable element. All RS1600s had an oil cooler adapter sandwiched between the pump and filter, complete with cooling radiator mounted upright in front of the water radiator, towards the nearside headlamp. It attached through the radiator fittings and with a small bracket bolted to the centre radiator support; pipework was fed between the radiator and offside inner wing.

ESCORT RS1600

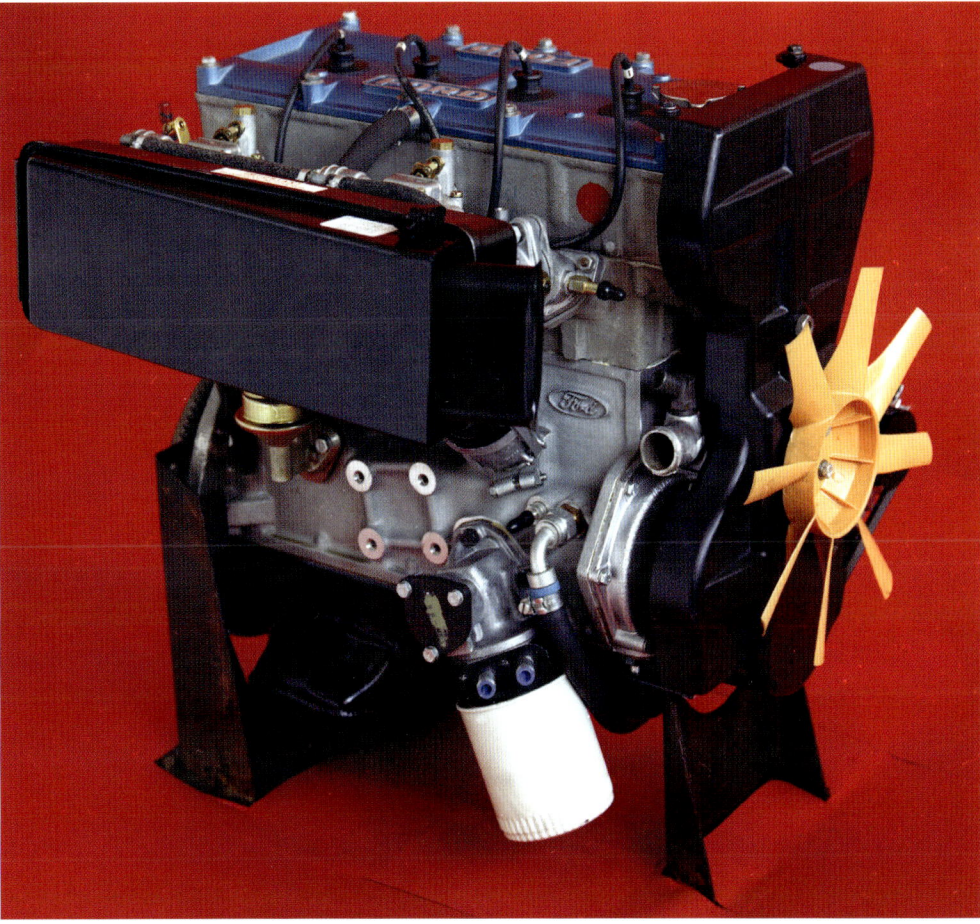

Ford studio shots of 1969 pre-production BDA, based on iron Crossflow 691M cylinder block. Note the early oil pump, non-production C40L dynamo and 18lb flywheel from the Cortina 1600GT.

Alloy-block BDA of 1972, wearing an unnaturally blue cam cover. Note the oil filler cap's lack of retaining wire and later oil pump.

Twin Cam-type big-header rad took care of the BDA's additional cooling requirements. Painted satin black, it wore a regular 13psi cap. Radiator top hose bore a horizontal red stripe.

Cooling System

The RS1600's high-capacity 12.5-pint (7.1-litre) cooling system was thanks to a radiator with extra-large header tank – like the Twin Cam's, featuring five notches across the faces of the tank and three along the bottom but with the angled metal brackets running straight down the centre of its sides rather than the edges. Painted satin black, the radiator had a regular 13psi Autolite or AC (after 1971) cap and an overflow outlet on the right-hand side, which on very early cars exited via a tube routed through a hole in the inner wing.

The radiator top hose had a horizontal red stripe; it ran to an alloy thermostat housing on the top left-hand side of the cylinder head above the exhaust manifold. Wire clips rather than Jubilee tytpes were usually fitted.

The BDA's water pump was similar to that of a Kent engine but slightly shallower. It had an eight-blade 12in fan in orangey-yellow plastic.

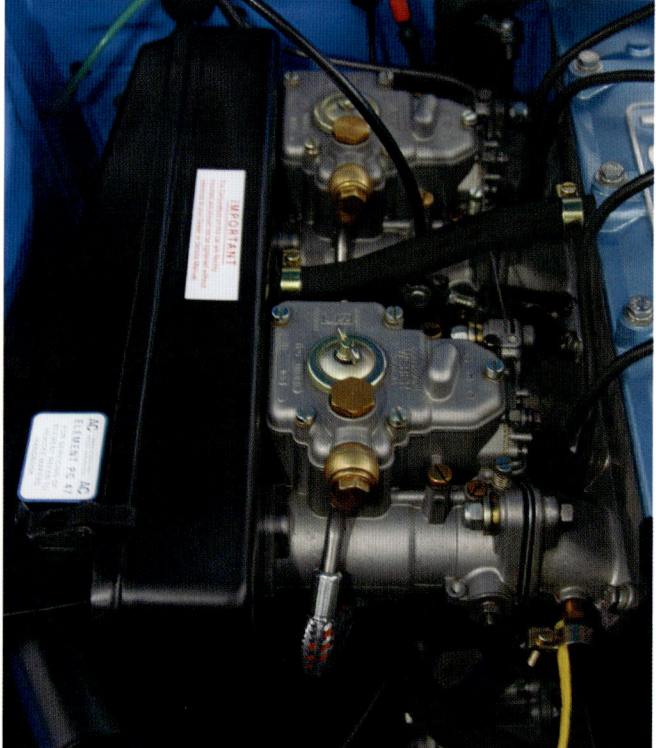

Dell'orto 40 DHLAE carburettors (above) replaced the RS1600's previous Weber 40DCOE 48s (right) in April 1972. All mated to the same clipped-together satin black air box.

Fuel System

Feeding fuel into the barking BDA was a pair of twin-choke side-draught carburettors on an alloy inlet manifold – unlike the Twin Cam, cast separately from the cylinder head. Early UK-spec RS1600s ran two Weber 40DCOE 48s; each had a metal identification tag attached to a float chamber screw plus a code on the flange where it met the inlet manifold; original carbs were Italian (not Spanish) made.

Exported RS1600s and all built from April 1972 onwards had Dell'orto 40 DHLAE carburetors. The satin black air box remained the same, its two halves clipped together and containing a paper filter.

A mechanical fuel pump was mounted on the right-hand side of the engine and operated by an auxiliary shaft. An AC pump (as fitted to the Twin Cam) was used with Weber carbs, which was swapped in April 1972 to a Mexico-type fuel pump.

Exhaust System

Right-hand-drive RS1600s had a tubular steel four-into-two-into-one exhaust manifold, while the four-branch fitted to left-hand-drive cars was of a four-into-one design; this part was carried over to all RS1800s.

The RS1600's large-bore exhaust system was made from mild steel, painted silver/grey. It featured a round centre silencer and oval rear box, with a double-loop rear silencer hanger welded onto the rearmost chassis rail, wrapped under the tailpipe and supported by two O-shaped rubbers.

Ignition and Electrical System

The RS1600's distributor was the Twin Cam's Lucas 23D440953A with mechanical advance and 6,500rpm rev limit. Motorcraft AG12 spark plugs were fitted until May 1974, when Motorcraft AGR12s were installed instead.

Cranking over the BDA lump was a job normally entrusted to a Lucas M35G starter, superseded in October 1972 by the Lucas M35J. Early cars used the Twin Cam solenoid setup, mounted high on the bulkhead alongside the brake/clutch reservoir. AVO machines had the solenoid moved down to

Tubular steel four-into-two-into-one exhaust manifold, as found on right-hand-drive RS1600s; left-hookers had a four-into-one design.

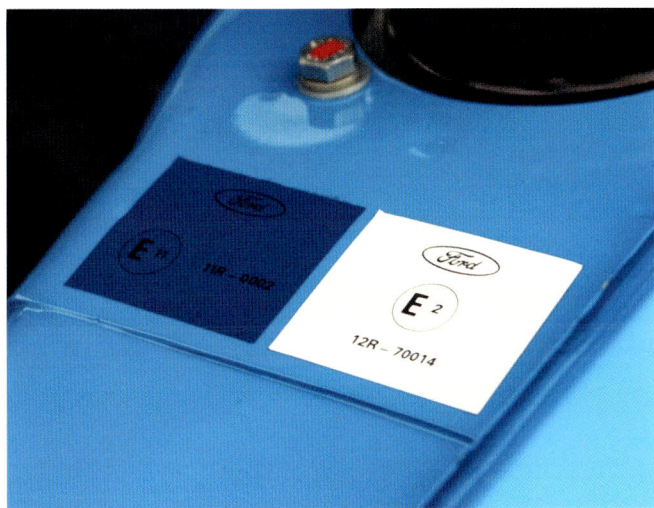

Blue and white lighting stickers were a frequent fitment to the strut tops of RS1600s when halogen headlamps were specified.

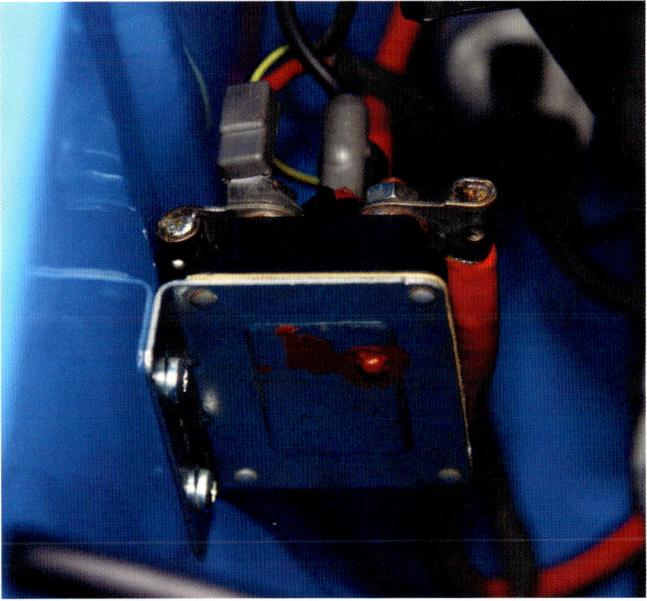

This flat-type starter solenoid was found towards the front of the offside inner wing. Around October 1972 it was swapped for a round version, mounted in the same position.

Lucas 6RA fused headlight relay was fitted to the RS1600's nearside inner wing, fed by grey-taped wiring from the main loom.

the inner wing, with the early flat type replaced around October 1972 by the Lucas round version. RS1600s with an optional (or cold-climate) pre-engaged starter motor had a direct-mounted solenoid. A boot-mounted Motorcraft 38Ah battery provided the power, substituted for a 57Ah in cold climates.

Initial RS1600 prototypes were equipped with dynamos but production models had a Lucas TRS 17ACR 35-amp alternator in silver with a black plastic back housing. It was mounted on a straight bar on the lower left-hand side of the engine, with a white nylon adjuster bracket.

An RS1600's wiring loom was similar to mainstream Escorts of the period, wrapped in grey tape and often featuring a paper tag strapped just beneath bulkhead entry into the fuse box. RS1600s were always fitted with the later-type Escort seven-fuse setup with clear plastic cover. Screwed onto the passenger-side bulkhead, it had internal connectors plus an extra lower spade terminal for accessories.

The ballasted ignition coil was identical to the part used on the Mexico, in a stock Escort bracket.

Transmission

Like the Twin Cam and subsequent Mexico, the RS1600 used a 2000E gearbox – the common name for Ford's Type 3 four-speed with three-rail shift mechanism and remote change.

The cast iron gearbox casing (painted black or very dark green) came from Halewood but was added to the RS1600 at Aveley, with suitable dressing back of the transmission tunnel, particularly near the uprated mounting brackets. The mounting looked similar to a standard Escort part, relieved to give extra access for the speedo cable. The tunnel stiffener was trimmed and a plate welded in place of the original gearstick hole to move the RS1600's lever further back. The chrome gearstick was found at the rear end of the tail casing. The reversing light switch was found in a tapped hole on the driver's side, in the gap between the front of the alloy top and the bellhousing.

Unlike the single-rail Cortina Type 3 'box with alloy tail housing, the Escort's was iron. It also had a separate bolt-on bellhousing (with 105E in the casting) and cast alloy top cover. Inside, there were 28 teeth on second gear and 23 on third – compared with the 21 of a standard wide-ratio unit and the 24 of a Lotus Cortina's gearbox. The proper 2000E ratios were first: 2.972:1, second: 2.010:1, third: 1.397:1, forth: 1.000:1, and reverse: 3.324:1.

A hydraulic Borg and Beck 8.09in diaphragm-spring single dry plate clutch was connected to the engine bay-mounted master cylinder by a pushrod. A short red flexible hydraulic clutch pipe was attached to a fitting on the bulkhead, with a rigid steel pipe following the bellhousing (affixed to the rear

FACTORY-ORIGINAL SPORTING MK1 ESCORTS

RS1600 top mounts were satin black, swapping from the bulbous early type to these waisted mounts from 1973.

of the engine with two big P-clips through the bellhousing bolts) before connecting into the slave cylinder.

The RS1600 featured a single-piece propshaft, without the central support connecting it to the floorpan. Most cars had a 3.777:1 differential in a satin black Timken rear axle (which had revised damper mounting points from November 1973) with uprated half-shafts. But, of course, Ford's competitions department offered several special build options, including Atlas rear axle, ZF five-speed gearbox and Salisbury limited-slip differential.

Steering and Suspenison

Based so closely on the Escort Twin Cam, the RS1600's underpinnings were almost identical. Its Capri-sourced satin black Macpherson strut front suspension had a green colour code, with Armstrong oil-filled damper inserts, a rubber bump stop and shroud covering the piston rod.

The dampers remained largely unchanged until 1973, when the piston diameter was altered to accompany new smaller top mounts with waisted middles, rather than the previous tiered type. According to parts lists, the dampers were swapped in November 1973 and the top mounts from June 1974 (along with another damper revision) but RS1600s were certainly seen with waisted mounts much earlier during 1973.

The suspension top mounts were satin black, with coloured paint splashes on each nut to confirm they'd been tightened by the factory to the correct torque settings.

RS1600 front coil springs were 5.3in diameter, rated at 100lb and dabbed with a green paint splash. The end of each coil was coated in black plastic.

Underside of RS1600, showing stone deflector, rear axle and multi-leaf springs. Underseal was commonly applied from new, and enabled the survival of many fortunate Escorts.

Like its predecessor, the RS1600 used a 20mm front anti-roll bar, mounted wider than standard and equipped with round, black rubber bushes from the Twin Cam. The front crossmember (shared with the Mexico) was essentially similar to a normal Escort part but reworked on the RS1600 for negative camber. It's possible that some late RS1600s received RS2000-type strengthening plates around the crossmember welds. A six-tooth pinion Burman steering rack with 17.5:1 ratio bolted to the crossmember. Pretty much everything underneath was covered in satin black paint.

A similar story continued on the RS1600's rear end. Black 51mm-wide semi-elliptic 97lb three-leaf springs (with blue and red colour code) were held on U-bolts over the back axle. A moulded rubber pad and metal U-shaped saddle sat between spring and axle to keep everything in place. If Ford's parts lists are to be believed, the RS1600 took on the RS2000's 85lb leaves during October 1973; by this point, of course, very few standard RS1600s were being produced anyway.

Naturally, a pair of radius rods located the RS1600's rear axle. They were altered from straight (well, there was a slight bend in the middle) to angled arms in October 1973, when the rear shock absorbers switched from 65.5-degree inclined Armstrong hydraulic telescopic oil-filled dampers to vertical types; the rear axle mountings were also altered to fit. Each was black with a yellow and white identification code. Early models had a black shock absorber mounting beam underneath, but the tops of later dampers instead protruded through the boot floor. There was no rear anti-roll bar.

Masses of suspension upgrades were available for the RS1600 from Rallye Sport dealers, optional from the factory or as part of the Special Build Programme. For example, the Clubman Pack offered uprated springs, gas dampers and roller bearing front top mounts fitted at AVO. Meanwhile, Ford's competitions department accessories list included a quicker steering rack and even a rear turret kit for serious rallying. Needless to say, without original paperwork it's impossible to guarantee the exact suspension settings of any RS1600 before it left the showroom.

Brakes

Stopping a screaming rally-bred 16-valve monster was no easy task for 1970 saloon car technology, but the RS1600 retained Capri/Twin Cam-sourced anchors throughout its production run.

Girling 9.625in front discs and pads were used, along with Girling 16P calipers; each had 54mm pistons, imperial fittings, big dust seals, a pale gold finish and satin black disc guards. From February 1972 the calipers were swapped for visually very similar Girling 16PBs.

RS1600 rear brake drums were 9x1.75in Girling HL3As until around June 1973, when supply difficulties often led to the use of Lockheed 9in assemblies instead.

Bilstein dampers were a very useful option; pre-October 1973 inclined shocks were mated to this black beam under the boot floor.

Early RS1600s used a Girling Powerstop AHV 550 Mk2A remote servo, positioned on a triangular silver bracket at the nearside front of the engine bay in place of the regular Escort's battery tray. The Mk2A servo had a semi-gloss black body with flat silver front cover bolted on. A steel connection

Girling Powerstop AHV 550 Mk2B remote servo, as fitted from 1972. The connection pipe was now rubber, running over the timing belt cover rather than the slam panel.

FACTORY-ORIGINAL SPORTING MK1 ESCORTS

The first Aveley RS1600 rolls off the line while Ford bigwigs share a joke. Note this Maize machine's Twin Cam-type steel wheels, starting handle grommet and oil cooler behind the grille.

pipe was clipped into place across the bonnet slam panel's rear edge. Original factory photos never showed a model identification sticker on the RS1600's servo, so it's doubtful they were ever used.

The servo was updated around January 1972 with the 550 Mk2B remote servo, featuring a black two-piece body and rubber connection pipe running over the engine timing belt cover rather than the slam panel.

Left-hand-drive RS1600s had neither of these servos; instead they used the same Girling Hydrovac in-line unit found on post-October 1972 Escort Mexicos.

RS1600 brake lines comprised Bundy mild steel tubing and ribbed flexible rubber hoses, with metal clamps and UNF fittings.

Wheels and Tyres

RS1600s rolled on a variety of steel or alloy wheels, depending on build date and options specified.

Halewood-made RS1600s and the first Aveley cars came with Lotus Cortina/Twin Cam plain steel wheels; painted silver, they were fitted with regular Escort stainless steel domed hub caps and UNF open-ended wheel nuts wound onto studs with dished ends. In June 1971 they were swapped for 5.5x13in pressed steel ventilated disc wheels – essentially the same as before, but now featuring cooling slots on their faces.

From September 1972 until September 1973 the standard RS1600 wore these 5.5x13in Silver Fox-painted spoke-style sports steels. Later models had the centres sprayed Pearl Grey, a period Ford colour.

RS four-spoke alloy wheels were often specified for road-going RS1600s. This is the proper colour scheme: polished rims, with dark grey spokes and backs. The RS centre caps pushed through from behind.

From September 1972 until September 1973 the RS1600 wore Silver Fox-painted 5.5x13in spoke-style sports steels, similar to the wheels found on lower-spec Escorts (which were always 5x13in), Cortinas (with different offset) and Capris. Lacking date stamps on the spokes, the RS wheels used 7/16 UNF chrome closed-ended nuts (as seen on the Escort Sport). After September 1973, the same sports steel wheels were updated with metallic Pearl Grey centres.

Alloy wheels were available as motorsport extras from launch, in the form of magnesium Tech Del Minilites, in sizes from 5.5x13in to 9.25x13in. But it wasn't until the RS four-spoke that alloys became a mainstream factory fitment. Launched in January 1971 and available through Rallye Sport dealers, the RS four-spoke alloy wheel became an optional extra on new RS1600s during March that year. Made by GKN Kent Alloys, they featured a 70mm centre hole, chrome and black RS caps (pushed through from behind), chrome nuts and valves.

Originally, their spokes were completely plain, but from around October 1972, the flat face within the spokes gave the 5.5Jx13 size and part number – H71AB-1007-A-C. The rims and spoke edges were polished but the spoke centres and rears of all Mk1 RS alloys were painted dark grey – not Pearl Grey, as is commonly assumed. April 1973 brought a dark grey centre cap.

From March 1971 the Special Build Programme and Rallye Sport dealers also offered 6x13in RS four-spoke alloys, again with chrome or grey centre caps depending on build date. Don't assume they were the same as the 6x13in four-spokes found on Mk2 Escorts, because later wheels featured a different offset and were stamped with H76 part numbers.

The first RS1600s wore India Autoband 165SR13 tyres, then Dunlop SP68s or SP44 rally tyres. After October 1972 low-profile 175/70HR13 rubber became standard, in Goodyear G800, Pirelli CN36, or Dunlop SP68 guise. When 6x13in alloys were specified, wider 185HR70x13s were used instead.

Body

With no lairy look-at-me stripes, the road-going RS1600's appearance was much like any other Escort. And while its slower AVO counterparts gained go-faster decals, the RS1600 simply got on with its job – of getting places quickly. Okay, a triple coachline came as part of the Custom Pack (from 16 October 1971) and a black vinyl roof was included in the Custom Pack after November 1973; hand-fitted after the bodywork was painted, the vinyl roof was attached with contact adhesive, had seams at either side and stopped above the door pillars.

Otherwise, the only telltale was a set of subtle badges, saying RS1600 in blue and silver on the front wings (admittedly, prototypes retained Twin Cam badges). Meanwhile, the boot lid wore a simple round blue-and-silver RS badge next to the Escort script on the right-hand side. In March 1973 it

Well-used Twin Cam-based RS1600 press machine. As you'll see, there's a non-dipping rear-view mirror and central jet for the windscreen washers.

By and large, only the passenger's door step featured a small Ford oval; the driver's side was usually blank.

Starting handle grommet was fitted until the hole was deleted around October 1973. Look closely and you'll see the RS1600's oil cooler radiator mounted vertically behind the grille.

FACTORY-ORIGINAL SPORTING MK1 ESCORTS

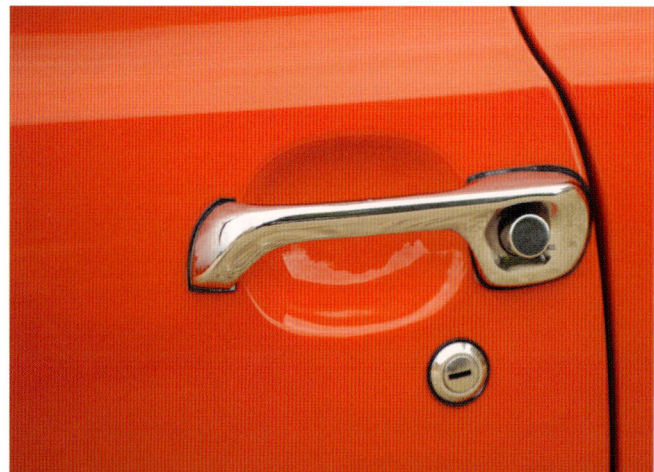

By the time of RS1600 production, all Escort bodyshells came with later-type handles and anti-burst locks.

A Lucas two-speed wiper motor was always used, along with stainless wiper blades. Many RS1600s left the factory with Trico Speedblades, but the parts shown are regular Escort kit.

was deleted in favour of a rectangular RS1600 badge (identical to the front wing badges) on the boot lid's left-hand side.

Of course, the RS1600's Type 49 two-door bodyshell meant front wings with flared wheelarch lips. It always came with a round-headlamp front panel, generally with starting handle hole (bunged with a black rubber grommet) until around October 1973. The Twin Cam's Escort van-sourced chromed quarter bumpers were fitted too.

A regular Escort aluminium radiator grille was present, with the usual bright metal alloy polished surround and satin black middle. It was attached with nine screws, and the bodywork behind the grille was painted satin black.

RS1600s almost always had the later-style Escort bonnet, although Twin Cam-based cars and any built before April

In Tawny Brown with RS four-spokes and gold triple coachline, this 1972 press shot of an early RS1600 Custom Pack has a small yellow and red sticker at the bottom of the windscreen, denoting a laminated version; toughened 'screens had a blue or green sticker instead.

No-nonsense cockpit of the RS1600 went through a variety of spec changes. This is the post-October 1972 layout, with padded GT-type seats.

Although early RS1600s had the Twin Cam's silver-faced instrument surround, most received plain black clocks, with flat faces rather than dished dials from January 1973. This car's imperial oil pressure gauge was replaced by bar readings in mid-1973.

changed from October 1972 until October 1973 for grey Beta cloth. After October 1973 the Custom Pack gave black RS recliners with round RS badges, chrome levers and optional roll top head rests. They were trimmed in black Beta cloth, with block pattern running vertically.

Back seats in an RS1600 were always linked to the fronts. Until October 1970 the cars had a GT-type contoured rear bench in black vinyl, replaced by a basic L-spec seat from the start of AVO production. After October 1972 it reverted to the padded bucket-effect.

Custom Pack RS1600s had cloth-trimmed rear seats to match the fronts but when a Clubman Pack or competitions department buckets were ordered, the back seat stayed standard.

RS1600 door cards were the padded Super-type until September 1970, when they were replaced by poverty-spec L-type parts; October 1972 saw them switched back. Rear quarter cards changed from black plastic to fibreboard after September 1970; all had push-round ashtrays but only Super trim levels featured plastic rear armrest extensions.

The RS1600's window winders and door release handles

FACTORY-ORIGINAL SPORTING MK1 ESCORTS

Contour seats were optional on the RS1600, here trimmed in pre-October 1972 grey herringbone. Note this RS1600's Springalex steering wheel, a very popular option.

were always the flat, textured type. Until August 1973 there were slimline internal lock buttons, but later cars had fatter mushroom-headed pins.

The RS1600 started life with the Twin Cam's silver-faced six-clock instrument surround with plastic-chrome rings and dished dials; after September 1970 the surround was black.

Twin Cam, RS1600 and early Mexico shared the same pedal box, with clutch and brake master cylinders mounted above. Note the silver accelerator lever and small, square pad.

The RS1600's AC-made instruments featured black faces and thin white lettering, white needles and chrome bosses. They comprised large 140mph speedometer (incorporating main beam warning light) and 8,000rpm rev counter (with 6,500rpm red line) plus small fuel gauge, battery charge indicator, oil pressure gauge and water temperature gauge; circular warning lights for alternator failure and direction indicators were mounted between the two main instruments.

After January 1973 the dished dials were swapped for flat-faced gauges with 130mph speedometer and 7,000rpm rev counter without a red line. Up to mid-1973 the oil pressure gauge had imperial lettering but it was phased out in favour of empty blocks with bar readings.

Early RS1600s featured a deep-dished 14in steering wheel as standard, which was generally swapped for a leather-rimmed Springalex with black or polished spokes. From January 1972 until around November 1972, the later Escort flat padded 'safety' three-spoke wheel with black leather rim and alloy/silver spokes was specified, but it's probable that all RS1600s contained a Springalex instead. Later cars had a flat, black RS three-spoke steering wheel with leather rim as standard.

A single column stalk was used for indicators, headlamp

Seat belts were a compulsory extra. The same stalks were used for later static three-point belts and inertia reels, with black plastic coating and silver push buttons. The handbrake lever was stock Escort. The chrome gear-stick and black plastic knob looked similar to an Escort GT's, but on the RS1600 reverse was marked back towards the driver's seat. It was also mounted further back in the transmission tunnel.

Leather-rimmed three-spoke steering wheel was standard-fit on RS1600s after winter 1972. It came compete with legendary RS-logo centre cap.

dipping/flashing and horn, with chrome button. There was a single-tone horn, but dual-tones were available (as usual, fitted behind the front grille, probably from September 1973).

Halewood-made RS1600s housed an early Escort dashboard layout, with swivelling, non-adjustable air vents (they rotated but had no flaps, so couldn't be turned off), lower fascia panel including ashtray with horizontal ribs, choke knob (black plastic, with silver and black insert) and chunky black plastic rocker switches with chromed plastic surrounds. The heater controls always had the same black plastic levers, alloy surround and black Mazak diagram.

Adjustable air vents and thinner rocker switches were fitted from October 1970, when the lower fascia panel was revised to the later Escort type; early cars had slots only to the right of the grained ashtray but from summer 1971 there were five holes in the panel, with blanking plates for unused positions. The usual switch layout, from right to left was: two-speed wiper, two-speed heater, brake test (where fitted), heated rear window (where fitted), hazard warning light (where fitted). Until December 1972 the heated rear windscreen switch warning light was red, after which it was amber. The headlamp switch was mounted under the main instruments, unless the car had an earlier dashboard (when it was near the ashtray).

FACTORY-ORIGINAL SPORTING MK1 ESCORTS

Black headlining was an AVO identifier, with Halewood-built RS1600s featuring white Lodestar pattern. The passenger sun visor gained a mirror as standard in October 1972.

RS1600 rear seats mirrored the style up front. Here is the black vinyl GT-type contoured rear bench.

Optional or dealer-supplied lamps and accessories required additional toggle or rocker switches; where fitted they were mounted in black plastic panels beneath the fascia. Likewise, an RS1600's optional radio would be slipped into a plastic housing affixed to the fascia or attached under the driver's or passenger's dashboard. A selection of push-button or manual radios and eight-track tape players was available; they were accompanied by a single Ford 2.5W speaker mounted under a round black speaker grille in the parcel shelf, with protective cover underneath. Along with the radios, aerials were often dealer-fitted, usually roof-mounted with a cable running inside a windscreen pillar. Speaker wiring would run beneath the rear seat and down the nearside inner sill.

From October 1972 the RS1600 was given hazard flashers as standard, complete with warning light on the dashboard. Alongside it sat the cigar lighter, which would be moved to the centre console on late-spec Custom Pack cars (when wood trim covered the dashboard hole).

No centre console was fitted to the RS1600 as standard, but two different types were offered. From October 1970 a black plastic coin tray was optional (as fitted to the later 1300E, complete with PVC gaiter and detachable ice scraper), plus pod-mounted round Kienzle clock with orange hands as an accessory. This console was included with the Custom Pack until October 1973. After this date, the RS1600 Custom Pack came with full height RS2000-type console, including clock (black bezel and red/orange hands), radio aperture, slots/holes for a cigar lighter and spot light switches. At the same time, the Custom Pack added polished wood veneer dashboard cappings, which were never fitted to RS1600 doors. It also included a fold-down glovebox panel within a surround screwed to the passenger-side under-dash shelf.

Another popular option was a Butlers flexible dash-mounted map reading light – it came as part of the Custom Pack from October 1971 until being transferred to the Rallye Pack in November 1973.

Under the RS1600's dashboard was a pair of black cardboard parcel shelves, attached with plastic-headed brass clips into black metal brackets. Beneath them on each side was a black cardboard kick panel, with a vinyl map pocket stitched onto the driver's side.

The RS1600 used a Twin Cam pedal box with clutch and brake master cylinders mounted above. Early models had three black pedal levers with block-pattern rubbers, while later cars had a silver accelerator lever and small square pad with rectangular block pattern. A floor-mounted satin black button to the left of the pedal box was for the foot-operated windscreen wash/wipe.

A black, loop-pile, two-piece carpet was fitted to the earliest RS1600s, but the first Aveley-built machines (from September 1970) made do with a black one-piece rubber floormat instead. In August 1972 the RS1600 reverted to carpets, now a black one-piece looped-pile version. The original October 1971 Custom Pack also added a black looped-pile carpet, along with sound insulation kit of absorbent panels at known reverberation points. The carpet changed slightly in November 1973 to make way for floorpan alterations.

Above the RS1600's transmission tunnel sat a 2000E chrome gearstick and black plastic knob (similar to a normal Escort's but with reverse marked back to the right and towards the driver's seat), black metal handbrake lever with bare steel push button and seat belt clasps or stalks.

The belts were a compulsory extra – static Wingards with two-handed fasteners and black, textured metal clasps, Wingard inertia reels (with large silver buckles mounted on the transmission tunnel) or the late-type inertia-reels from

Unless he saw these badges, the average 1970s sports car driver would be asking his mechanic why a little Ford Escort left him standing. Even then, the subtlety of the RS logos meant the RS1600 was a tiger in a tabby's clothing.

1970 had an early bonnet with single washer nozzle hole. The bonnet release was operated remotely from a lever underneath the dashboard, which swapped from passenger's to driver's side in late 1970.

Like other Escorts, all but the very earliest RS1600s had copper washer nozzles sticking through the riveted and screwed scuttle vents. A self-parking Lucas two-speed windscreen wiper motor was fitted, normally along with twin-wire Trico Speedblades but possibly standard Escort wipers if factory supplies were low. A wiper arm spoiler was a dealer accessory from November 1973.

AVO RS1600s were usually (if not always, from July 1971 onwards) equipped with a Triplex laminated front windscreen as standard but it's probable that early cars had

RS1600s featured a flush-mounted petrol cap rather than the early protruding neck. A chrome locking cap was a dealer accessory, sometimes with the black plastic centre shown here.

Plain glass was fitted in the back of a standard RS1600, although a heated rear screen was part of the Custom Pack from October 1971.

This RS1600 is lacking its original rain gutter trims, which risk paintwork damage when refitted after restoration work.

Twin Cam-based, Halewood-built RS1600s had an early-style chassis plate, unusual radiator overflow and passenger-side bonnet release. Cars equipped with the Mk2A remote servo had this steel connection pipe running across the slam panel.

toughened 'screens from the factory. Toughened windscreens wore a blue/green Triplex sticker, while laminated versions had yellow and red.

The rear windscreen was plain unless a Custom Pack was specified, when a heated rear window was fitted. It was optional on non-Custom Pack cars after September 1970 and eventually made standard – probably around April 1974.

The RS1600's side windows were plain, although tinted windows were a rare export option. Opening front quarter lights were sometimes fitted to overseas-bound RS1600s, and optional in the UK. Opening rear quarter windows were available at extra cost from September 1970. Window rubbers were the usual black Escort items with chrome inserts, while the rear side rubbers swapped from plain to ridged – probably from around September 1972.

Like mainstream Escorts of the period, RS1600s had later-style doors with separate locks and two-stage latches. The quarter window pillars were body-coloured until October 1973, after which they were satin black. The handles always looked identical, but were replaced by Mk2 van-style versions with hollow backs from 1974. Door and boot locks shared the same key, which never corresponded to the steering column lock. The keys were in an all-metal finish.

Door mirrors were never standard, but could be factory-fitted when specified or for foreign markets. Aluminium scuff plates were attached to the sills, and a small metal Ford oval in blue and silver lived on the passenger-side door step – although sometimes they were also found on the driver's side. Meanwhile, RS1600 rear wheelarches were crudely (probably with a hammer) rolled under by AVO to clear the chunky tyres.

Everything else externally was standard Escort. A stainless steel trim was attached to the rain gutters on either side of the roof, which changed to chrome-look plastic trim in early 1973. There was a flush body-coloured petrol cap (a chrome locking cap was a dealer accessory). The chrome rear bumper was straight until December 1972, when it received a central cutout for the single-bulb number plate light.

Underbonnet

The RS1600's howling BDA powerplant was fitted into a mildly modified Escort engine bay. The inner wings were regular reinforced Type 49 items, complete with spot-welded suspension top plates. The only adjustments were made to the bulkhead – typical of an AVO product, it featured some rather, er, artistic modifications.

At the back of the engine, a section of bulkhead lip was cut and rolled down by hand (presumably with a big hammer) and roughly coated with seam sealer. Normally there was no bulkhead drain tube but some early RS1600s were fitted with a Twin Cam part; likewise the engine stabiliser bar.

A CV combined brake and clutch reservoir was mounted on the RS1600's bulkhead, sitting on a crudely-welded body-coloured bracket and attached with a screw clamp. Twin feeds were taken through the bulkhead from the reservoir to master cylinders on the pedal brackets, using a pair of rubber hoses in black with a yellow horizontal stripe.

Beside the pipes the RS1600's speedometer cable ran through the upper bulkhead within a black grommet; occasionally it was held on a bracket attached to the bulkhead. Further towards the offside, a Twin Cam throttle cable was clipped to a body-coloured bracket welded (or screwed) to

Combined brake and clutch reservoir sat on body-coloured bracket. Note the throttle cable and speedometer cable running through grommets in the bulkhead. The twin hoses ran to master cylinders above the pedal box; originally, each had a horizontal yellow stripe

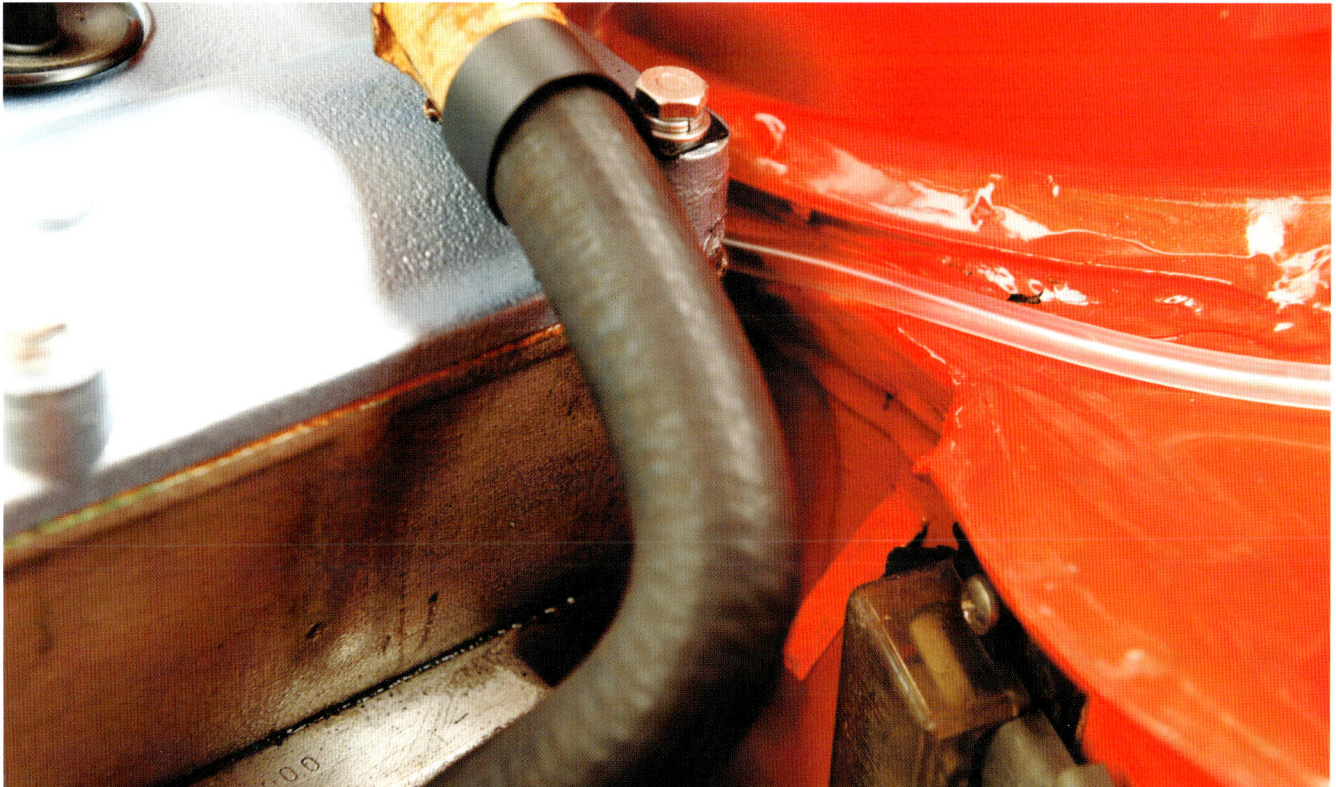

Engine too big to fit the hole? No worries: AVO's trick was to hack away the bulkhead lip and slap on a load of seam sealer. Problem solved.

the bulkhead; on some cars this was a separate bracket fastened to the rearmost strut top bolt.

Further down the bulkhead, the RS1600 had a sealed clutch cable tube on the brake reinforcement plate but after mid-1971 a flush automatic transmission-style plate was used instead. The choke cable ran through the bulkhead in a hole beside the heater hoses. The brake pedal-to-servo hole was sealed.

When it comes to RS1600s, there's no set rule about which washer fluid reservoir was fitted from the factory. By and large, RS1600s received the original off-white 'cheese wedge' washer bottle attached to the nearside bulkhead on three body-coloured pins – possibly because Ford felt the later-type washer bottle would be affected by its proximity to the BDA engine. Often, AVO would weld on the pins, even when the bodyshell had provision for a later bottle, such as a spot-welded bracket for the late-model Escort bottle, or screws for the type of reservoir fitted to regular Escorts from around 1970 until the start of 1972.

That said, even early RS1600 press cars from the same production run had a mixture of bottles, so who really knows what happened?

From January 1974 a Trico electric washer motor was an optional extra; it would be screwed onto the heater dome flat spot and operated by a dash-mounted flick switch.

Halewood-built RS1600s had a radiator overflow exiting through the offside inner wing, along with early-style chassis plate (which was moved to the slam panel for AVO production). The very first RS1600s also featured a deflector panel in front of the radiator.

Like lower models, the unpainted bonnet prop had a clear/white plastic retaining clip connecting it to the bonnet. A release cable ran along the nearside inner wing with handle underneath the passenger-side dashboard; from late 1970 it was swapped to the driver's side, and a black plastic-coated cable was fitted around the end of 1972.

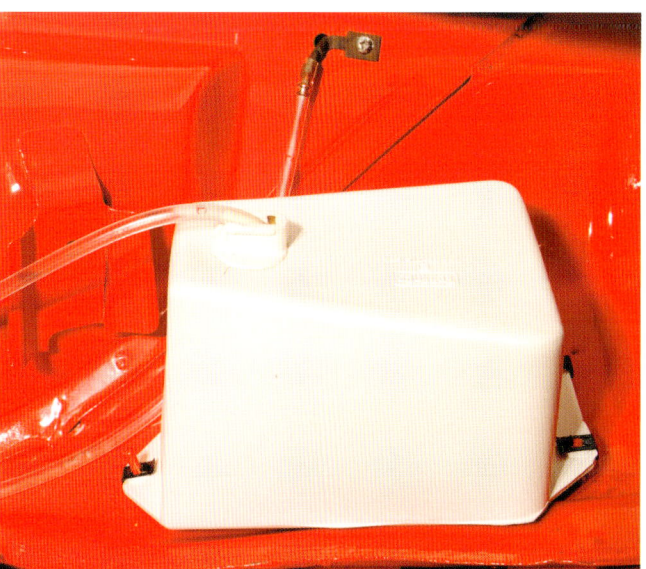

Cheese-wedge washer bottle was fitted to the vast majority of RS1600s, long after mainstream Escorts switched to slide-on tanks – as can be seen by the bracket spot-welded to this car's bulkhead before the bodyshell arrived at Aveley.

The familiar Lucas 6RA fused headlight relay was fitted to the RS1600's nearside inner wing. Its wiring ran from the main loom in grey tape, while a short brown earth wire attached to one of the relay screws.

Separate blue and white lighting stickers were a frequent fitment to the strut tops of RS1600s when halogen headlamps were specified; later cars had a single white sticker.

Like other Escorts, the RS1600 usually had a white-and-black coolant sticker on the slam panel (normally the nearside, but not necessarily) and a negative earth sticker attached somewhat randomly – maybe to an inner wing or in the boot near the battery.

Lighting

Round headlamps were always found on the front of an RS1600 – in Lucas 75/50W 7in circular sealed-beam form as standard until September 1973, followed by Cibie H4 55/55W sealed-beam halogens (as found on the RS2000). Twin-bulb quartz-iodine Carello (until December 1971) or Cibie (until October 1973) "biode" headlamp conversions were also optional. Giving 110 watts on main beam, the Cibies had a separate reflector positioned against the main reflector.

Underneath the headlamps were regular Escort indicators,

Halogen headlamps were commonly specified as optional extras. These rare Cibie Biodes were favoured by rally boys for their superior performance.

with amber plastic lenses and chrome trim. In late 1974 the chrome was dropped on some cars. Several export markets had clear white lenses, which were also available from British Ford dealers.

The Rally Lighting Pack offered twin Cibie quartz iodine long-range driving lamps and quartz fog lamps (with grey backs) on sturdy brackets, which became part of the Clubman Pack from July 1971.

RS1600s featured the usual Escort back lights with chrome surrounds and black plastic seals. A single-bulb number plate lamp was mounted on the rear panel but export cars had twin bulbs.

Reversing lights weren't fitted until October 1970, after which they were an optional extra. From early 1971 the styled-in units became standard fit – Ford-branded with plastic lenses, stainless lens surrounds and black plastic backs.

A rear fog lamp was a dealer option, mounted to the driver's-side rear bumper bracket; it could come with a toggle switch or an official Ford rocker switch.

An RS1600's interior light was the regular Escort courtesy lamp operated by buttons in the A-pillars. The switches were swapped in March 1972 from protruding pins to a smaller, round, rubber-encased type.

Interior

An RS1600's cabin was always black (admittedly, the doors and rear quarter metalwork was painted body colour) but trim levels were swapped on a relatively regular basis.

Halewood-built RS1600s were little more than re-engined Twin Cams, so the first cars had full Super/GT-style interior with early dashboard and switch layout. They also featured padded fixed-back PVC seats with smooth vinyl outer sections and perforated inners; they tipped forward using a round button on the plastic-surrounded base at the rear of the cushion. From August 1970 the lever was moved up to the backrest.

When production switched to Aveley in October 1970, the RS1600's trim was downgraded to L-spec. Its black PVC front seats were the flimsy fully-tilting types, complete with backrest-mounted lever.

From October 1972 until October 1973 the front seats became fully-tilting padded XL-type items with levers on their backrests; after October 1973 their bases were fixed to the floor but the backrests tipped forward.

Contour seats were optional on the RS1600, generally available from Ford's competitions department as a non-matching pair of fixed bucket seat for the driver and recliner for the navigator. Trim options were black vinyl, grey herringbone (until October 1972), grey Beta cloth (October 1972 until October 1973) or black Beta cloth thereafter.

The optional Custom Pack of October 1971 included low-back Contour semi-bucket seats in grey herringbone cloth,

ESCORT RS1600

around March 1973, which had stalks on the tunnel featuring black plastic coating and silver push buttons.

Above an RS1600 driver's head was usually a black roof lining, although Halewood-built RS1600s had Cortina white Loadstar pattern headlining with matching sun visors. Later visors were black vinyl; the passenger side received a vanity mirror with the Custom Pack, although this was made standard from October 1972.

The first RS1600s featured a white non-dipping rear-view mirror, although an ivory/white dipping version was available as a dealer accessory. The dipping mirror was standard from September 1970 – generally a grey Wingard shaped mirror, followed in October 1973 by a black dipping mirror with black stalk. The few RS1600s built after October 1974 may have received a black Mk2-type flat-sided mirror head on a black Mk1 stalk.

Halewood-built machines featured a pair of white coat hooks at the tops of their B-pillars, while the first AVO cars had three rear grab handles in black; the rear handles had black sliding hooks. Later models had only the two rear handles.

Like normal Escorts, the RS1600's rear parcel shelf gained larger domed screw caps in late 1971, and lost its metal edging strips in November 1973. It was always black cardboard.

Always matching the interior trim level, RS1600 door cards were XL-type (L-design shown here) from October 1972 onwards. At the door tops are the correct slimline door lock pins.

Full-size steel spare wheel took up most of the RS1600's boot compartment. It was secured with a long bolt through the boot floor.

FACTORY-ORIGINAL SPORTING MK1 ESCORTS

Normal Escort nine-gallon tank bolted into the right-hand rear wing. Early and late RS1600 petrol tanks were satin black, with primer grey used in the interim.

Inside Boot

Like the Twin Cam and early Mexico, the RS1600's boot compartment contained its battery on a tray in the spare wheel well, clamped in with a satin black bracket. A negative earth decal was often stuck to the nearby inner wing or wheelarch, sometimes at a wonky angle. It's likely that many early RS1600s left the factory with the Twin Cam's cardboard battery cover, which would then be topped with the negative earth sticker. The battery negative lead was earthed to the well, while the positive cable ran alongside the inner arch and down through a crudely-drilled hole in the boot floor, just in front of the back seat bulkhead. From there it went underneath the car and crossed the transmission tunnel above the propshaft, held in place with clips riveted to the floorpan.

On the opposite side, a nine-gallon petrol tank was bolted into the right-hand rear wing. Early cars had either primer grey or satin black tanks (press cars of various ages were photographed with both) but most later cars had grey. It's worth noting that even the black tanks were grey on the hidden side, sprinkled with black overspray.

The RS1600's Motorcraft battery lived on a tray in the spare wheel well; here's its original earth strap.

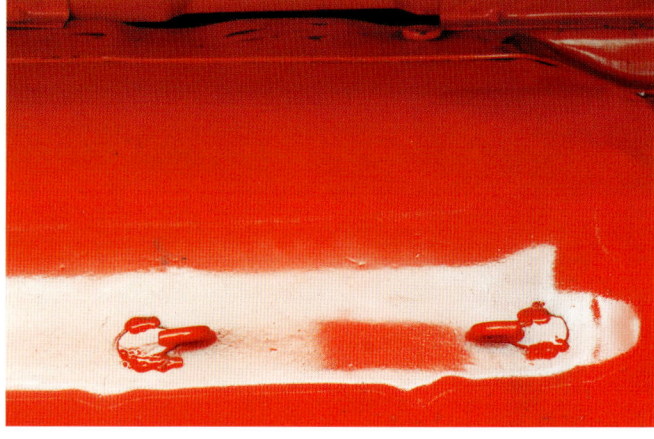

Body-coloured hooks were spot-welded to the boot floor and used to strap down the standard tool kit.

ESCORT RS1600

The usual negative earth sticker was often placed near to the battery – in this case a sensible spot on the inner wheelarch. Original decals were often fitted in a somewhat haphazard manner.

A spare 13in wheel (steel or alloy, depending on the rest of the car) was mounted to the boot floor with one long stud and nut through a bolt hole; this could be a wheel nut welded onto the bolt or a long stud, threaded on both ends.

Body-coloured hooks welded to the floor were used to strap down the standard tool kit – a normal grey vertical jack (mid-blue with red-on-white sticker in later cars) and satin black wheel brace in fawn muslin bag. The regular Escort black Hardura rubberized carpet was fitted, along with holes for the hooks; the mat became shorter in October 1973 when the upper damper mountings poked through the floor.

The boot floor was body-coloured, bearing eight studs for the satin black stone deflector fitted underneath. The guard was dropped as standard after 1972, and optional thereafter, but the bolts were always in place.

A boot light was standard throughout production, a boot latch cover may have found its way onto some of the very last RS1600s, and the rear light protectors were black plastic until autumn 1974, after which they were clear.

Colour Schemes

Colour	Code	Introduced	Discontinued	Coachline colour (with Custom Pack)
Ermine White	B	January 1970	July 1972	Red
Maize Yellow	T	August 1970	July 1971	-
Sunset Red	J	August 1970	July 1972	White
Tawny Brown	S	August 1971	July 1972	Gold
Le Mans Green	M	August 1971	July 1973	Black
Electric/Monza Blue	U	August 1971	July 1973	White
Black	A	August 1971	January 1975	Gold
Daytona Yellow	T	August 1971	January 1975	Black
Copper Brown	7	August 1972	July 1973	Gold
Diamond White	B	August 1972	January 1975	Red
Sebring Red	N	August 1972	January 1975	Black
Stardust Silver	3	August 1973	January 1975	Black
Olympic Blue	E	August 1973	January 1975	Black
Modena Green	M	August 1973	January 1975	Black
Vista Orange	V	August 1974	January 1975	Black
Special order	Y			

FACTORY ORIGINAL SPORTING MK1 ESCORTS

ESCORT MEXICO

Maize Yellow was one of three colours offered to the first Mexico buyers – the others being Sunset Red and Ermine White. This July 1971 Mexico still sports its factory-fitted semi-matt black decals, and even the original "We brought it back from Mexico" rear windscreen sticker. A one-owner car until 2008, it was hardly used between 1978 and 2003. Apart from a new nearside front wing in 1974 and a driver's door skin in 1977 (both due to minor accidents), this Escort has never been welded. It was fitted with optional reversing lights from new, plus Springalex steering wheel, Cibie lamps and twin fuel tanks around 1972. Current owner Mark still has the Mexico's original purchase invoice, service book and handbook, along with Magard sump guard and Contour recliners, which were added when the car was just one month old. Mark recently stripped back Ziebart from the engine bay, revealing the original stickers, brake pipes and paintwork.

For the average Ford enthusiast, the Escort Mexico has an iconic status – a rallying superhero that was also king of the pub car park. In contrast, some hardcore Escort fans see the Mexico as the baby of the Rallye Sport range, little more than a run-of-the-mill Mk1 but with a Cortina engine. The reality? Well, it was a bit of both.

Introduced in November 1970, the Escort Mexico was named in celebration of Ford's victorious attack on the 1970 World Cup Rally – a tough six-week, 16,000-mile sprint from London to Mexico. Rather than running a fleet of frantic but fragile RS1600s or Twin Cams, Ford chose to forsake outright power in favour of reliability and easy upkeep. A set of seven well-proven Escort motorsport shells were fitted with uprated 1834cc versions of the simple overhead valve Kent Crossflow engine, pushing out 140bhp. Hannu Mikkola's now-famous FEV 1H finished the rally in top spot, followed by similar Escorts in third, fifth, sixth and eighth places.

ESCORT MEXICO

Finding a mint, low-mileage Mexico might sound impossible today, but when Mark Harper uncovered this one-owner Escort in 2008, it had recorded only 25,000 miles from new. Built in June 1974, this Sebring Red Mexico was ordered with delete-stripe option; it was dealer-fitted with Custom Pack and head rests before delivery.

Ziebart protection was applied soon after purchase, which no doubt helped the car's almost-perfect preservation. It's never been welded, retains all the factory-fitted panels and paintwork, even including the AVO-applied runs… Other than minor service parts, Mark has changed very little of his Mexico's originality. He's added the Ford mud flaps and headlamp protectors, plus period Dunlop SP Sport Aquajet tyres on refurbished steel wheels; the shade of grey's darker than standard, but everything else is spot on.

For the showrooms, Ford stayed faithful to the philosophy of installing an affordable mainstream motor into a purebred package. Yes, the Mexico's 1.6-litre powerplant was sourced from humdrum Fords of the period. And yes, it lacked an RS badge. But the rest of the car was pure Rallye Sport.

Built around the heavy-duty Type 49 bodyshell, the Mexico was the first all-new model developed by Ford's then-new Advanced Vehicle Operations facility at Aveley in Essex.

In fact, the phrase all-new model is a bit misleading – like its rallying ancestors, the Mexico was an RS1600 but for the bit under the bonnet, now an 86bhp 1599cc Crossflow from the Cortina GT. Everything else remained.

That meant a four-speed Type 3 2000E gearbox, identical to the RS1600's transmission. The suspension and brakes were essentially those developed for the Twin Cam from Lotus Cortina and Capri 3.0 components, while the 13in steel wheels were lifted from the Mk2 Lotus Cortina.

The Mexico's bodywork was identical to the RS1600, benefiting from the flared front wheelarches, Type 49 strengthening points and round-headlamp front end. Likewise, its purposeful interior offered little more than basic vinyl seats, rubber floor mats and the traditional six-dial instrumentation.

But that didn't detract from the Mexico's immediate success. Besides its innate driver appeal, a stroke of marketing genius developed a distinctive set of bold stripes that ran along the sides, over the roof and across the boot lid. This extrovert scheme was a delete option, but appealed to thousands of buyers who found the Mexico filled the perfect spot between everyday Escort GT and troublesome RS1600.

Like its bigger brother, the Mexico was built on the Aveley production line, where painted and trimmed shells were delivered by transporters from Halewood before being fitted with all the important AVO components – including a Swansea-sourced back axle and the Halewood-made gearbox. Officially, the first Mexico chassis number was BFATK_23264.

At the start of 1971 around 70 Mexicos had been manufactured, but by the end of that year another 1,800 were on the roads. The initial colours of Sunset Red, Ermine White and Maize Yellow had been joined by a full range of shades, while an important batch of options were now available.

The July 1971 Clubman Pack in particular pinpointed the Mexico's target market, providing the ideal kit for a generation of upcoming rally drivers to hone their skills.

In contrast, the Custom Pack (from 16 October 1971) added a touch of luxury, with extras including cloth seats, carpets, heated rear window and triple coachline.

The most significant change to the Mexico's spec came around October 1972 with the chassis number of

FACTORY ORIGINAL SPORTING MK1 ESCORTS

From behind, a Mexico was much like a normal Escort, with no satin black back panel and no aluminium boot edge trim. A straight chrome rear bumper was fitted until December 1972.

BFATM_00113, when its battery was moved from a tray in the boot to the standard Escort position under the bonnet; its previous remote brake servo was swapped for an in-line item, as fitted from the outset to left-hand-drive cars. Meanwhile, all Mexico interiors were upgraded from L to XL level.

Officially, the Mexico was only available as a two-door saloon, but there were ten-or-so exceptions.

Three Mexicos were made as estates for evaluation purposes; each was built in 1972 on a normal estate bodyshell but with Type 49 strengthening. Two cars were Daytona Yellow, while the other was converted to RS2000 specification around 1974. All three had vinyl roofs.

Similarly, Aveley built one van with full Mexico spec and BFAV chassis number. It was apparently Copper coloured.

A further six (or so) Mexicos were built using Type 49-style strengthened four-door bodyshells. One was kept by Ford for appraisal, at least one was sold to a customer and four were used as police cars in Jersey. Each was full Mexico specification, with 1.6-litre Crossflow engine, 2000E gearbox, radius rod rear axle and Aveley chassis number (beginning BFAF).

Many other four-door Mexicos were rumoured to be built, but the majority were fakes or, possibly, from a batch of around 20 1600cc four-door Mk1s made for Liverpool police. These Escorts were manufactured at Halewood (with BBAF chassis numbers) using export-spec four-door bodyshells, two-dial dashboards, heavy-duty rear suspension, flared front wheelarches and 5.5in steel wheels. Legend has it that the order was cancelled and the cars were sold privately through Ford dealers, some of whom applied Mexico badges. It's not known whether these cars used a 2000E gearbox and hydraulic clutch.

Mexico production came to an end in January 1975, with the final vehicle number BFATRC00442. By then, 10,352 Mexicos had left the lines. None were officially marketed in Australia or Germany, although other European countries took a fair few. Nevertheless, the majority were sold through Ford's UK network of Rallye Sport dealers.

Its name lived on – with considerably less success – in the Mk2 RS Mexico.

Type 49 shell was part of a Mexico's DNA, complete with flared front wheelarch lips and crudely rolled-under rear arches to clear the chunky tyres.

ESCORT MEXICO

Engine – Block, Head and Sump

Taken from the Cortina GT, 1600E and Capri 1600GT, the Mexico's 1599cc Crossflow engine always used a cast iron 711M cylinder block, identifiable by the 711M-6015-B-A in raised letters on the side of the crankcase near the starter motor. Between the core plugs there was also a T-number cast onto the side of the block, generally between T12 and T20; despite popular myths, this had no bearing on cylinder wall stiffness. The block was semi-gloss black.

A unique engine number was hand-stamped into the top of the block below the cylinder head between exhaust manifold ports one and two. It read 711M6015BA followed by digits corresponding with the numerical part of the chassis number on the car's VIN tag.

With a 9.0:1 compression ratio, the Mexico used a standard 1600HC crankshaft and cast alloy 1600GT pistons, with three rings (one oil and two compression) and valve cutouts. Likewise, the 1600GT camshaft had more overlap than a standard 1600HC engine.

A semi-gloss black, cast iron, eight-valve, flat (non-

It was only a Cortina engine, but the 1599cc Crossflow nestled between the AVO Escort's inner wings meant lively performance. Most of what's under this Maize Mexico's bonnet has remained unchanged since the '70s.

Few revisions were made to the Mexico's engine during production. The biggest underbonnet alterations were repositioned battery and brake servo – now in normal Escort places.

Cortina engine was adapted for Escort crossmember and sump, which moved the dipstick position. Mexico's 1600GT unit had an extended dipstick tube.

The Mexico's 12-pint cooling system stayed the same throughout production, featuring black high-top radiator and black rubber hoses with wire clips.

chambered) cylinder head was fitted, with four individual inlet ports on the right and four exhaust on the left. Otherwise identical to a regular 1600HC Crossflow head, the Mexico's part housed bigger valves, with face diameters of 38mm (inlet) and 31.5mm (exhaust). The basic shape looked externally similar to other 1300cc and 1600cc Crossflow heads, with the number 37 cast into the top, visible under the rocker shaft or under the inlet ports.

In October 1973 Ford introduced another method of identifying the cast iron cylinder head; this involved stamping the 1600GT engine code (L7) near the top rearmost exhaust manifold stud.

A semi-gloss black Crossflow long-neck rocker cover was screwed to the head, wearing a red-on-silver 1600GT sticker and black plastic oil filler cap with Ford oval logo and moulded part number starting in 71. Well, that was the normal setup, but an original AVO factory photo showed a Mexico sporting a silver filler neck...

The Mexico used a regular Crossflow 35-40psi oil pump and gasket, externally mounted under the distributor, with a spin-on cartridge type filter. An RS1600 oil cooler was available as a factory-fitted optional extra, mounted behind the grille and with hand-drilled holes through the panelwork.

Like mainstream Escorts, the breather system was modified in late 1973, swapping to a smaller setup with internal plunger, reducing its overall size. The Mexico's sump was a crudely-welded steel big-wing 3.96-litre item in semi-gloss black, as used on the Twin Cam and RS1600; a Tech-Del magnesium sump guard was an official factory option.

Unlike the Cortina engine on which it was based, the Mexico's dipstick (part number 711M 6750 AA) went through the back of the block. All Escort Crossflow engines had similar dipsticks with bare alloy handles but the Mexico's 1600GT unit had an extended dipstick tube sited higher than the 1300's. A revised oil pick-up pipe was added in late 1972.

Cooling System

Without the Twin Cam or RS1600's highly-stressed powerplant, the Mexico wasn't deemed demanding enough to warrant a radiator with big header tank. Instead, an enlarged version of the regular Escort design was used, having a black-painted angular copper tank topped with a 13psi, standard reach cap (Autolite on early cars but AC after 1971). There was a regular aluminium water pump and an 88-degree wax thermostat in a bare alloy housing. The cooling system's capacity was 12 pints.

Like all Crossflows, the Mexico came with black rubber hoses, made by various suppliers – so there were no specific markings. Generally, wire clips were used rather than Jubilee types. An orange seven-blade plastic 9in fan was mounted on the front of the engine.

Fuel System

Keeping the Mexico accessible and practical for the man in the street meant sticking to a single downdraught carburettor rather than its predecessors' dual sidedraughts. Therefore a twin-choke Weber 32/36 DGV-FA was bolted to the Ford alloy inlet manifold, as found on the 1300GT (part number 711F 9424 HB until June 1972 and 711F 9424 HC thereafter); the carb's identity was found on a metal tag attached to one of the float chamber screws plus

ESCORT MEXICO

The Mexico's AC oval metal airbox came in hammered silver finish until October 1972 when a blue air cleaner housing was fitted. But there was certainly a crossover where battery-up-front Mexicos still had the silver airbox.

Double-loop rear silencer hanger wrapped under the tailpipe and was supported with two O-shaped rubbers.

Mexico exhaust comprised tubular steel four-into-one exhaust manifold and large-bore mild steel system.

a code on the flange where it met the inlet manifold. Original Webers were stamped as being made in Italy.

The Mexico wore an AC oval metal air cleaner housing with an adjustable intake for summer or winter running; it had a hammered silver finish, including the rubber joint. The airbox was affixed to the inlet manifold's front bolt on one black support bracket, while its top cover was held in place with a pair of nuts and washers. Inside was a paper element.

Sometime around October 1972 the silver airbox was repainted in light/medium gloss blue. Again there was an adjustable intake but now the rubber joint was also painted blue. Although the change coincided with the Mexico's battery relocation, Ford's habit of phasing in components meant a few cars were fitted with a combination of blue airbox and underbonnet battery.

An AC mechanical diaphragm fuel pump sat under the inlet manifold on the side of the cylinder block. It had a bare steel finish, gauze screen and inverted sediment bowl. Black braided fuel lines were used, along with a Motorcraft UFO-style fuel strainer.

Exhaust System

The standard Mexico exhaust system comprised a tubular steel four-branch manifold in gunmetal grey, mated to a large-bore mild steel exhaust pipe in silver/grey.

Like the RS1600, the Mexico's system featured a round centre silencer and oval rear box. A double-loop rear silencer hanger was welded onto the rearmost chassis rail, wrapped under the tailpipe and supported with two O-shape rubbers.

The original four-into-one exhaust manifold was sometimes replaced by high-performance four-into-two-into-one manifolds, which were offered as Rallye Sport extras; it's reckoned some early Mexicos left the factory with such parts as standard.

Ignition and Electrical System

Being built around the RS1600 meant the early Mexico had its battery mounted in the boot on a tray in the spare wheel well. It was usually a Motorcraft 38Ah square-post battery but a 57Ah version was available for cold-climate export markets. From October 1972 it was found under the bonnet, clamped onto a stock Escort tray on the nearside inner wing. To complicate matters, left-hand-drive Mexicos always had their batteries in the right-hand front corner – but not in an inner wing recess like regular LHD Escorts.

The standard Mexico starter motor was a Lucas M35G inertia type, but a pre-engaged unit was optional in the UK or fitted for cold climates. In October 1972 the M35G was swapped for a Lucas M35J, although the pre-engaged unit remained available.

Early models had a flat-type solenoid affixed to the offside inner wing, while the M35J was accompanied by a Lucas round bobbin version. Pre-engaged starter motors were equipped with a direct-mounted solenoid.

A Motorcraft nine-volt ballast resistor coil was mounted on the usual Escort bracket attached to the offside inner wing. It had an aluminum finish, with blue label. It linked to an Autolite distributor with mechanical and vacuum advance plus a big black cap. The model number was cast into the distributor's body – from November 1970 until July 1971 it was 71EB 12100 JA, and from July 1971 onwards 71BB 12100 BFA. Many were simply stamped 71BB BFA followed by several extra characters.

The Lucas (Rist) plug leads were black siliconised rubber with black caps and bore the Ford oval printed in white, along with a black-on-white numbered sticker on each. They slipped onto Autolite AG22C or Champion N4 spark plugs.

Early Mexicos (until October 1971) were fitted with a Lucas 15 ACR 28-amp alternator, superseded by a Lucas TRS 17ACR 35-amp unit. From November 1972 an AC Delco 35-amp part took its place, but in June 1973 there was a return to the Lucas TRS 17ACR 35-amp alternator.

The alternator was mounted on the lower left-hand side of the engine on a silver-coloured triangular mounting bracket, with a satin black adjuster bar; Mexico belts were plain rubber, usually marked as Motorcraft or Ford.

The regular Escort fuse box lived on the Mexico's engine bulkhead, with seven plastic continental fuses, additional lower spade terminal and clear plastic cover. The wiring loom – wrapped in grey tape – was the same from late 1970 until the battery went up front, although the first few Mexicos had an earlier-style grey and red loom connector. The loom differed slightly from standard Escorts, having thick, single yellow and white headlamp connections at the fuse box.

Transmission

The Mexico's chrome gearstick linked to what was colloquially known as a 2000E gearbox – a close-ratio Type 3 unit with three-rail shift mechanism and remote change, as fitted to the Twin Cam, RS1600 and Corsair 2000 V4 GT.

The big, cast iron casing (all in black or very dark green) was encouraged to fit the Mexico with a mild hammering (mainly near the floorpan mounting brackets), a trimmed-back tunnel stiffener, welded-in plate and a new hole cut into the tunnel further back. The rear gearbox mounting position was the same as a regular Escort (with uprated RS1600 support) but it was modified to make room for the speedo cable, then marked in orange.

A genuine Mexico gearbox had a separate bolt-on bell-housing with 105E in the casting, a cast alloy top cover and

Before October 1972 a Mexico's square-post battery lived on a tray in the spare wheel well. This car's cardboard battery cover wasn't standard, but was a Ford accessory

Most noticeable difference under the post-October 1972 Mexico's bonnet was the battery clamped onto a stock Escort tray. Left-hand-drive cars kept their batteries in the right-hand front corner.

iron tail casing with the gearstick located at the back. The reversing light switch was fitted into a tapped hole, found in the gap between the alloy top and bellhousing on the driver's side.

The ratios were first: 2.972:1, second: 2.010:1, third: 1.397:1, forth: 1.000:1, reverse: 3.324:1. Under the top cover, second gear had 28 teeth; third gear (the next one forward, after the synchro hub and selector fork) had 23 teeth – whereas a standard wide-ratio box had 21 teeth and a Lotus Cortina gearbox (which had an alloy bellhousing and tail casing) had 24 teeth.

The Mexico used a normal 1600HC flywheel coupled to a 7.54in diaphragm-spring hydraulic clutch. Like the RS1600, a short, red, flexible hydraulic clutch pipe attached to a fitting on the bulkhead, with a rigid steel pipe following the bellhousing before mating into the slave cylinder; the metal pipe was secured to the back of the engine with two large P-clips through the upper bellhousing bolts.

A single-piece propshaft was used, with no metalwork in the tunnel to take a centre mounting. It turned a 3.777:1 differential (number of teeth on the pinion/crown wheel: 9/34) inside a satin black Timken rear axle. A 4.44:1 ratio was also available, with the number of teeth on the pinion/crown wheel being 9/40. A limited-slip differential was available as a factory option by 1974.

Everything stayed the same throughout Mexico production, but the axle casing was altered in November 1973 for the revised rear suspension layout.

Brakes

Like the RS1600, the Mexico used Girling 9.625in front discs, Girling 16P calipers with 54mm pistons, imperial fittings and large dust seals. The calipers had a pale gold or silver finish, while the discs had satin black guards. From February 1972, Girling 16PB calipers (still with imperial fittings) were fitted instead.

On the back, the Mexico had Girling HL3A 9x1.75in drums, as fitted to the Capri 3.0, Escort Twin Cam and RS1600. Late models (probably all those made after June 1973) used Lockheed Mk2-type rear drums with a two-piston wheel cylinder.

A Girling Powerstop remote brake servo was fitted to early Mexicos at the nearside front of the engine bay, where a non-AVO Escort had its battery. It was attached to the inner wing on a silver-coloured triangular bracket.

The first Mexicos had an AHV 550 Mk2A servo, featuring a semi-gloss black body with bolted-on front cover in silver.

A Girling Powerstop remote brake servo was fitted to early Mexicos – the first had this AHV 550 Mk2A servo (far left), swapped around January 1972 (until October 1972) for the 550 Mk2B. Period servos have been spotted with Girling Powerstop 5204 stickers (above).

FACTORY ORIGINAL SPORTING MK1 ESCORTS

Girling Hydrovac in-line vacuum servo appeared in October 1972, although left-hand-drive Mexicos always had this setup. This late-spec Mexico has RS2000-style dual-circuit brake system, fitted as standard from November 1973.

A metal connection pipe was clipped into place across the rear edge of the bonnet slam panel. It's unlikely that these servos left Ford with any identification stickers.

From around January 1972 until October 1972 it was replaced with the 550 Mk2B remote servo, featuring a black two-piece body. This servo connected to a rubber pipe running behind the radiator rather than across the slam panel. Mk2Bs were sometimes fitted as replacements for Mk2As under warranty; could the use of aftermarket units explain why some original-looking servos feature "Girling Powerstop 5204" stickers?

A big change came in October 1972, with a swap to a direct rather than remote brake servo; although, to confuse matters, it's worth noting that left-hand-drive Mexicos always had this setup. The satin black Girling Hydrovac in-line vacuum servo was mounted on an extended mounting bracket bolted to the bulkhead pedal box reinforcement.

The Mexico had steel brake lines in Bundy tubing, UNF fittings, ribbed flexible rubber hoses and metal fittings. In November 1973 the Mexico was upgraded with an RS2000-style dual-circuit brake system. The reservoir featured a red plastic cap rather than the single-circuit system's clear/white cap.

Suspension and Steering

A Mexico's purposeful stance was thanks to its RS1600 underpinnings. The Mexico's AVO crossmember was much the same as a normal Escort's but reworked to produce negative camber. It used the RS1600's round rubber engine mounts, with a thicker rubber and longer mount on the driver's side. Two different steering racks were fitted during production – Cam Gears (with five-tooth pinion) or Burman (six-tooth pinion).

The front featured Capri-sourced Macpherson struts and Armstrong oil-filled dampers with a green paint splash, rubber bump stop and shroud covering the piston rod. Dampers were mainly unchanged until sometime in 1973 (probably around October), when the inserts changed diameter, along with waisted top mounts rather than the earlier

All Mexicos – without exception – had Type 49 bodyshells, the most obvious modification being suspension reinforcing plates. The strut top mounts were semi-gloss black.

Late-type Macpherson strut top mount had waisted middle. Factory-stamped chassis number was done by hand after the car was painted.

ESCORT MEXICO

tiered "beehive" design; top mounts were semi-gloss black.

The struts were equipped with 100lb 5.3in diameter coil front springs, again with a green paint splash. Like all AVO-built Escorts, the Mexico used a Twin Cam 20mm anti-roll bar with wider mounts and black rubber bushes at each front corner.

Mexico rear suspension used semi-elliptic 97lb three-leaf springs with 51mm-wide leaves featuring blue and red paint splashes. The springs were held on U-bolts over the rear axle, with a moulded rubber pad between the spring and axle. There's a strong chance the Mexico's spring rates were brought into line with the RS2000's during October 1973 – decambered 85lb leaves with blue and red colour code.

Until November 1973, the Mexico had Armstrong hydraulic inclined telescopic oil-filled rear dampers in black with a yellow and white identification splash. They were mounted to a black mounting beam attached under the rear floorpan but in November 1973 were replaced by upright shock absorbers that poked up through the boot floor.

There was no rear anti-roll bar, but Mexicos used twin radius arms to locate the rear axle; these rods were straightish until the rear shock absorber change in November 1973, when they were replaced by angled arms; the rear axle mountings were also modified to suit.

Various uprated suspension components were available factory-fitted from the options list, as Rallye Sport accessories or from Ford's Special Build Programme, including gas dampers, roller bearing top mounts, a rear turret kit and uprated front springs – yellow rally springs were 96lbs, red springs were 135lbs and black race springs were rated at 160lbs.

Wheels and Tyres

AVO offered a wide choice of wheels from the factory, with several changes throughout production. Early cars (until June 1971) came with Mk2 Lotus Cortina/Twin Cam 5.5x13in pressed steel wheels, in silver, with plain stainless steel hubcaps taken from normal Escorts, Cortinas and Anglias; they used 7/16 UNF open-ended wheel nuts on studs with dished ends. Then, until September 1972 similar rims were fitted but with cooling slots machined around their faces.

Spoke-style sculptured steel wheels appeared in September 1972; the design was similar to lower-spec sporting Escorts but the Mexico's were wider at 5.5x13in. There were no stampings on their faces. Until September 1973 the wheels were painted Silver Fox; after then they had metallic Pearl Grey centres. All wore stainless centre caps and 7/16 UNF chrome, dome-ended wheel nuts.

Alloy wheels were always available to order. From launch, the Mexico could be supplied with Tech Del Minilite magnesium wheels in a variety of sizes.

In January 1971 RS four-spoke alloys were launched; they were available from Rallye Sport dealers or as an

The first Mexicos featured Twin Cam plain steel wheels (left), followed in June 1971 by rims with cooling slots (below). Dunlop tyres were usually supplied.

Spoke-style steel wheels came in September 1972; painted at first in Silver Fox, then from September 1973 two-tone with metallic Pearl Grey centres (similar to the photo but a lighter shade).

FACTORY ORIGINAL SPORTING MK1 ESCORTS

The first 50 Mexicos were Sunset Red, with white stripes painted by hand; 3M plastic decals were introduced before December 1970. The next cars were Ermine White with red stripes. After the initial batch, Maize Yellow was added to the range, boasting semi-matt black decals as a delete option. Eventually, an extensive range of shades could be specified, with a metallic finish offered at extra cost. The Sunset Red Mexico in this 1971 shot also boasts a host of options – including Lighting Pack, Contour seats and RS four-spoke alloys; these wheels were a paler shade of grey than production versions.

FORD badging was like every other Escort. Smooth boot lock stayed until the very last cars.

optional extra on new cars after March 1971. Made by GKN Kent Alloys, early four-spokes had a 70mm centre hole, RS centre caps in chrome and black (pushed through from behind), polished rims, chrome nuts and valves. The spokes were plain (without part numbers), with their recesses and backs finished in dark grey (not Pearl Grey, as commonly thought; this was a Ford colour and the wheels were out-sourced).

From October 1972, lettering on the flat face of the spokes gave the 5.5Jx13 size and part number H71AB-1007-A-C; it's worth noting that the similar Capri four-spokes had a different number and centre bore. After April 1973 the centre cap was dark grey.

RS four-spoke alloy wheels were also available in 6in width through the Special Build Programme or Rallye Sport dealers; they had a different offset from Mk2 6x13in alloys, and no part number on the spokes. Again, the centre caps were dark grey after April 1973.

Early Mexicos were equipped with 165SR13 tyres, usually Dunlop SP68s but generally Goodyear G800 from around October 1972. Dunlop SP44 open-tread rally tyres or low-profile 175HR70x13s were optional.

Body

To many people's eyes, an Escort wasn't a proper Mexico unless it had the bold, bright sticker kit. That's nonsense, of course, but the showy stripes were undoubtedly a big reason why the Mexico sold so well.

The well-loved Mexico decals were a delete option; if you chose to go without them the car would be completely plain, and nothing on the chassis plates would highlight the change.

Although the first 50 Mexicos were Sunset Red with hand-painted white stripes, Ford switched to 3M transfers for mass-production. A set of nine broad stickers was used – three down each side, a boot decal 5mm from the bottom edge and roof stripes 32mm from the rain gutter. Decals didn't wrap into door shuts, but tucked under window rubbers after the glass was fitted.

Decals came in red, semi-matt black, white and yellow; yellow was only seen on Electric Blue cars, to coincide with the Mexico's launch in Sweden. No blue Mexico decals were ever produced, and white was dropped in August 1973. Neither Tawny nor Black Mexicos automatically came with decals but they were available on request.

The Custom Pack of October 1971 deleted the broad stripes, instead adding a triple coachline in a contrasting colour. The ends of the coachline wrapped around door skins, into door shuts and under the rear light clusters.

Badges were always fitted to the front wings. Theoretically a broad-striped car had 1600GT badges on the wings, while plain or Custom Pack cars said Mexico instead. But there's good reason to believe a buyer could have whichever badges he preferred.

A Mexico's purposeful stance was thanks to its RS1600 suspension and wide steel wheels. This car's nearside fuel filler connects to an additional petrol tank – a period mod for continental touring.

Broad decal kit made a bold statement. Rear wheelarches were rolled under from the factory.

FACTORY ORIGINAL SPORTING MK1 ESCORTS

Badges were always fitted to the front wings. Broad-striped cars usually said 1600GT, while plain or Custom Packs read Mexico instead. Custom Pack deleted broad decals in favour of triple coachline. The ends wrapped around door skins, into door shuts and under rear light clusters.

Some early Mexicos had toughened windscreens, but most were laminated, complete with this yellow and red sticker. Note the twin-wire Trico Speedblade wipers.

Most standard Mexicos came with plain glass rather than optional heated rear window. This car's rear sticker is a Ford original.

Rear bumper received central cutout around December 1972. Reversing lights were now standard kit. From February 1973 a Mexico badge was on the boot lid regardless of stripes (or lack of).

Black vinyl roof was part of Custom Pack (not on its own) from November 1973 – meaning a vinyl-roofed car never boasted broad decals.

FORD badging was like every other Escort's, across the bonnet and boot lid. On the back was also the usual Escort script, but no model-designating boot badge was fitted until February 1973. It always said Mexico, regardless of stripes (or lack of).

A black vinyl roof covering was standard as part of the Custom Pack (not on its own) from November 1973, meaning a vinyl-roofed car always had the triple coachline and never broad decals.

Where fitted, the vinyl had seams on either side, around 5in from the rain gutter. The coverings were hand-fitted with contact adhesive, and ended at the top of the A-pillar. Post-August 1973 Mexicos had chrome-look plastic gutter trim rather than earlier cars' stainless steel.

Naturally, a Type 49 bodyshell was always part of a Mexico's DNA, complete with flared front wheelarch lips and

Initially the starting handle hole had a black rubber grommet but the hole disappeared in October 1973.

FACTORY ORIGINAL SPORTING MK1 ESCORTS

Flush-mounted petrol cap was body-coloured unless fitted with broad decals – in which case the cap matched the stripe colour.

Twin-wire Trico Speedblade wipers were usual. Stainless steel wiper arm spoiler was a popular Rallye Sport dealer accessory, available from November 1973.

AVO stone deflector was fitted to the underside of the early Mexico's boot floor, with eight bolts protruding through.

On the later car you can clearly see the Mexico's studded boot floor; the accompanying stone deflector had been dropped as standard-fitment after 1972 but every car kept the eight bolts.

ESCORT MEXICO

crudely rolled-under rear arches to clear the chunky tyres.

Chrome van-sourced bumpers were fitted to the front corners on AVO brackets. The aluminium radiator grille had a polished surround and satin black middle; it was attached with nine screws. Behind the grille was satin black paintwork.

A round-headlamp front panel was always fitted to Mexicos, with starting handle hole and black rubber grommet until around October 1973. After this point, the panel was plain, but the changeover was gradual – probably depending on what Halewood had in stock. A front spoiler was offered as a Rallye Sport accessory for the 1974 model year.

Every Mexico had the late-style Escort bonnet without a washer nozzle hole. Instead, two copper washer nozzles poked out through the riveted-and-screwed scuttle vents. Mexicos had a Lucas two-speed self-parking wiper motor, with twin-wire Trico Speedblade wipers; some AVO-built cars had normal Escort wipers instead, presumably when Speedblade stocks were low. A stainless steel wiper arm spoiler was a popular Rallye Sport dealer accessory, available from November 1973.

A toughened windscreen was found on early Mexicos, but most cars from around July 1971 were supplied with a laminated 'screen. Toughened windscreens had a small blue or green Triplex sticker across the bottom, whereas laminated versions had a yellow and red sticker.

Mexico doors were standard Escort parts, with small locks and two-stage latches. Until October 1973 the quarter light pillars were body-coloured, after which they were satin black. The door handles always appeared identical but for the 1974 model year had hollow backs (like Mk2 vans and estates). Door mirrors were never standard, but one for the driver was commonly specified as a dealer accessory.

The door sills were fitted with aluminium scuff plates and a small metal Ford oval in blue and silver, usually only on the passenger side. A raised badge was fitted until late 1971, when a flat version was used instead.

Mexicos had fixed quarter windows, but opening fronts were offered on export models and opening rears were a rarely-specified extra.

The side window rubbers were smooth basic-spec but on later Mexicos – probably during the autumn 1972 upgrades – they were replaced with ridged items. The front and rear 'screen rubbers remained the same, with plastic-chrome strips and chrome finishing insert.

The back windscreen was plain, although a heated rear window was an optional extra. It became of the Mexico's standard kit in 1974 – probably around April. It was also included as part of the Custom Pack from October 1971.

A flush-mounted petrol cap was fitted, with a chrome locking cap offered as a dealer accessory. The non-locking cap was body-coloured unless fitted with broad decals – in which case the cap matched the stripe colour.

All Escort boot lids were the same, but on very late cars the

Mexico decals were almost legendary, if a little lairy. A delete option on standard cars, there was nothing on the chassis plate to highlight the change. Custom Pack of October 1971 deleted broad stripes in favour of a triple coachline.

Doors, handles and locks were all regular post-1969 Mk1 Escort. Quarter window pillars were body-coloured until October 1973.

No telltale boot badge appeared on the Mexico until late February 1973. Mexico rear lights were the same as any other Escort's.

FACTORY ORIGINAL SPORTING MK1 ESCORTS

Four Cibie Oscars and Super Oscars were optional extras as the Rally Lighting Pack, later as just a pair, part of the Rallye Sport option pack or Clubman Pack.

Cibie H4 headlamps were standard kit from October 1973. Front indicators lost chrome rims during 1974. Headlamp protectors fitted to this Mexico were a Rallye Sport accessory.

lock changed from flat to having a recessed key aperture. The boot and door locks shared the same all-metal key, but the very last cars probably had a Mk2 Escort-type ignition key with black plastic handle.

A straight chrome rear bumper was used until December 1972, after which the whole Escort range had a central cutout section for the number plate lamp. No overriders were fitted.

Lighting

By the time the Mexico made production, Ford had finally settled on using round headlamps for its sports machines. In the Mexico's case they were Lucas 75/50W 7in circular sealed-beam units until September 1973, superseded by the Cibie H4 55/55W sealed-beam halogens found on RS2000s. Twin-bulb quartz-iodine headlamps were optional, in the form of Carellos until December 1971 (some very early Mexicos received these units as standard) and Cibies until October 1973, which supplied 110 watts on main beam. The Cibies had separate reflectors positioned against the main reflectors.

Four quartz-halogen Cibie Oscars and Super Oscars were optional extras as the Rally Lighting Pack, later as just a pair, part of the Rallye Sport option pack or Clubman Pack. Cibie backs were stove enamel grey (like a glossy primer colour) and appeared on sturdy cadmium plated brackets. When factory fitted, they had Ford rocker switches in the fascia or an addi-

ESCORT MEXICO

tional separate plastic panel.

Front indicators were amber plastic with chrome rim, although on some Escorts they became completely plain during late 1974. Some export markets had clear white lenses; such models also featured (1300E-type) side repeaters hand-fitted on each front wing.

Mexico rear lights were the same as any other Escort, having chrome surrounds and black plastic seals. The number plate lamp was a single bulb with glass lens, mounted on the rear panel; only export models had twin lamps.

Reversing lights were initially a Mexico optional extra (listed on the car's build plate), made standard from early 1971. They were Ford branded, with plastic lenses, stainless surrounds and black plastic backs; the holes were hand-drilled.

An additional fog lamp was a dealer option, accompanied either by the official Ford rocker switch or an aftermarket toggle switch.

Underbonnet

All Mexicos had Type 49 bodyshells, the most obvious modification being reinforced suspension strut top plates welded onto the inner wings. Oh yes, and on cars built before October 1972, the lack of battery tray in the engine bay –

Mexico was sold in numerous export markets. This Sunset Red left-hand-drive example displays its clear front indicators and extra side repeaters. It also sports laminated windscreen and dual-circuit braking system. The car was built at Aveley in 1972, sold in Italy, brought back to the UK in 1999 and rebuilt during 2010 by Jonathan Evans.

Underbonnet shot of a 1972 left-hand-drive Mexico. Note the standard inline brake servo and battery position – the same on all left-hand-drive examples.

FACTORY ORIGINAL SPORTING MK1 ESCORTS

Aveley 1970, and a very early Sunset Red Mexico. Note the silver-painted oil filler spout – was the entire rocker cover this colour?

which was replaced by a Girling remote brake servo. Export models were the exception, featuring an inline servo and battery in the normal Escort position under the bonnet.

Until October 1972 the Escort Mexico had a CV combined brake/clutch reservoir, attached with a screw clamp to a crudely-welded body-colour bracket on the bulkhead. A pair of holes was made for twin hoses (in black rubber with a yellow horizontal stripe) to run from the reservoir to master cylinders on the pedal brackets.

When the Mexico gained an inline brake servo in October

Combined brake/clutch reservoir was used until October 1972. You can still see a trace of yellow stripe on these original hydraulic hoses.

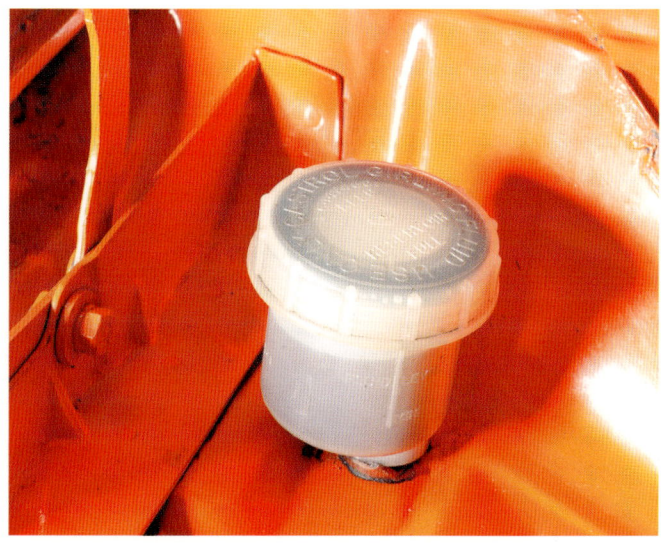

When the Mexico gained an inline brake servo in October 1972, a small Girling clutch reservoir was fitted, mounted through the bulkhead.

ESCORT MEXICO

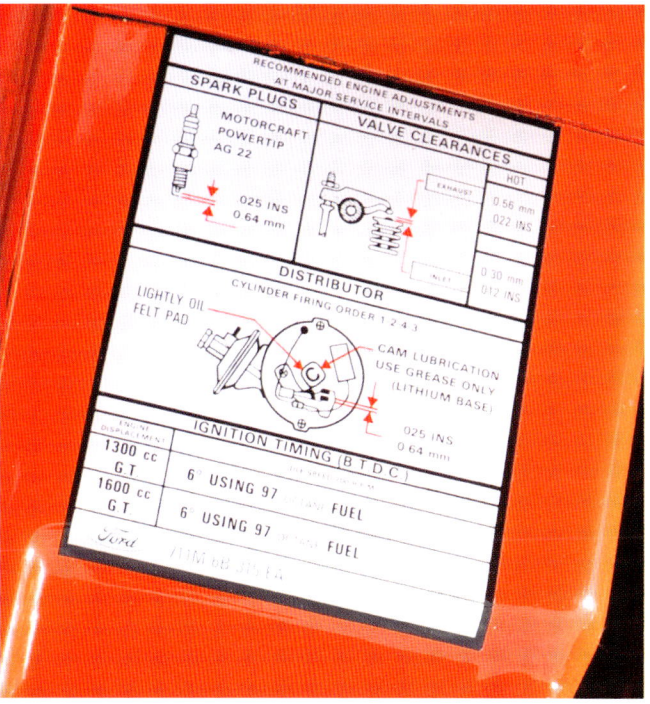

Early Mexicos had this yellow tuning sticker – the 2737E part number across the bottom means it was intended for imperial engines rather than the Mexico's metric unit. A silver 711M adjustment sticker replaced the previous yellow decal.

1972, it also swapped the large combined brake/clutch reservoir for a small Girling clutch reservoir mounted through the bulkhead and a conventional Escort brake master cylinder with integral reservoir on the front of the servo unit.

Unlike lesser Escorts, there was no hole in the bulkhead brake reinforcement plate for a clutch cable. Until mid-1971 there was a sealed clutch cable tube, after which a flush automatic transmission-style plate was used instead. The brake pedal-to-servo hole was also sealed up.

On early Mexicos the speedometer cable can through a black bulkhead grommet beside the brake/clutch reservoir similar to the RS1600; some cars even had the cable attached to the upper bulkhead flat panel on a bracket. During 1971 the speedo cable was moved down to poke through a grommet above the brake reinforcement plate (in the normal Escort position; earlier cars just had the grommet) but some cars retained the upper hole well into 1972. The choke cable ran in the regular route from beside the fuse box.

Some (not all) Mexicos built between March 1972 and early May 1972 had an RS1600-style cut-and-rolled/hammered-down bulkhead lip (designed to clear the rear of the twin-cam engine); it's very likely that all these Mexicos also had the RS1600 radiator support panel with holes punched through for oil cooler pipework plus an upper

Remarkably straight for original stickers, these coolant decals were commonly fitted to the nearside inner wing, or sometimes the bonnet slam panel.

FACTORY ORIGINAL SPORTING MK1 ESCORTS

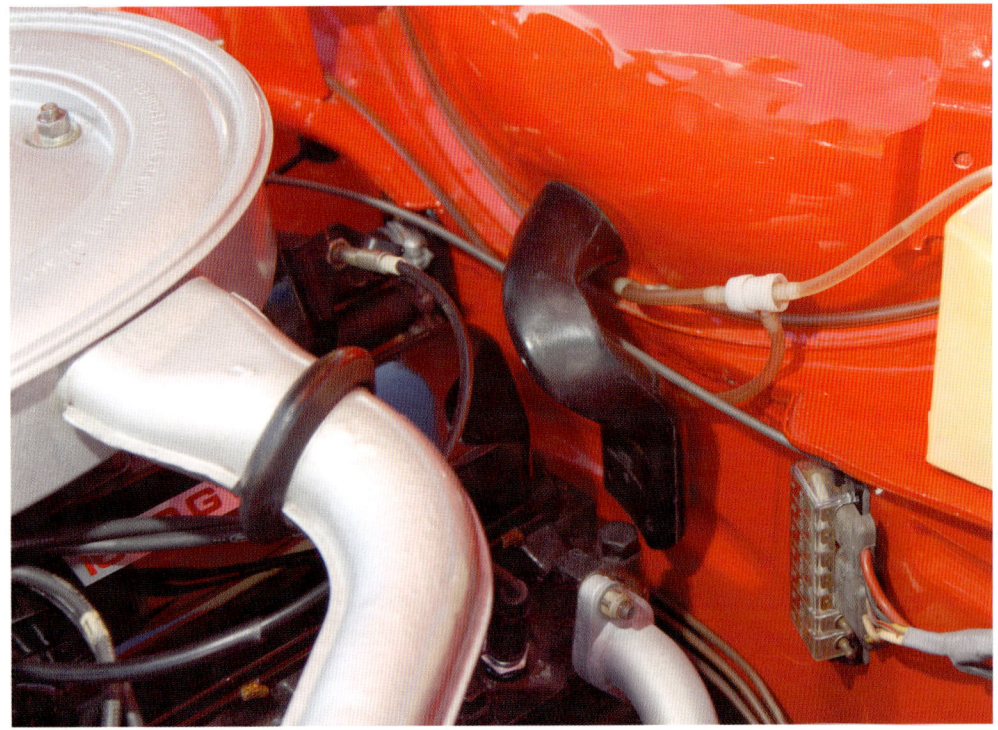

RS1600-style hammered-down bulkhead lip, as found on some Mexicos built between late March 1972 and early May 1972. Most had the Twin Cam bulkhead drain, but this shot shows the regular Escort part.

bulkhead hole for the speedo cable, along with an L (for Twin Cam) on the body plate, rather than G or X.

Mexicos were generally fitted with the normal twisted-shape Escort black plastic bulkhead drain tube with FoMoCo lettering. But some Mexicos – a few very early cars and those built with shells designated for RS1600s with bashed-down bulkhead – had the wide, flared-out Twin Cam-style plenum drain.

It's worth noting that a handful of very early (1970) Mexicos were said to come with a Twin Cam engine stabiliser bar and plate welded to the bulkhead – presumably because they were built using leftover Twin Cam bodyshells.

Mexicos were fitted with three different types of washer bottle, and on early cars it's almost impossible to say which was used on a particular date. The original Escort off-white "cheese wedge" reservoir was found on some Mexicos, attached to the nearside bulkhead on three body-coloured pins.

Many Mexicos were instead fitted with a slide-on washer tank, featuring a water outlet on the left-hand side and a mounting bracket screwed onto the bulkhead; from late 1971 a similar bottle with central outlet was used, slid onto a bracket spot-welded onto the bulkhead. Clear plastic washer pipes with a white plastic T-piece replaced the previous barrel type.

Several early 1972 Mexicos had fittings for early and later types of washer bottle (as did all Mexicos with the RS1600-style bashed-down bulkhead lip), with pins and bracket.

An electric washer pump was available from January 1974; made by Trico, it mounted onto the flat spot on the heater dome, operated by a dashboard-mounted flick switch.

The bonnet cable and release handle moved from the passenger's to driver's side around the end of 1970. Early cables were bare but from late 1972 they had a black plastic coating. Under the bonnet, the prop was attached with a clear/white plastic retaining clip connected to a welded-on loop; the prop was plain metal. Bonnet hinges and fixings were always body-coloured.

Mexicos were fitted with a fused Lucas 6RA headlight relay on the nearside inner wing, identical to other AVO cars. Wiring ran from the main loom, with an additional short brown earth wire to one of the relay screws. One or a pair of

Early Mexicos were fitted with two types of water reservoir – the original Escort off-white "cheese wedge" bottle or the later slide-on washer tank with left-hand-side water outlet. The electric pump in the left-hand photo is an aftermarket addition.

lighting decals was sometimes applied to the nearside strut top area – one white and one blue.

A white/black coolant sticker was positioned on the nearside inner wing or slam panel in front of the battery – although it could just as easily have been placed across the other side. The well-known negative earth decals were attached even more randomly – sometimes to the nearside inner wing, occasionally the offside, or in the boot of early cars, near the battery on the inner wing or wheelarch.

Mexicos usually also wore an engine adjustment sticker towards the front of the offside inner wing. Somewhat inexplicably, early cars had a yellow decal, which related to imperial engines; the silver 711M sticker (for metric engines) wasn't used until around 1972.

Interior

The Mexico interior was always black, although a handful of special order colours were believed to exist. Interior metalwork featured a satin black dashboard and A-pillars, with the doors and rear quarters in body colour.

All Mexicos had a six-dial metal dashboard pressing with a padded black vinyl top plus round, black plastic, adjustable air vents. The heater control panel had black plastic levers and an alloy surround containing stuck-on black Mazak diagram.

Beneath the dashboard was a black plastic fascia panel housing the swivel ashtray (with grained finish) flanked by rocker switches and black plastic choke knob. Behind the panel was the heater box.

Other than Mexico prototypes (with pre-October 1970 dashboard layout), two different fascia panels were used – until summer 1971 there were two switch slots to the right of the ashtray and none to the left; after this date the fascia had five switch holes with blanking plates for any unused. The exceptions were cars with hazard warning flashers, which always had the five-slot panel.

The black plastic rocker switches featured chromed plastic surrounds; from choke cable to ashtray they were: two-speed wiper switch, two-speed heater switch, brake test switch (where fitted), heated rear window switch (where fitted) hazard warning light switch (where fitted). The Mexico's headlamp switch lived under the main instruments.

Hazard flashers were optional until made standard in October 1972, with a warning light indicator recessed into the dashboard. Up to December 1972 the heated rear windscreen switch had a red warning light, after which it was amber.

A deep-reach cigarette lighter was optional on the Mexico

Even in 1971 this was a no-nonsense environment. The black PVC seats and door cards came directly from the Escort L. This car's seat belt stalks and passenger-side gauges are aftermarket additions.

FACTORY ORIGINAL SPORTING MK1 ESCORTS

Like the front seats, the Mexico rear bench was basic L-specification in black PVC until October 1972.

Contour bucket seats were available from Ford's competitions department. The head rests were an additional option.

From October 1971 until November 1973, the Custom Pack came with a flexible dashboard-mounted map reading light.

Desirable Springalex dished steering wheel was popular Mexico option.

You didn't get carpets inside a standard Mexico until October 1972. Instead, there was a black one-piece rubber floor mat.

Dished six-dial instruments were fitted until January 1973.

Traditional black headlining was in every Mexico, along with black sun visors. Early models lacked passenger vanity mirror.

and would be fitted into the dashboard panel; the car would have the letter X on its build plate. Custom Pack cars also featured the lighter.

Supplementary dealer-fitted switches for rear fog lamp or Cibie spot lamps had no set position, so could have used toggle switches or rockers in a separate black plastic housing.

Every Mexico was fitted with six-dial instruments in an all-black surround with plastic-chrome rings, although the very earliest cars had a Twin Cam silver-finished inner surround.

Until January 1973 the Mexico's AC-made gauges had dished black faces, with thin font, white needles, chrome bosses on the speedo and rev counter needles. The instrument panel comprised a large 140mph speedometer (incorporating main beam warning light) and rev counter (marked to 8,000rpm with 6,500rpm red line) plus four smaller dials for fuel, battery level, oil pressure and water temperature. Round warning lights for alternator charge and direction indicators were mounted between the two main instruments.

The dished dials in the black surround stayed until January 1973, when they were replaced by flat-faced dials with 130mph speedometer and 7,000rpm rev counter with no red line. Up to mid-1973 the oil pressure gauge had LB/IN lettering but this was phased out in favour of empty blocks depicting bar.

Officially, the standard Mexico steering wheel was a regular Escort part – until January 1972 the dished GT 14in wheel in black plastic with a silver Escort badge. From January 1972 until November 1972 the later Escort flat three-spoke 'safety' wheel was used, featuring a black vinyl pad over silver spokes, a grey Escort badge and padded black leather rim.

It's likely, though, that AVO equipped most Mexicos with the optional Springalex dished steering wheel – usually with black spokes, a black leather rim and centre boss featuring the Ford oval logo. Other symbols were also used, including a white Springalex badge, black with crossed flags, a Ford Sport logo and so on.

Around November 1972, the now-familiar flat RS three-spoke steering wheel became standard, in black with black with leather rim.

FACTORY ORIGINAL SPORTING MK1 ESCORTS

All black as before, the Custom Pack's cockpit was vastly more inviting than the standard Mexico. Pure luxury, compared to the poverty-spec rubber mats of old.

Post-October 1973 Custom Packs gained this RS2000-type full height console. The cigarette lighter was moved from its previous position in the dashboard.

One steering column stalk was fitted for indicators, headlamp dipping/flashing and horn, with a chrome button on the end. The Mexico was fitted with a single horn, positioned behind the front grille, but dual-tone horns were available, probably fitted from September 1973.

The Mexico's trim level began as a basic, no-nonsense affair, ready to be ripped out for rallying. But before long it could be specced-up beyond all recognition.

Until October 1972 the standard Mexico had black PVC L-spec seats with vertical stitching, fully tilting frames and a lever on the backrest. The rear bench was a basic item to match. Instead of carpets, a black one-piece rubber floor mat was used. Buyers of early cars were offered a Plush Pack upgrade, which added wicker-style Contour bucket seats and optional head rests.

Vinyl, padded XL-specification seats (front and rear) were fitted to the Mexico with the October 1972 trim upgrade, including broad side bolsters and an inner panel of narrow horizontal perforated bands. Until October 1973 the fronts were fully-tilting, with backrest-mounted lever, after which the seat bases were fixed and only the backrests tipped forward. Head rests were available at extra cost.

Mexico door cards were also L-spec until October 1972, when they were swapped for padded XL parts; meanwhile, the black fibreboard rear quarter panels gained plastic arm rest extensions on each side; all had push-round plastic ashtrays. Internal door handles and winders were the flat, textured type. Until March 1973 the Mexico had slim black door lock buttons, but later cars featured black mushroom-headed versions.

Carpets came along as Mexico standard fitment in October 1972, in one piece and tucked under aluminium strips along the bottom of each door aperture.

Before then, though, a black looped-pile carpet was part of the Custom Pack from October 1971, along with a sound insulation kit of absorbent panels at known reverberation points. The carpet was altered in November 1973 for the revised seat runners and floorpan.

Early Custom Pack Mexicos benefited from Contour cloth low-back bucket seats – in grey herringbone until October 1972, then grey Beta cloth until October 1973. After that, the Custom Pack switched to black Beta cloth-trimmed recliners with round RS badges, chrome levers and optional driver and front passenger seat roll top head rests; the Beta cloth pattern ran vertically down the seats and head rests.

Custom Pack cars came with a cloth-covered rear seat to match the fronts – in grey until October 1973 and black Beta thereafter. The Custom Pack also added plastic armrest extensions into the rear quarter panels.

Various optional seats were available for the Mexico from Ford's competitions department, often Contour buckets in black vinyl, black or grey cloth. It was normal for the driver's seat to be a fixed-back bucket and the navigator's to be a recliner. The Clubman Pack (from 23 July 1971) offered Contour buckets as a matching pair, with standard PVC rear bench.

The Mexico's satin black six-dial metal dashboard pressing changed little during production. From October 1973 it added 1300E-style wood cappings – notably lacking cigarette lighter hole.

Although the later Mexico lacked a remote brake servo, the same pedal box stayed at the driver's feet. Now it gained a different brake pedal, lacking the master cylinder.

Seat belts were a compulsory extra, offered as static or inertia-reel three-point belts with fixed stalks, black plastic coating and silver push buttons. Inertia-reel belts became standard around March 1973.

FACTORY ORIGINAL SPORTING MK1 ESCORTS

Sporty RS three-spoke steering wheel with leather rim became a firm fixture on sporting Escorts. Dished dials were dropped in favour of flat faces from January 1973; rev counter had no red line, and wording was removed from the oil pressure gauge.

The shaped remained the same, but the earlier grey dipping mirror was swapped to black in October 1973.

Black vinyl sun visors matched the PVC headlining. A passenger vanity mirror came standard from October 1972.

Black Beta cloth-trimmed recliners were known as "roll tops" thanks to these optional head rests. Part of the October 1973 Custom Pack, they replaced the earlier Contour low-back buckets.

October 1972's improved trim included padded XL-spec rear seat, again in black vinyl. Custom Pack cars came with a cloth-covered rear seat to match the fronts.

From October 1971 until November 1973, the Custom Pack came with a flexible dashboard-mounted map reading light, clipped up the pillar or horizontally in front of the passenger.

No centre console came as standard but the October 1971 to October 1973 Custom Pack provided a black plastic coin tray, as fitted optionally to the GT and standard on the subsequent 1300E. Incorporating a detachable ice scraper, it ran from underneath the heater panel to the back of the handbrake lever (a standard Escort part, in black metal with a bare steel push button).

Later Custom Packs gained a four-piece RS2000-type full height console, including clock (with black bezel and orange hands), radio aperture (to take the optional five-push-button Ford device), positions for optional spot light switches and cigarette lighter – automatically moved from its previous position on the dashboard.

The October 1973 Custom Pack also added 1300E-style light American cherry veneer dashboard cappings – notably lacking a dashboard cigarette lighter hole, and never accompanied by matching wood on the doors. Like the 1300E, the Custom Pack included a wooden glovebox with fold-down panel within a surround screwed to the passenger's under-dash shelf.

Otherwise there was no glovebox, but the Mexico featured normal Escort black cardboard under-dash shelves on both sides, attached with plastic-headed brass clips into black metal brackets.

A push-button radio was optional in the Mexico, usually attached to the heater panel cover in a plastic mount. The radio had a single Ford 2.5W round speaker under a black speaker grille in the rear parcel shelf, with a protective cover underneath. Speaker wiring ran under the rear seat and down the nearside inner sill, sometimes taped to the wiring loom but often loose. The aerial tended to be dealer-fitted, so could be anywhere – in the nearside front wing or (most often) roof mounted, with the lead running inside a windscreen pillar.

The cardboard rear parcel shelf was always black; from autumn 1971 the domed screw caps were larger and after November 1973 the shelf was a single piece without metal strips on either side.

The traditional black vinyl AVO headlining was fitted to every Mexico, along with black sun visors. Early models lacked a vanity mirror on the passenger visor, but this came as part of the Custom Pack and was standard from October 1972. Early cars had three black grab handles with chrome end caps; each rear handle had a black sliding coat hook. Later Mexicos had only the two rear handles.

The interior light was regular Escort. There were two main types of courtesy light switch, although variations of each were used. Officially, the switches were updated in March 1972 from the protruding pin to a smaller, round, rubber-encased type.

October 1972 upgrade from L to XL-spec brought padded door cards. Until March 1973 there were slim door lock buttons, but later cars featured these mushroom-headed versions.

Until October 1973, Mexicos were equipped with the standard Escort grey plastic dipping rear-view mirror with tapered sides. In October 1973 it swapped to black. A year later, a black Mk2-type flat-sided mirror was attached to the black Mk1 stalk.

Seat belts were a compulsory extra, offered as Wingard statics (with two-handed fasteners and black, textured metal clasps), early Wingard three-point inertia-reels (with large silver buckles mounted on the transmission tunnel) or later inertia-reel (with fixed stalks on the tunnel, featuring black plastic coating and silver push buttons). By around March 1973 inertia-reel belts were standard. Very late cars had Mk2-type gold push buttons and square Mk2-style inertia reel mechanism.

The first Mexicos featured a Twin Cam/RS1600 pedal box, with clutch and brake master cylinders mounted above. Early cars had three black pedal levers, with normal Mk1 horizontal block-pattern rubbers.

From October 1972 the same pedal box stayed at the driver's feet, now with a new brake pedal and obviously lacking the hydraulic brake cylinder. The clutch and brake levers were black, with horizontal block pattern rubbers. The accelerator pedal now had a silver lever with small square pad, changing in November 1973 for a larger pedal, angled inwards. It received a new pad in June 1974.

To the left of the pedal box was the usual floor-mounted button for windscreen wash/wipe, in rubber with a circular satin black metal surround. In each footwell was a black cardboard kick panel, with vinyl map pocket stitched onto the driver's side after October 1972. It's possible that the last few Mexicos had Mk2-type plastic kick panels.

FACTORY ORIGINAL SPORTING MK1 ESCORTS

Inside Boot

The early Mexico's battery-in-boot setup meant the spare wheel was mounted to the boot floor, with one long stud and nut through a bolt hole; this could be a wheel nut welded onto the bolt or a long stud, threaded on both ends. Body-coloured hooks welded to the floor were used to strap down the standard tool kit – a regular Escort vertical jack (grey on early cars; mid-blue on later models, complete with red-on-white sticker) and satin black wheel brace in a fawn muslin bag.

A nine-gallon fuel tank was bolted to the right-hand inner wing, painted satin black on some early cars, then later a satin/matt shade of grey; it's notable that only the inside face of the tank was sprayed black – the hidden half was grey and peppered with overspray. The very last Mexicos may have received black tanks too.

In the regular Escort spare wheel well was the Mexico's battery clamped onto an AVO-welded tray (with a small, satin black bracket), sometimes with a negative earth sticker on the nearby inner wing or wheelarch. The battery cable ran along the inner wheelarch, through a crudely-drilled hole in the boot floor and down the transmission rtunnel; it crossed the tunnel above the propshaft, with

Not much room for luggage - the early Mexico's battery-in-boot setup moved the spare 13in wheel to the boot floor. Twin tanks (pictured) were an aftermarket fitment.

Later Mexicos had more boot space than pre-October 1972 machines, thanks to the repositioned battery and spare wheel. It cleared the way to use the black Hardura boot mat.

clips riveted to the floorpan. The Twin Cam's fibreboard battery cover (in 38ah or 57ah sizes, with FoMoCo embossed on the underside) was found on early cars, although it's likely that many went without. Where fitted, the cover would be topped with a negative earth sticker instead of its wheelarch position.

The Mexico's spare 13in wheel was steel as standard, or alloy when RS four-spokes were specified. From October 1972 it was mounted at an angle in the wheel well, with lengthened strap and bracket (bolted to the boot hinge support) holding it in place. The tool kit was moved from the boot floor to behind the spare wheel.

There was a normal Escort black Hardura boot mat, made smaller in November 1973 for the revised shock absorber layout. Lifting it up would reveal eight bolts protruding through the floor, used to attach the AVO satin black stone deflector fitted to the underside. It was dropped as standard after 1972 but remained optional, so every car kept the eight bolts.

A boot light was always listed as standard Mexico spec, but may have been lacking from some early cars. Rear light protectors were black plastic until late 1974, after which they were clear. There was a black rubber boot latch cover, fitted to some cars from autumn 1974.

Spare 13in wheel was steel as standard, or alloy when RS four-spokes were specified. From October 1972 it was mounted in the wheel well.

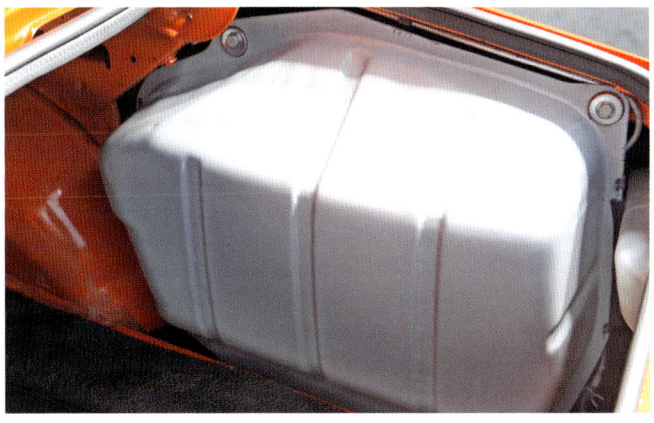

A nine-gallon petrol tank was bolted into the Mexico's right-hand rear inner wing. The tank on most later Mexicos was primer grey.

Mexico colour schemes

Colour	Code	Introduced	Discontinued	Decal colour (where fitted)	Coachline colour (where fitted)
Maize Yellow	T	August 1970	July 1971	Black	
Ermine White	B	August 1970	July 1972	Red	Red
Sunset Red	J	August 1970	July 1972	White	White
Tawny Brown	S	August 1971	July 1972	Black	Gold
Le Mans Green	M	August 1971	July 1973	Black	Black
Electric/Monza Blue	U	August 1971	July 1973	White or yellow*	White
Black	A	August 1971	January 1975	White or red	Gold
Daytona Yellow	T	August 1971	January 1975	Black	Black
Copper Brown	7	August 1972	July 1973	Black	Gold
Diamond White	B	August 1972	January 1975	Red	Red or black (rare)
Sebring Red	N	August 1972	January 1975	Black	Black
Stardust Silver	3	August 1973	January 1975	Black	Black
Olympic Blue	E	August 1973	January 1975	Black or yellow*	Black
Modena Green	M	August 1973	January 1975	Black	Black
Vista Orange	V	August 1974	January 1975	Black	Black
Special order	Y	August 1970	January 1975		

* Swedish market

ESCORT SPORT

An almost permanent feature of Ford shows nationwide, this Diamond White machine has become synonymous with the Sporting Escort Owners' Club thanks to being inseparable from SEOC leaders Peter and Geraldine Ridgewell. Bought by the couple more than 30 years ago, their June 1974 Sport was built for export in a heavy-duty bodyshell, complete with reinforced suspension top plates. When the order was cancelled it remained in the UK. The car's spec also included optional vinyl roof, heated rear window and alternator. The door mirrors were original accessories but its rear fog lamps are an aftermarket addition. Restored in May 1990 and again in May 2002, this Sport lays claim to being one of the most driven Escorts still in existence. Despite having over 300,000 miles on the clock and assorted European tours under its radials, much of the original car remains.

If you could pinpoint one overriding reason for the existence of Ford's sporting Escorts, the answer would probably be a bit disappointing.

Forget the romantic notions of enthusiasts in sheds working weekends to build legendary machines. Never mind the bitter inter-manufacturer rallying rivalry and desire to scoop innumerable championship victories. And as for the notion of bringing high-performance motoring to a nation of working men, well that was just a happy side-effect.

Nope, the real reason Ford put its money behind fast Escorts was one of economics. Spreading a halo effect across the rest of the Blue Oval brand simply meant more cars were sold.

So when Roger Clark rocketed through forests in his RS1600, motorsport fans looked for the road-going equivalent. When the trendy chap down the street pulled all the girls in his striped-up Mexico, the family man next door bought a 1300L.

It's a marketing trick at which Ford excels, in some cases creating a new niche where none was apparently needed.

ESCORT SPORT

Such times can produce very memorable cars.

When the Escort Sport was launched in October 1971, Ford's range of fast Escorts seemed to want for nothing. The products of AVO catered for hardcore motorsport and weekend rally drivers, while the GT was a more affordable option for the sales rep in a rush.

But what about an alternative for the young, fashion-conscious motorist? Something sporty-looking and fun to drive that could impress the neighbours yet still go easy on the wallet…

Slotting neatly into the Escort range as a low-cost, low-spec version of the GT, the Sport was very much built down to a price. But it was clearly a winning concept, mixing basic Escort trim, GT mechanicals and enough choice parts to resemble a Rallye Sport machine.

In short, image was everything. If it wasn't needed, it wasn't included. Like contemporary Escorts exiting AVO, the Sport had an all-black interior with flimsy vinyl seats and rubber mats rather than carpets. There were 13in rims under flared front wheelarches, chrome quarter bumpers and good-

By the time of this Sport's June 1974 build, the model had moved further up the Escort range in place of the defunct GT. With the now-standard triple coachline, sports steel wheels, optional vinyl roof and heated rear window, there were even hints of the executive 1300E.

Why did a matt black back panel make an Escort look sporty? It worked, whatever the reason. And for the Sport it was a permanent feature. Note this car's central bumper cutout, made standard from late 1972.

107

A relatively high ride height on GT suspension and chunky 165SR13 tyres gave the Sport something of an unusual handling experience, mixing body roll with impressive grip.

old round headlamps – the recipe required for brochures to declare, "The hot looking Escort with performance to match… Externally the Sport resembles the RS1600."

Yet underneath the hype, Ford bosses were reputedly unimpressed by what amounted to a sheep in wolf's clothing. With GT running gear and 165x13 tyres, the rubber's bigger rolling radius knocked the edge off the Sport's performance; the 72bhp 1300GT engine and early GT's 4.125 final drive ratio remained, but acceleration was hampered.

Even so, Ford's brochure quoted 0-60mph in 12.8 seconds and a, "Top speed of around 99mph… All of which adds up to a very hot car."

But it wasn't all bark and no bite. The Sport competed in price-bracketed saloon car racing, blessed with homologated goodies like limited-slip differential and beefier exhaust manifold. Ford even included a special class for Sports in the media-friendly Mexico Rally Championship.

The marketing worked. The image was spot on. Buyers didn't care that the Sport wasn't especially fast. It was fun, and it looked great. And when trim upgrades came along in the Escort range-wide revamp of August 1972, the Sport started knocking nails into the GT's coffin.

Until then, the Sport's cabin was completely that of a standard Escort but with an aftermarket-type rev counter slapped onto the dash top. After the update it was swapped for the GT-type six-dial arrangement, all in black like an RS cabin. Meanwhile, hazard flashers were added and the wheels were exchanged for sculptured sports steels. No wonder the market now favoured the Sport over the pricier GT.

Production of the Escort Sport started long before launch (around July 1971 from chassis number BBATL_07049), although manufacturing of Sport parts began in May 1971, the prototype was made in June and Ford's press cars left the factory in August.

The Sport was built as a mainstream model in the UK (always Halewood – never Aveley) and Germany, and it was made in right-hand-drive or left-hand-drive form, using standard or heavy-duty bodyshells. That said, British Sports almost always had the normal shell, and even foreign cars never used AVO chassis strengtheners – although early Sports used an RS1600/Mexico boot floor. The Sport lasted until the Mk1's demise in December 1974.

Today the Sport is a real rarity, with few cars surviving in their original guise. Because of their cheap and cheerful nature, many Sports were thrashed and discarded while reasonably new. And now, sadly, most of the remaining examples have been converted to resemble their AVO counterparts. Still, that was really the idea all along.

Engine – Block, Head and Sump

The Sport's 1297cc, four-cylinder OHV powerplant was pure Escort GT – the tried-and-tested Crossflow unit with Metric 711M block. Painted semi-gloss black, the block had a raised 711M-6015-A-A cast onto the crankcase plus a T-number between the core plugs (often, but not always, T12); despite popular rumours, this probably had nothing to do with cylinder wall thickness. There was a unique engine number hand-stamped into the top of the block between manifold ports one and two, comprising two letters to represent the year and month of manufacture, followed by five numbers that matched the car's chassis number. A white paint splash was found on a lug near the bellhousing and starter motor.

Inside the Sport's Kent engine was the usual mildly-balanced GT crankshaft, drilled through the webbing. All 1300cc connecting rods were the same. The pistons were normal 1300HC Crossflow parts, in cast alloy with valve cutouts, one oil ring and two compression. Despite Ford's claims, this meant the Sport had a 9.0:1 compression ratio rather than the quoted 9.2:1.

Normally there was a 272-degree duration CA camshaft, but owing to supply problems some GT engines contained standard 1300 Crossflow CC-type cams, which weren't as happy to rev round to the red line.

Above the block was a normal flat 1300HC Crossflow cast iron cylinder head, with four inlet ports on the right and four exhaust ports on the left. The inlet valve faces were relatively large at 38mm diameter, while the exhaust valves were 31mm. The head could be identified by a number 37 cast under the rocker shaft – the same as a 1600cc version. From October 1973, characters corresponding to the engine code were stamped into the head near the top rearmost exhaust manifold stud – on a Sport's GT engine it was J3, as opposed to the standard 1300HC's J2.

Atop the head was a semi-gloss black 1300cc Crossflow long-neck rocker cover with airbox bracket and red-on-blue 1300GT sticker. From November 1974 the decal was deleted. Inside the filler spout was a black plastic oil cap with Ford oval logo and part number beginning in 71.

A standard Crossflow bare alloy dipstick was slotted into an extended tube bracket, reading from a regular Crossflow black sump. The oil pump was a standard Ford 35-40psi part mounted externally under the distributor, usually black but sometimes bare metal. A spin-on cartridge filter was fitted beneath.

The original breather system was changed in late 1973, when its external plunger was swapped for an internal version, resulting in a smaller component.

Under the Sport's bonnet was the usual metric Escort GT engine, pumping out 72bhp. Like the regular Crossflow lump, the cast iron block and head were black, the only visible difference being a 1300GT sticker on the rocker cover.

FACTORY ORIGINAL SPORTING MK1 ESCORTS

Regular Escort 1300 12-fins-per-inch radiator provided ample cooling for the Sport. Fan was GT's seven-blade beige plastic part.

Cooling System

The Sport came with the usual small Escort 1300cc radiator with 12 fins per inch and angular copper top painted black. Occasionally Sports left the factory with an Escort 1100 nine-fins-per-inch radiator. There would always be an AC 13psi cap.

The Sport's water pump was the normal Crossflow part in bare aluminium, turning a beige seven-blade plastic fan. Similarly, an 88-degree wax thermostat lived inside a bare alloy or black housing but from November 1974 it was always painted black in readiness for Mk2 production.

Coolant hoses were the same as those on other Crossflow-engined Escorts, in black rubber with wire clips rather than Jubilee types.

Fuel System

Fuelling a Sport's 1300GT powerplant was a job for the familiar Weber 32DGV downdraught dual-choke carburettor with throttle cable bolted onto the throttle linkage.

It was mounted onto a 1300GT Ford alloy manifold specific for the two-bolt throttle linkage. Above the carburettor was a round metal airbox with adjustable intake for summer or winter running. At first the airbox was painted in a hammered silver effect (including the rubber joint) but for the 1972 model year the airbox became mid-blue. Most said AC on top, but late versions in 1974 were simply stamped with the Ford logo. Inside was a paper filter.

The Sport was equipped with an AC mechanical fuel pump in bare steel finish, with gauze screen and inverted sediment bowl. It was positioned under the inlet manifold on the side of the cylinder block. There were black braided fuel lines and a Motorcraft UFO-type fuel strainer.

Exhaust System

Like other 1300GT-engined Escorts, the Sport boasted a tubular steel exhaust manifold. A four-into-two-into-one design, it clamped adjacent to the gearbox and flowed into a slightly larger bore system than found on normal 1300s. There was an oval centre silencer and round rear box, in steel finish from the factory. Such systems didn't last long, and official Ford replacements were silver-grey or blue-grey.

After late 1973 the exhaust had revised profiles around the downpipe and over the rear axle.

GT air pan was painted mid-blue from 1972. It sat atop a Weber 32DGV twin-choke carburettor.

Tubular four-branch exhaust manifold was carried over from GT. It fed a larger-bore exhaust system, often painted silver-grey.

Ignition and Electrical System

Everything under the Sport's bonnet was taken from the 1300GT, so there was a conventional battery arrangement in the passenger-side front corner. Usually a Motorcraft 38Ah in black rubber or white plastic, it had flat bolt-on terminals; alternatively, Sports bound for cold climates came with a Motorcraft 57Ah battery.

On early cars it was charged by a Lucas C40 dynamo (with large, black regulator on the bulkhead) or optional Lucas 16ACR alternator, which became standard in October 1973. There was a plain rubber drivebelt, often marked as Motorcraft or Ford.

The Sport's starter motor was a 12-volt Lucas M35J, which was date-stamped some time before the car's build. A pre-engaged starter motor was an optional extra, often standard on export models. Otherwise, a solenoid was attached to the nearside inner wing – a flat, square type until late 1972, when it was replaced by a Lucas round version.

An Autolite/Motorcraft 9-volt ballasted ignition coil clamped into a bracket screwed to the offside inner wing. Normally it had a bare aluminium finish with blue label.

Plug leads were made by Rist/Lucas, printed onto the black siliconised rubber in white with a Ford oval logo. Their caps were black rubber, which clipped onto Motocraft AG22 spark plugs. The other ends attached to a terracotta or black plastic standard Crossflow FoMoCo/Motorcraft distributor cap. The Sport's distributor was the 1300GT type (71-EB or 71AB part number) with a blue colour splash on the sealed vacuum advance module.

The Escort Sport used a basic Escort fuse box, screwed onto the passenger-side bulkhead with internal connectors, a clear plastic cover and seven plastic continental fuses. Nearby, the wiring loom wore a green tag; throughout the car it was wrapped in grey tape.

Transmission

Although the Sport was criticised for its gearing, its transmission setup was a fairly good compromise of off-the-shelf Escort GT parts – the only drawback being the larger rolling radius of its bigger wheels.

The Sport's gearbox was the regular GT Type 2 close-ratio four-speed manual, including the following ratios: first 3.337:1, second 1.995:1, third 1.418:1, fourth 1.000:1 and reverse 3.867:1.

The black gearbox casing had a blue paint splash on the starter motor casting (the standard Escort's was yellow). A metal tag on the tail housing related to the speedometer drive gear – on a Sport it should have been F/F (23-tooth gear for 13in wheels) but sometimes the gearbox had a GT's E/F tag – meaning there were 25 teeth for 12in wheels.

The part number of a Sport gearbox began 69AB, 70AB, 69AG or 70AG, but from around November 1974 some began with 75AB or 75AG – these were Mk2 Sport gearboxes, featuring a one-piece tail housing and different gearstick thread.

Within the Sport's bellhousing was a normal Escort 1300 cable-operated 7.5in diaphragm-spring single dry plate clutch and slim 16lb lightweight flywheel.

Linking to the gearbox was an Escort 1300 two-piece propshaft with rubber-mounted centre bearing, all in black. It turned a regular Escort differential with 4.125:1 axle ratio – as found standard on the early GT and optional on later models; a tag on a diff bolt read 4.125. The differential was fitted into a black Timken one-piece axle. From autumn 1973, there was a heavy-duty differential with stronger bearings, slotted inside an updated axle casing with anti-roll bar links.

Suspension and Steering

Underneath a Sport it was business as usual. The entire GT running gear was used, all in satin black with black rubber bushes.

The front end featured the usual Escort crossmember, square metal/rubber engine mounts and 3.5-turn lock-to-lock steering rack with 17.5:1 ratio. It was suspended with Macpherson struts containing Sachs Ford-branded shock absorber inserts; each strut had red and blue paint splashes to denote GT spec, while their glossy black top mounts had a beige paint splash, with bright-coloured dabs on each bolt to confirm it had been correctly tightened. From autumn 1971 the tiered top mounts were swapped for slightly smaller versions with waisted middles. Two types of waisted mounts were found on normal Mk1s – small hole and large hole. Large hole mounts were used from autumn 1973, along with beefier shock absorber inserts.

Sport front springs were 100lb with a blue paint splash,

Sport's GT distributor had standard Crossflow black or terracotta plastic distributor cap with black Rist/Ford leads.

FACTORY ORIGINAL SPORTING MK1 ESCORTS

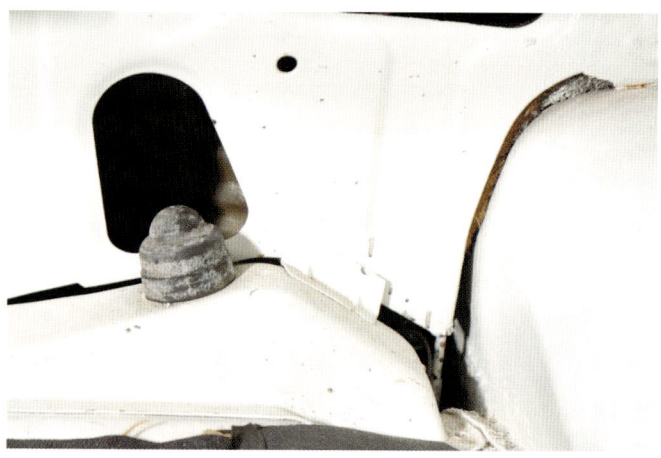

Underneath the Sport was exactly what you'd find under a run-of-the-mill machine, mostly painted black. The front crossmember and steering rack were regular Escort parts.

Late 1973 saw the rear dampers moved to this upright position, with their tops poking through the boot floor. This suspension modification applied across the Escort range.

swapping to softer 88lb parts with red colour splash after October 1973; the coil ends were coated in black plastic, top and bottom. The standard Escort front anti-roll bar remained, including yellow paint dabs on the brackets.

A Sport's rear suspension was GT specification, including blue metallic (Armstrong) or black (normal Ford) shock absorbers. Early cars had them mounted at an angle from a black crossmember attached to the floorpan, but from October 1973 they were virtually upright, with their upper mountings poking through the boot floor.

They worked with semi-elliptical 116lb four-leaf rear springs, probably bearing a beige colour code. They linked to the axle with twin U-bolts and rubbers either side.

The Sport never had radius rods, but a thin rear anti-roll bar was added in October 1973, alongside the entire mainstream Escort lineup.

Along with the upright dampers in October 1973 came this thin rear anti-roll bar, complete with new mounts onto the back axle. Late-spec Sport had revised front spring rates but the rear retained these 116lb multi-leafs.

ESCORT SPORT

Sculptured sports steel wheels were fitted for the 1973 model year, complete with satin black sections for that Minilite-style spoke effect. The design was essentially similar to contemporary AVO wheels but 5in rather than 5.5in wide.

Girling brake servo came straight from the GT, accompanied by 8.6in front disc brakes.

Brakes

Sport stoppers were lifted straight from the Escort GT, featuring 8.6in solid front discs, Ferodo or Mintex pads and Girling twin-piston calipers in satin black or burnished gold. On the rear were 8x1.75in rear drums in black painted cast metal.

Servo assistance was always standard on the Sport, using a Girling Hydrovac in-line vacuum unit on a bracket attached to the driver's side inner wing. There were no identification stickers, but the servo's drum had a yellow stamp. Attached to it was an aluminium Girling 75 master cylinder that wore a clear plastic cap.

The Sport had a single-line braking system, bare Bundy steel pipework, UNF fittings, ribbed flexible rubber hoses and bare metal fittings.

Wheels and Tyres

Looking like a Mexico meant a Sport needed larger wheels than any other regular Escort, so the car received 13in rims. Like the first Mexico, the early Sport's were plain, pressed steels, painted Silver Fox and wearing the same stainless steel hubcaps as other normal Escorts. Unlike the Mexico, though, the Sport's wheels were only 5in wide. They were attached with 7/16 UNF open-ended wheel nuts on studs with dished ends.

With the Sport's 1973 model year update in August 1972, its wheels were swapped for 5x13in sculptured sports pressed steel wheels, painted silver with satin black sections to produce a spoke effect. They wore aluminium centre caps, stamped Ford inside. Until December 1972 the centres were painted plain black, later swapping to black with a chrome ring.

Holding the wheels onto the car was a set of 7/16 UNF chrome domed nuts, as found on AVO models with steel rims.

Early Sports were equipped with Goodyear G800 165SRx13 radials, which were later replaced by 165SRx13 Michelin ZXs.

A basic 1300 badge was accompanied by the bold Sport script – always in black but usually surrounded by a white outline.

FACTORY ORIGINAL SPORTING MK1 ESCORTS

Late-model Escort door handles were visually identical but had hollowed rather than solid backs. Escort Mk1 door locks were this small circle with horizontal key slot. Sport coachline ended neatly before the shuts.

Added as an official accessory, this Sport's door mirrors were identical to those found on the 1300E. Rare passenger-side part originated from export market.

Body

Although it boasted the appearance of an AVO machine, the Sport's bodywork was simply a standard Escort with a couple of RS bits bolted on. Various overseas markets used the heavy-duty export shell, but the Sport was always built around a two-door saloon body on a normal production line.

There was a round-headlamp front panel, generally fitted with starting handle hole until around October 1973. Unlike Aveley-built Escorts, there was no grommet in the hole. But there was a pair of chrome front quarter bumpers, taken directly from the back of an Escort van and identical to those used on the RS1600 and Mexico. They sat beneath an aluminium radiator grille with polished surround and satin black middle; behind the grille, the front panel was sprayed satin black.

Most importantly, the Sport featured flared front wheelarches, using RS1600/Mexico wings. Everything else was

Sport coachlines were unique to the model, fitted standard from August 1973 in orange and black or white and orange. The chrome hockey sticks and boot trim were by now standard Escort bling.

Heated rear window was an optional extra, always accompanied by an alternator rather than the Sport's standard dynamo. This car's black vinyl roof was optional too, joined here by chrome drip rail trim otherwise missing from the Sport.

ESCORT SPORT

Satin black grille was always fitted, with polished outer rim. The starting handle hole had been dropped from presses by the time of this Sport's 1974 build date.

regular Escort kit.

The Sport's bonnet had no hole for a washer nozzle (the copper jets protruded through the scuttle vents). There were late Mk1-style doors with body-coloured quarter light pillars until October 1973, after which they were satin black. Exterior mirrors were never factory-fitted, but wing or door mirrors could be specified as dealer accessories.

The door handles were chrome, and solid until the 1974 model year, when their backs were hollowed out. There were small separate locks with key matched to the boot lock but

By 1972 the rear bumper was still straight (with no cutout) and the black back panel had gained chrome hockey sticks – not that they were fitted neatly, even on this press car.

Le Mans Green was a classic Sport colour for look-at-me Mexico wannabes. This 1972 example still had body-coloured door window channels and drip rails.

115

FACTORY ORIGINAL SPORTING MK1 ESCORTS

Very early sport in Sunset Red with optional opening rear quarter windows and factory aerial in front wing. Note there's no AVO-type grommet in the starting handle hole.

different from the ignition barrel. Keys were all-metal until late 1974, when the ignition key gained a black plastic handle. The boot lock was smooth until November 1974, when the barrel became recessed.

The early Sport had one-speed windscreen wipers, but from August 1972 it was fitted with a self-parking Lucas two-speed motor. The wipers were normal Escort chrome arms and stainless steel blades, and never fitted with an RS spoiler or twin-wire Tricos.

The wipers swept a Triplex Zebrazone toughened glass front windscreen, which featured a small green or blue decal in the lower centre, stuck to the inside and facing out. By 1973 a laminated windscreen was an optional extra.

The side glass was standard Escort, although opening rear quarter windows were optional from launch. Likewise, a heated rear 'screen was optional (only when accompanied by an alternator) from October 1972.

Sport window rubbers were standard Escort, although all had chrome inserts around the front and rear, while late models had ridged side rubbers. A stainless steel roof gutter moulding was used until around August 1972, when it was dropped altogether in line with basic models receiving chrome beading around the side windows. A black vinyl roof was available for extra cost from early 1974, accompanied by a chrome plastic drip rail trim.

The sills of a Sport were always body-coloured, with no external trims. Inside, of course, there was a small metal Ford oval in blue and silver on the passenger doorstep; the raised badge was replaced by a flat version during late 1971.

Despite its 13in wheels, the Sport's rear arches weren't rolled under like its AVO counterparts. The petrol cap was mounted on the driver's-side rear wing – body-coloured and flush-mounted, although a chrome locking cap was a popular dealer accessory.

On the tail of a Sport was a satin black-painted back panel,

Retro-fitted H4 headlamps are a definite improvement on the Sport's standard sealed beams. Like its bigger brothers, the Sport's front quarter bumpers were taken from the back of an Escort van.

The reversing lights were optional extras on the down-specced Sport. This car's fog lights are aftermarket accessories.

which had an aluminium boot edge trim and hockey sticks added in September 1972. The rear bumper was chrome, without overriders. On early Sports it was completely straight but in December 1972 it gained a central cutout for better spread from the number plate light.

The Sport had normal FORD lettering on the bonnet and boot lid, along with the usual Escort script on the offside at the back. The front wing badges simply said 1300, but alongside each was a Sport decal in black and white. From August 1973 a triple coachline was fitted as standard, in orange and black or white and orange.

Lighting

Ford's trick of getting the Sport to look like an AVO model was made much easier by basing the car around a standard low-spec Escort. This meant circular 7in Lucas 60/45-watt sealed beam headlamps rather than the GT's rectangular units. No, they weren't halogen, but from ten paces away, who could tell the difference?

Under the headlights was a pair of indicators with amber plastic lenses; their chrome rims were deleted towards the end of production, although even some of the last cars still had the chrome parts.

The Sport's rear lights were standard Escort components, featuring chrome surrounds and black plastic seals. A single-bulb number plate lamp was mounted in the middle of the back panel.

Reversing lights were an optional extra, when they'd be hand-fitted in the standard Escort position beneath the back lights. A single fog lamp was also available, generally dealer-fitted. In such cases it was a Ford-branded part, mounted to the driver's side rear bumper bracket; in theory a toggle switch with warning lamp would be added under the instrument cluster, but in practice they were fitted in a variety of places.

Inside the Sport was a normal Escort courtesy light with override switch. It was triggered by buttons on both A-pillars, updated in March 1972 from the protruding pin design to a round, rubber-encased type.

Underbonnet

Popping the bonnet of an Escort Sport was disappointing for anyone expecting to see something resembling an RS. The battery was on a tray in the front corner, there was a regular disc-braked Escort servo and, unless the car was an export model based on a heavy-duty shell, the inner wings lacked AVO-style strengthening plates. What the Sport buyer received instead was mainly Escort GT.

The Sport's bulkhead was standard Escort but for the oil pressure pipe running through a hole drilled in front of the driver. The bonnet hinges were body-coloured (including their retaining bolts) and there was a normal twisted-shape black plastic bulkhead drain tube.

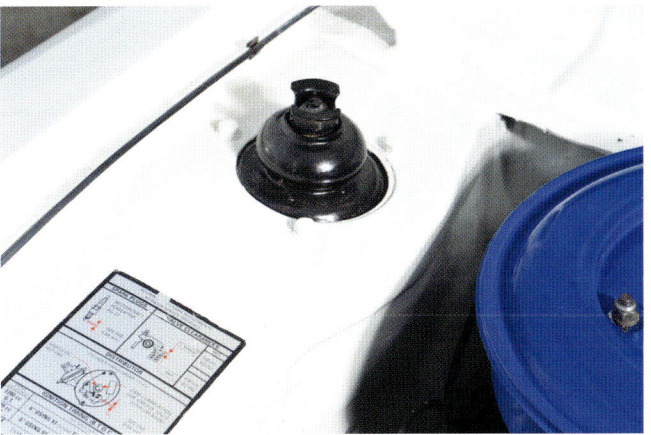

Export-spec Sport featured heavy-duty bodyshell with AVO-style suspension top reinforcing plates welded to the inner wings; suspension tops were black, with waisted design from 1973. Giving information on engine service settings, the silver 711M sticker was often found on the Sport's offside strut top.

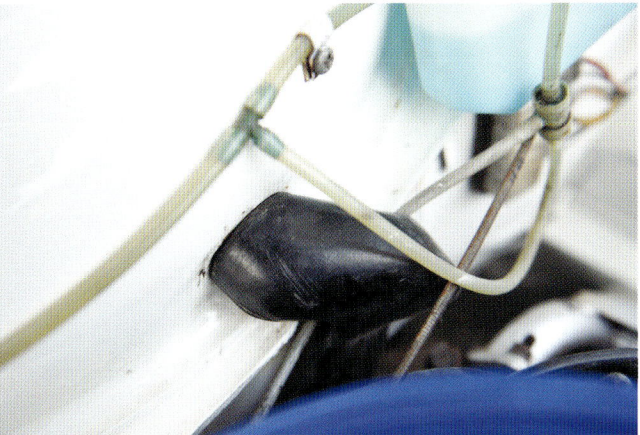

The usual Escort bulkhead drain was this black plastic, twisted shape. Washer pipes were clear tubing with white plastic T-connector.

An export-market 1971 Sport, with typical left-hand-drive battery and brake servo positions. Note silver airbox and early 70AB washer bottle.

FACTORY ORIGINAL SPORTING MK1 ESCORTS

This is the mid-term Sport steering wheel, with unpadded leather rim and stitching on the bottom. Earlier type had aluminium-effect spokes while very late versions had stitching at the quarter-past-three positions.

Early Sport interior with two-dial dash, here in left-hand-drive layout. Note the padded steering wheel with silver spokes and export-spec half-cloth seats.

VDO rev counter stuck to the early Sport's dashboard like a marketing department afterthought. In reality, it probably was.

ESCORT SPORT

Early Sports had a 70AB rounded-edge windscreen washer reservoir (with water outlet on the left-hand side) slid onto a bracket on the nearside bulkhead. It was gradually replaced in winter 1971 by the 70AG washer bottle – a similar design but with central outlet and mounting bracket spot-welded (rather than screwed) to the bulkhead. Both types were opaque plastic with clear plastic tubing and clear T-piece connector.

The Sport's bonnet prop was usually plain metal, although occasionally could be body-coloured. Under the bonnet was a white plastic retaining clip. There was a release cable running down the driver's-side inner wing top, connected to a handle under the dashboard. It gained a black plastic coating in late 1972.

A negative earth decal in white/black was placed on the nearside inner wing, there was a coolant sticker in white and black on the slam panel (in any position but commonly the nearside) and sometimes a silver engine servicing label stuck around the offside strut top. Application was somewhat random, though, so there's no way of telling what was originally fitted at the factory.

Interior

Like the AVO machines it emulated, the Sport was offered only with a black cabin including sombre seating, plastics and so on. Mainstream Escort harmonised interiors were never offered to buyers of the Sport.

Still, anyone who'd looked at the poverty-level cockpit of an early Mexico wouldn't have been especially disappointed by the Sport – it had the same black rubber floor mats rather

Inside a Sport, the greatest giveaway that it was a mainstream rather than AVO machine was its putty-coloured headlining. The Sport's passenger sun visor never left the factory with a mirror.

Regular cable-clutch Escort pedal box had silver accelerator after October 1973. Carpets in this car were fitted after production.

Flat-faced gauges with black surround were similar to late-spec RS but with 110mph rather than 130mph speedometer. The rev counter had no red line after December 1972.

FACTORY ORIGINAL SPORTING MK1 ESCORTS

The 1972 Sport interior – still featuring the earlier steering wheel. Cloth seat option now provided padded GT type in charcoal brushed nylon.

than carpets, and identical basic PVC seats. The fronts were fully-tipping with vertical stitching and a backrest-mounted lever. Then, from October 1973 they featured fixed bases and tipping backs, again operated by a lever on the backrest. Reclining seats weren't available but cloth upholstery was optional – when fitted, the Sport housed padded XL-style seats with horizontal stitching but without their plastic runner surrounds, although they were added on later models. Until autumn 1972 the covers were charcoal brushed nylon, superseded by charcoal Beta cloth until November 1973, when black Beta was used. Export-market Sports were available with half-cloth upholstery, having black vinyl covers with charcoal fabric centre sections.

In the back of a Sport was the standard vinyl Escort bench, but a padded XL-type seat was fitted when cloth was specified. The Sport's rear seat crossmember was body-coloured until November 1973, after which it was painted black. It lacked the PVC cover that accompanied carpeted cars.

Sport door cards were always the basic unpadded type in black vinyl. Window winders and door handles were the usual parts in chrome, with black plastic rotating knobs on the winders. The door lock pins had slim black buttons until August 1973, after which they were mushroom-shaped. Sport rear three-quarter trims were black fibreboard with push-round black plastic ashtrays and no armrest extensions.

The most noticeable difference within an early Sport's

Much of the Sport interior was basic Escort, without even the luxury of a cigar lighter. Most Sports had only two switches on the fascia – the hazard flashers came in August 1972 and this car's heated rear window was an optional extra.

Round plastic speaker grille in rear parcel shelf accompanied optional factory-fitted radio or tape player.

Back seat matched the fronts – standard Escort kit in black vinyl.

cabin was the absence of a proper sporting Escort six-dial instrument cluster. Until August 1972 the Sport featured a two-clock binnacle taken from the Escort L (including speedometer, fuel and water temperature gauges) in black with chrome-look rings. A separate VDO rev counter was found in a textured black pod mounted on the padded dash top between the dials and A-pillar.

Thankfully for Sport sales, a full six-dial GT instrument assembly was fitted in August 1972, finished in black like an AVO cluster. It featured large speedometer and tachometer plus small gauges for fuel, battery level, oil pressure and water temperature. All had flat black faces and white needles, plus chrome bosses on the speedo and rev counter. Until December 1972 there was a red line at 6,300rpm, after which it was deleted. Up to mid-1973 the oil pressure gauge had

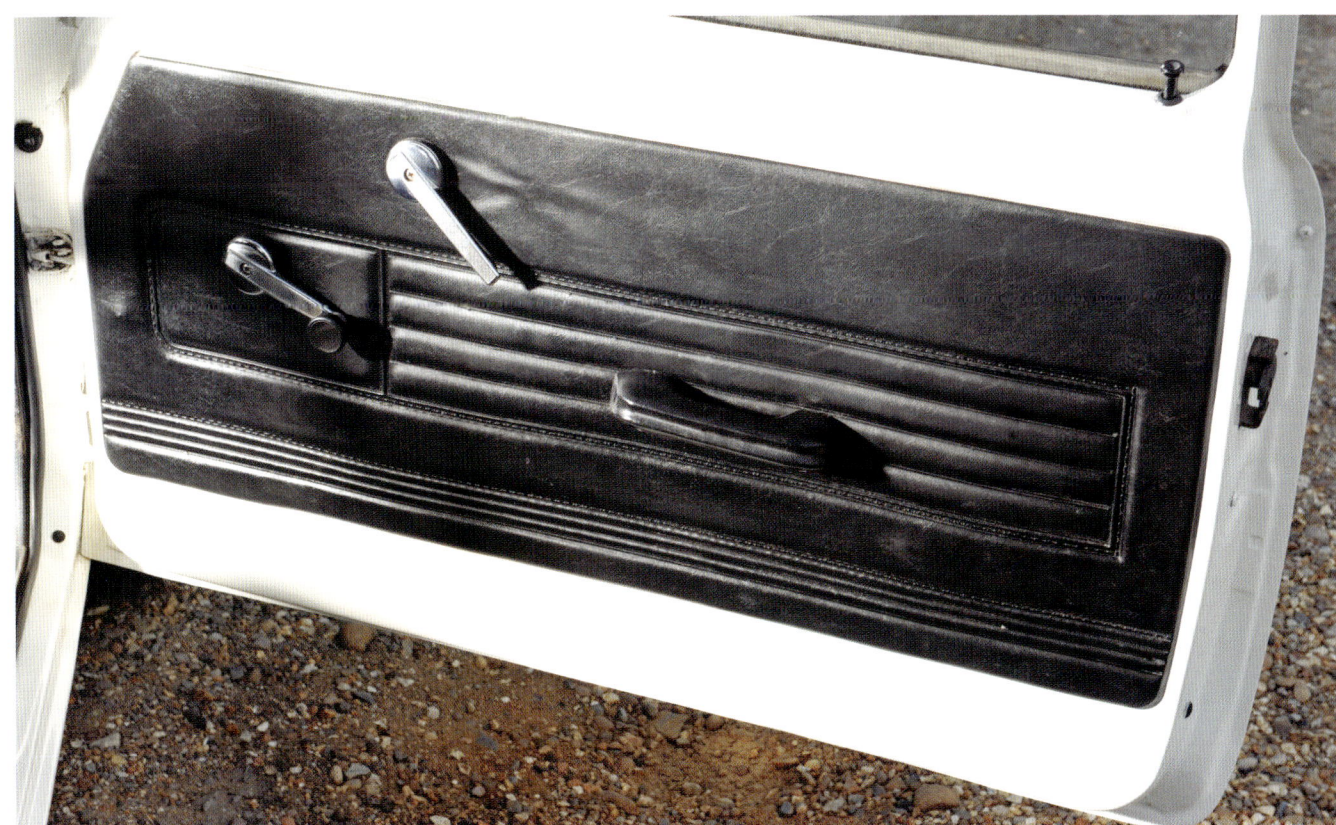

Sport door cards were basic Escort spec, always in black vinyl. Here are the mushroom-headed lock pins, seen from August 1973 onwards.

imperial lettering but empty blocks for bar were gradually introduced.

Of course, the black, padded dashboard top was swapped to accept the larger instrument cluster but everything else remained. There were round, adjustable air vents and heater controls with black plastic levers, metal surround and black Mazak glued-on diagram.

The Sport's black plastic fascia housed an ashtray (with grained finish) flanked by rocker switches (for wipers and heater) and black plastic choke knob. The first Sports had two slots for switches, but from late 1971 there were five holes, some with blanking covers.

August 1972 brought hazard warning flashers as standard, when an accompanying switch was added to the fascia; from right to left they were: two-speed wiper switch, two-speed heater switch, blank, ashtray, blank (or heated rear window switch if fitted), hazard warning light switch. There was also a circular dashboard-mounted hazard warning light in orange with chrome surround; from April 1974 it gained a transparent red lens.

August 1972 also moved the headlamp switch from the dashboard (on the right of the instrument binnacle) to the GT-type position under the main instruments.

The Sport had a black cardboard parcel shelf under the passenger-side dashboard, attached with plastic-headed brass clips into black metal brackets; from late 1973 the driver got a shelf too. In the footwells were black cardboard kick panels, without the map pocket found on higher-spec cars.

There was no cigar lighter and no option of a centre console, but a push-button radio was available, mounted in a holder under the fascia and coupled up to a round speaker in the black cardboard rear parcel shelf.

The Sport's steering wheel was taken from the Capri GT. It closely resembled the mainstream Escort padded three-spoke part with grey badge in the middle, but was improved thanks to a cushioned leather rim and brushed aluminium-effect spokes. From around October 1973 the spokes became black and the leather lost its padding. From late 1974 the steering wheel gained stitching at the quarter-past-three position, rather than one joint at the bottom. Like other Mk1s, there was a single column stalk, complete with chrome horn push.

The Sport shared its pedal box with all other cable-clutch

This wasn't the usual combination – early Sport had spare wheel on boot floor, with no mat; later model had wheel in well plus the carpet. All had grey primer petrol tank.

Escorts. It had black metal levers and black rubbers with moulded horizontal lines. From October 1973 there was a larger accelerator pedal, with bare metal lever that gained a pad in late 1974. A foot-operated wash/wipe was fitted to the left of the pedal box after autumn 1972.

Like the GT from which the Sport took its transmission, the gearstick was chrome; the gaiter and plastic four-speed gearknob were standard Escort parts. Behind the gearstick was a black metal handbrake lever with bare steel push button. The last few cars received a black push button and Mk2 lever with more ratchets. Static three-point seat belts were fitted at extra cost, with later cars offered inertia reels too.

One area in which the Sport never looked like an AVO machine was under the roof skin; here there was always a mainstream Escort putty-coloured headlining, matched with padded sun visors. There was no vanity mirror for the passenger, nor were there any grab handles.

Until autumn 1972 the Sport was fitted with a fixed rear-view mirror, which was then replaced by a grey dipping version. From October 1973 until October 1974 there was a black plastic dipping rear-view mirror with tapered sides, which finally gave way to a black Mk2-type flat-sided mirror head on a black Mk1 stalk.

Inside Boot

If an Escort Sport owner wanted to convince you he was driving a proper RS, all he had to do was lock you in the boot. That's because the early Sport's 13in steel spare wheel was mounted on the boot floor, with one long stud and nut through a bolt hole. There was also a body-coloured hook for the tool roll to the top right of the spare wheel, and some early Sports even featured a complete AVO-style boot floor, complete with bolts for the stone deflector (not fitted).

From around November 1973 the spare was moved to an upright position in the wheel well, along with angled bracket and woven strap, extended by about an inch. From this point the tool kit was moved too – generally a mid-blue screw jack and satin black wheelbrace in fawn muslin sack. During November 1973 the jack was painted dark blue, lacking a winder knob. The very last cars had a black bag.

True to its humble origins, the Sport had no luggage compartment light, and a mat was not officially standard until November 1973, although they were fitted to press cars.

The Sport's petrol tank was generally primer grey (not glossy), although after October 1974 many were satin black. The rear light protectors were black plastic until autumn 1974, after which they became clear.

Sport colour schemes

Colour	Colour code	Introduced	Discontinued
Ermine White	B	Launch	May 1972
Pearl Grey	2	Launch	August 1972
Evergreen	6	Launch	August 1972
Tawny	S	Launch	August 1972
Sunset	J	Launch	November 1973
Sapphire	1	Launch	December 1974
Le Mans Green	M	Launch	December 1974
Daytona Yellow	T	Launch	December 1974
Electric/ Monza Blue	U	Launch	December 1974
Diamond White	B	May 1972	December 1974
Copper Brown	7	August 1972	December 1974
Sebring Red	N	August 1972	December 1974
Purple Velvet	F	December 1972	December 1974
Stardust Silver	3	October 1973	December 1974
Flame Orange	4	October 1973	December 1974
Jade Green	5	October 1973	December 1974
Sahara Beige	C	October 1973	December 1974
Olympic Blue	E	October 1973	December 1974
Modena Green	M	October 1973	December 1974
Arizona Gold	Q	October 1973	December 1974
Vista Orange	V	October 1973	December 1974
Royal Blue	G	November 1973	December 1974

FACTORY ORIGINAL SPORTING MK1 ESCORTS

ESCORT 1300E

A true barn find but now restored, Rich Farrell's Modena Green 1300E had covered only 8,670 miles when he unearthed it in 1991. The following year it was refreshed with new front wings, shot-blasted front panel, repaired nearside rear wheelarch, resprayed bodywork and renovated engine bay. A full mechanical overhaul returned this machine to factory-fresh driveability – so no wonder it's now covered 26,000 miles. Despite remaining unused in recent years, the 1300E retains its better-than-new condition, complete with original tyres and factory-optional clock, radio, aerial and speaker.

The early 1970s were difficult times for British motor manufacturing, and even the mighty Blue Oval could feel the squeeze. With a worldwide fuel crisis slowing down sales and the specialist plant at Aveley struggling to show worthy profits, Ford needed a quick trick to weather the storm.

The solution was a small economy car with high-class accoutrements, aimed at appealing to downsizing drivers. Ford bigwigs demanded a luxury Escort, and entrusting its development to the ailing Advanced Vehicle Operations (AVO) in Aveley made perfect sense.

Using a combination of parts-bin components and a coat of fancy paint, Ford fell back on a familiar formula. The firm's concept of creating an upmarket saloon first saw success as the Zodiac Executive, swiftly followed by the Corsair 2000E and Cortina 1600E, which mixed sporty underpinnings with a plush interior and traditional British wooden dashboard. Naturally, the equally-equipped Escort version followed suit: it was named the 1300E – because it was a 1300cc machine with the E standing for Executive. Simple, eh?

Whether you call it a cynical marketing makeover or genuine enthusiast's Escort is a matter of opinion, but there's no denying the 1300E was a cracking package. Indeed, in spite of its thrown-together nature, it was in many ways the

ESCORT 1300E

Sport suspension and 13in wheels gave the 1300E a lofty ride height and firm yet comfy quality.

most complete mainstream Mk1 of all.

Primarily based on the Escort GT specification, the 1300E used the existing model's uprated Kent engine, close-ratio gearbox, stiffened suspension and front disc brakes, along with its high-spec interior and rectangular headlamps. Sport flared front wings and 5x13in wheels were joined by a compilation of components from foreign models, AVO and a selection of new designs.

Chrome driving lamps were bolted beside the headlights, Ford Accessories wheel trim rings were added, export-spec indicator repeaters were screwed onto the front wings, there was an AVO Custom Pack coachline, special badges and black vinyl roof. Inside were the cloth seats normally seen as extra-cost options on XLs and GTs, American walnut cappings on the doors and dashboard, GT option-fit centre console and leather-rimmed steering wheel.

Customers were offered a choice of modern metallic paint finishes, beginning with purple and two shades of gold (before eventually extending to a full range of solid colours).

Three 1300E prototypes were put together before proper production began on 12 December 1972, with a Purple Velvet machine bearing chassis number BBATMT00847. The 1300E's official launch was 1 March 1973, when it became available through Ford dealers nationwide. The first 1,000 were Purple Velvet, with Amber Gold and Venetian Gold available after February 1973.

Because the car was intended as a limited run rather than mainstream model (the initial target was 5,000 units) it was built in a typically chaotic manner. A 1300E started life in Halewood as an Escort Sport, where it was given a colour plate reading Special Campaign. It was then equipped with a rectangular-headlamp front panel, sprayed a suitable shade and furnished with an upgraded interior.

These all-but-completed Escorts were shipped down to Aveley, where an assembly facility was set up to add the 1300E's extra parts. The production line ran separately from

With full-width front bumper, overriders, rectangular head-lamps and vinyl roof, this was Ford's ultimate interpretation of an executive Escort.

FACTORY ORIGINAL SPORTING MK1 ESCORTS

Heated rear window and bumper overriders were standard 1300E kit. Central bumper cutout was seen on all but the very first 1300Es.

the AVO carousel, where workers who normally built RS1600s and Mexicos now turned their hands to the 1300E. Their role was to make paintwork corrections (to rectify runs and orange peel in the awkward metallic), and add the vinyl roof, coachline, driving lamps, badges, wheel trims, steering wheel and wood cappings.

Until October 1973 all 1300Es were completed at Aveley, where the model helped to keep AVO afloat. Today, these cars are commonly referred to as Series One 1300Es.

The Series Two followed immediately afterwards, now fully finished at Halewood, based on the Escort XL (or sometimes Sport) and offering a broader choice of paint schemes. A four-door version (always XL-based) was added to the line-up in April 1974, with the first example being painted Sahara Beige and bearing the chassis number BBAFPT33502.

Production of the 1300E ended on 16 December 1974, with the final two-door chassis number BBATPG50211. All were right-hand drive. Owners' club figures suggest 6,768 two-door 1300Es were manufactured, plus 4,022 four-doors.

The 1300E formula was successful enough for Ford to mirror the package for overseas markets, naming it the Escort GXL. The specification was mainly 1300E but with minor alterations including Wipac square-edged spot lamps rather than round-edged Lucas oblong units, centre console-mounted clock and part-cloth, part-vinyl seats.

The GXL was built in left-hand drive or right-hand drive from April 1974 until December 1974 in two- or four-door bodies, although most were four-doors. A heavy-duty bodyshell was optional but rarely specified, as was automatic transmission.

Although the 1300E never sold in the quantities of its Cortina counterpart (or captured the public's imagination in quite the same way) it filled a gap in the market, and maintained Ford's pursuit of producing small, sporty saloons with an executive touch. And even though the badge was dropped for the Mk2 range in favour of the extra-plush Ghia, the E concept continued for years to come.

Escort 1300E production often occurred in batches of the same colour. Most Modena Green examples (as seen here) were made during November 1973 and March 1974, and a last large run of 1300Es saw around 250 Modena Green two-doors built at the end of November 1974.

ESCORT 1300E

Engine – Block, Head and Sump

Based on the Escort GT, the 1300E used an unchanged version of the metric 1300GT Kent Crossflow powerplant. That meant four cylinders, 1297cc and 72bhp.

Its 711M cylinder block had 711M-6015-A-A cast in raised characters on the side of the crankcase, along with a T-number between the core plugs (often, but not always, T12). The engine block was semi-gloss black, with a white paint splash on a lug near the bellhousing and starter motor. A unique engine number was hand-stamped below the cylinder head between exhaust manifold ports one and two.

The 1300E's crankshaft was mildly balanced, with drillings through the crank webs. There were normal Crossflow connecting rods and 1300HC/GT alloy pistons with three rings and valve cutouts. They gave the 1300E a 9.0:1 compression ratio, although Ford literature claimed the 9.2:1 of earlier GT powerplants.

Usually, the 1300E was fitted with a 272-degree CA camshaft but there were supply difficulties from December 1973 until December 1974, when 1300HC-type CC cams were often used instead; visibly the parts were almost identical, but a CC-equipped engine would struggle to rev to the GT's 7,100rpm limit.

A 1300E cylinder head was the regular flat 1300HC item, with four individual inlet ports on the right and four exhaust ports on the left. The valve face diameters were 38mm inlet, 31mm exhaust. Under the rocker shaft, the cylinder head was cast with a number 37, which also applied to 1600cc heads – externally, when fitted to an engine, they were identical. After October 1973, characters corresponding to the engine code were stamped into the head near the top rearmost exhaust manifold stud – on a 1300E's GT engine it was J3, but the standard 1300HC said J2.

Above the head sat the usual long-neck Crossflow rocker cover in semi-gloss black with red-on-blue 1300GT sticker. But from November 1974 the decal was deleted, leaving the rocker cover completely plain. Regardless of year, the oil filler spout was bunged with a black plastic cap bearing a Ford oval logo and 71 part number.

The 1300E's dipstick was the standard bare alloy Crossflow part, slotted inside an extended tube bracket designed to clear the GT airbox. It dipped into a normal Escort Crossflow sump.

There was an externally-mounted Ford 35-to-40psi oil pump under the distributor, generally painted black or sometimes left bare. A cartridge-type filter screwed on underneath. The 1300E's breather system was updated during late 1973, from having an external plunger to an internal plunger, and was much smaller overall.

Under the bonnet was a full Sport setup, including 72bhp 1300cc GT engine and servo-assistance for the front disc brakes. The 1300E's inner wings were standard Escort, without heavy-duty strengthening plates.

FACTORY ORIGINAL SPORTING MK1 ESCORTS

Cooling came from a normal Escort 1300cc radiator and beige seven-blade fan. Some 1300Es of this age had a black, rather than bare metal, thermostat housing.

Original Ford sticker showing radiator part number.

Cooling System

Like the standard Escort Sport and XL on which it was based, the 1300E featured a small 12-fins-per-inch radiator, with a black copper top and black fins. Some 1300Es even inadvertently received a nine-fins-per-inch Escort 1100 radiator from the factory. The radiator cap was a regular AC 13psi standard-reach part.

A normal Crossflow bare aluminium water pump was bolted to the engine, along with a beige seven-blade fan. There was an 88-degree wax thermostat in a bare alloy housing. But during November 1974 (when Mk2-type engines were introduced) the housing was changed to black.

As you'd expect, the 1300E was fitted with standard Crossflow black rubber coolant hoses. They were made by a variety of suppliers, so the hoses had no specific numbers, marks or stamps. They were held on with wire clips, rather than Jubilee types (the only exceptions being breather and servo pipes, and even then it was unusual).

Fuel System

Fuel was fed into a 1300E engine with the traditional Ford GT Weber twin-choke carburettor – in this case a downdraught 32DGV with throttle cable bolted onto the linkage.

Above it was a round metal airbox with facility to change the intake angle for summer or winter running. On the 1300E the airbox was painted mid-blue, and contained a paper filter element. Early airboxes said AC on top but the lettering was deleted on later cars in favour of just the Ford oval.

The carb sat atop a Weber-specific Ford manifold, complete with casting lug for the two-bolt throttle linkage. An AC mechanical fuel pump lived under the inlet manifold on the side of the cylinder block. It had a bare steel finish, gauze screen and inverted sediment bowl.

There was a Motorcraft UFO-style fuel strainer and black braided fuel lines.

GT airbox in blue sat above Weber 32DGV carburettor. Late cars like this lost the AC lettering on the airbox lid, leaving the Ford logo.

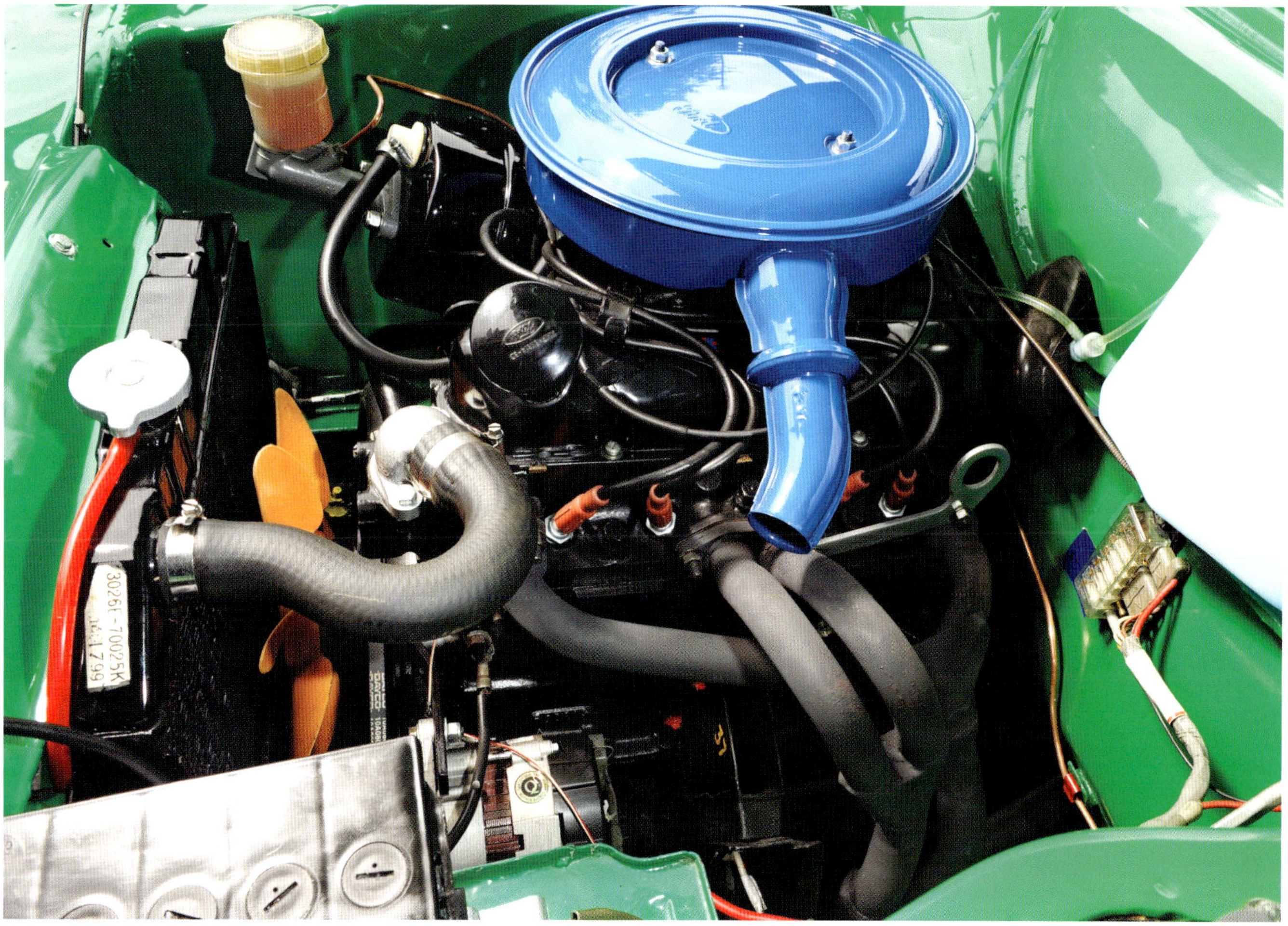

ESCORT 1300E

Tubular four-branch exhaust manifold was bare steel from new, but very prone to cracking.

Exhaust System

Getting gases out of a 1300E's engine was the work of a normal GT exhaust system. It included a tubular steel four-into-two-into-one manifold (clamped adjacent to the gearbox), large bore (1⅞in) pipework, an oval centre silencer and round back box held under the boot floor with an L-shaped bracket. From the factory the exhaust had a bare steel finish, but the inevitably frequent Ford replacements were blue-grey or silver-grey.

A mild change arrived during late 1973, when the exhaust gained revised profiles around the downpipe and over the rear axle.

Ignition and Electrical System

The 1300E's battery lived under its bonnet, clamped to a tray on the nearside inner wing. It was a Motorcraft 38Ah in black rubber or white plastic, with flat bolt-on terminals, red positive and black negative leads.

Cranking the engine was the job of a Lucas M35J 12-volt starter motor, date-stamped some months before the car's build date. A pre-engaged starter motor was offered as an optional extra. A round Lucas bobbin-type solenoid was attached to the nearside inner wing.

The ignition coil was an Autolite/Motorcraft 9-volt ballasted unit, in bare aluminum with a blue label and round terminals. A Motorcraft distributor was used (with 71-EB-12100-JA or 71AB-12100-JA part number), which had a blue colour splash on the sealed vacuum advance module. It was fitted with a standard Crossflow FoMoCo

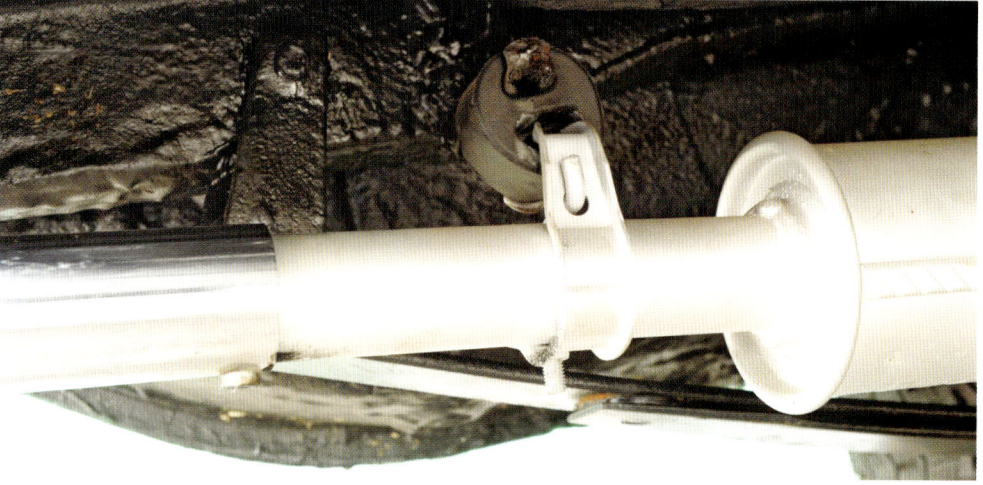

GT-spec exhaust system was mild steel – bare from the factory but silver-painted as Ford spares.

Regular Escort anti-roll bar was painted black. A cardboard undertray was fitted to all high-spec models, but most are now long gone.

or Motorcraft cap in black plastic.

The 1300E's HT leads were black siliconised rubber with black rubber caps. Made by Rist/Lucas, they had white lettering and a Ford oval logo printed on; although their part numbers were different from regular Crossflows, the leads were identical. The spark plugs were Motocraft AG22s.

Every 1300E came with a Lucas 17ACR 35-amp alternator, left bare aluminium with a black plastic back housing. The belt was plain rubber, usually (but not always) marked as Motorcraft or Ford.

Upright rear shock absorbers arived on Series Two. Armstrong units were blue, but Ford parts were black.

The 1300E featured the higher-spec Escort wiring loom, wrapped in grey tape; there was a green tag near the fuse box and a Ford or Motorcraft tag somewhere (anywhere) else. It was equipped for every conceivable Escort accessory, which also meant the 1300E's fuse box had an additional spade terminal at the bottom. The box was screwed onto the passenger-side bulkhead with internal connectors and wiring fed from behind. There were seven plastic continental fuses and a clear plastic cover.

Transmission

Beneath many 1300Es was an Escort Sport, so the complete transmission remained. That included a Type 2 close-ratio four-speed manual gearbox with the usual GT ratios of first 3.337:1, second 1.995:1, third 1.418:1, fourth 1.000:1 and reverse 3.867:1.

The gearbox casing was painted black, with a blue or red splash on the starter motor surround (as opposed to the yellow paint splash of a non-heavy-duty Escort 'box). On the tail housing was a metal tag, which contained the letters E/F or F/F. Technically, a 1300E should have had an F/F gearbox (relating to a 23-tooth speedometer drive gear for the Sport 13in wheels) but in practice some 1300Es had the E/F tag denoting 25-tooth speedo drive gear for GT 12in wheels.

The gearbox's part number generally began with 69AB, 70AB, 69AG or 70AG. But very late 1300Es were fitted with a Mk2 Sport-type gearbox with one-piece tail housing and different gearstick thread; these had a 75AB or 75AG part number.

All 1300Es had a normal Escort 1300cc cable-operated 7.5in diaphragm-spring single dry plate clutch, although it mated to a GT 16lb lightweight flywheel.

Like other 1300cc Mk1s it had a two-piece propshaft with rubber-mounted centre bearing and Timken one-piece axle with removable differential. Everything was painted black.

The rear axle ratio was the Sport's 4.125:1, with a tag on a differential bolt declaring 4.125. Series Two 1300Es had a heavy-duty differential with stronger bearings inside an updated axle casing built to accommodate a rear anti-roll bar.

Steering and Suspension

Sport underpinnings meant the underside of a 1300E looked very similar to a normal Escort, with satin black components and black rubber bushes. There was a standard crossmember, square metal/rubber engine mounts and 3.5-turn lock-to-lock steering rack with 17.5:1 ratio.

The 1300E's front suspension featured black Macpherson struts with red and blue paint splashes. Each strut had a Sachs Ford-branded shock absorber insert but Series Two dampers had chunkier tubes. The waisted-style top mounts were glossy black with a beige paint splash; their securing bolts had a coloured splash to confirm they'd been torqued to

ESCORT 1300E

factory settings – never especially neatly.

Series One 1300Es had 100lb front springs with a blue paint splash, while Series Twos had 88lb front springs with a red splash. Both types were black plastic-coated at the top and bottom of each coil. All 1300Es had a standard Mk1 Escort 20mm front anti-roll bar mounted on brackets dabbed with a yellow colour splash.

At the back, there were 1300GT-spec hydraulic shock absorbers – generally metallic blue Armstrong units but sometimes black Ford parts. Mounted ahead of the axle on U-bolt plates with rubbers either side, they were inclined by 60.5 degrees on Series One cars, attached underneath the car on a black crossmember beneath the boot floor. Series Two models had upright rear dampers, with their tops poking through the boot on a raised mounting.

All 1300Es featured semi-elliptical 116lb four-leaf rear springs in black with a beige paint splash.

Series Ones had no rear anti-roll bar, whereas the Series Two gained the late-spec Mk1 anti-roll bar, of smaller diameter than the Mk2 Escort type.

Brakes

GT-spec disc brakes were always fitted to the front of a 1300E, using Girling twin piston callipers in satin black or burnished gold, Ferodo or Mintex pads and 8.6in solid discs.

Drums were fitted to the rear axle, sized 8x1.75in and painted black.

Pedal pressure was hydraulically assisted, with a Girling Hydrovac in-line vacuum servo on a standard Mk1 Escort bracket attached to the driver's-side inner wing. Although there was no sticker on the servo, its round black drum was stamped in yellow. At the front was an aluminium Girling 75 master cylinder with clear plastic cap, which said, "Use FoMoCo brake fluid."

The UK-only 1300E featured a single-line braking system with bare Bundy steel pipework, UNF fittings, ribbed flexible rubber hoses and bare metal fittings.

Wheels and Tyres

Rather than reverting to the Cortina 1600E's Rostyle rims, the luxury Escort stuck to 5x13in sculptured sports pressed steel wheels direct from the Sport. Painted Silver Fox, they had satin black inner sections to give a spoked effect, along with chrome rim embellishers (as were optional on the Cortina 2000E).

The 1300E's centre caps were aluminium; the caps' middles were black painted with a chrome ring; they were stamped Ford on the inside. The wheels were fastened on with 7/16 UNF chrome domed nuts, as seen on the Sport and steel-wheeled AVO cars.

Michelin made the 1300E's 165x13 ZX radial tyres. A full-sized spare was squeezed into the standard Escort spare wheel well, lacking the embellisher and centre cap.

Sport 5x13in sculptured steel wheels were blinged up with trim rings from the accessories catalogue. Michelin ZX tyres were factory kit, but the red rear brake drums certainly weren't.

Bodywork

Cleverly, Ford's product planners designed an entirely new look for the 1300E, without doing much more than rummaging through various parts bins.

Being based around an Escort Sport meant a basic Escort bodyshell but with AVO-type front wings featuring flared wheelarches. Instead of the Sport's front panel, a rectangular-headlamp part was fitted, with or without a starting handle hole (depending on what Ford had in stock, no matter what year the car was built). Rumour has it that some 1300Es were converted from existing Sports long after the front panel was welded into place, and their round headlamp holes were cut into rectangles at the factory using a stencil; today you'd be very unlikely to find one or to prove the cutting was tackled on the production line…

Of course, there was a rectangular-headlamp grille, in satin black with polished surround. Behind the grille, between the headlamps, the paintwork was sprayed black. Beneath it was a full-width front bumper – identical to any basic Escort's but adding XL-type overriders in chrome with rubber inserts.

The 1300E always had the normal Escort bonnet without a washer nozzle hole – like all later cars, the copper tubes protruded through its riveted-and-screwed scuttle vents. A two-speed wiper motor linked to a pair of stainless steel arms and regular Escort blades. They swept a Triplex toughened

FACTORY ORIGINAL SPORTING MK1 ESCORTS

Standard black vinyl roof helped the 1300E's unique executive appearance. Fitted by hand after painting, it tucked under the top of the windscreen rubber.

The only Mk1 Escort to feature a standard exterior mirror, the 1300E had this upright Tex on a chrome boss affixed to the driver's door.

All late 1300Es had this big badge on the rear pillars, rather than the small 1600E-sourced emblem dropped in April 1974.

Factory aerial accompanied optional-fit radio. Base was stamped with Ford logo.

Front wing badge was unique to the 1300E Series Two. Earlier cars simply said 1300.

ESCORT 1300E

Regular Escort stainless wipers were found on the 1300E, rather than AVO favourite Speedblades.

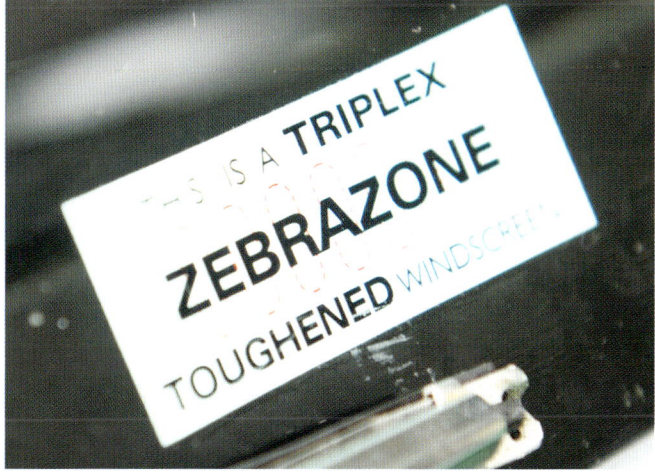

The 1300E's toughened windscreen had Triplex sticker on the inside facing out.

glass front windscreen, which had a small green or blue Zebrazone sticker in the lower centre, on the inside facing out. A Triplex laminated windscreen was an optional extra on Series Two 1300Es.

All 1300Es were equipped with a heated rear windscreen, usually with an earth cable on the driver's side; the wiring ran from the main harness in the boot. Some Series Twos had a red sticker in the rear window, saying Triplex Hotline.

The 1300E Series One had fixed side window glass, but the Series Two had opening rear quarter windows. Featuring stainless steel hinges with rubber inserts, the opening units sat directly against the rubbers. A chrome cap was fitted onto the outer retainer. The hinges were attached with Cyanoacrylate adhesive, which often failed; this led to windows falling out,

Opening rear quarter windows were standard-fit on the Series Two but were prone to dropping out. Many were replaced with fixed units in an official Ford recall.

Door handles looked the same, but late models had hollow backs. The bump protectors are genuine Ford accessories available from 1968.

Factory-fitted petrol cap was colour-coded to bodywork. AVO Custom Pack-type triple coach-line was trimmed a couple of millimetres before the stainless steel "hockey stick" trim.

FACTORY ORIGINAL SPORTING MK1 ESCORTS

Side repeaters were commonly found on export-bound Escorts but were standard on all British 1300Es.

Satin black back panel was carried over from Escort GT and Sport. Stainless steel boot trim and "hockey sticks" drew a dividing line while also acting as an effective rainwater storage device, often causing rust later.

GT-type Lucas headlamps were fitted in accordance with Ford's theory of linking rectangular lights with prestige motoring. Well, it kept the marketing men happy anyway.

and many were replaced under warranty with fixed glass. Standard Escort ridged window rubbers were used, with the usual chrome inserts and jointing cover.

Very early 1300Es had a stainless steel rain gutter trim, but this was replaced with chrome plastic prior to the model's official launch. Unusually, the 1300E also featured XL-type chrome beading around the window apertures.

A vinyl roof was part of the 1300E's unique appearance. Always black, it was hand-fitted with contact adhesive and joined just below the top of the windscreen rubber. A seam ran up either side, roughly 5in in from the rain gutter.

The 1300E used normal late-spec doors, with small locks under the handles. Series Ones had body-coloured quarter window pillars, while Series Twos had them sprayed satin black. No opening front quarterlights were offered. For the 1974 model year, the previously-solid door handles had hollow backs, as found on subsequent Mk2 vans and estates.

A single driver's door mirror was fitted to the 1300E – the only Mk1 Escort to include one as standard kit. Made by Denso (Series One) or Tex (Series Two), it was an upright rectangular mirror in chrome, with a chrome mounting boss attaching it to the door. Extra wing mirrors were offered as dealer accessories.

Along each of the 1300E's sills was an aluminium trim, with recess featuring a black pinstripe through which pop rivets attached it to the car; they were fitted by hand, so there were no set positions or quantity of rivets. Unlike the similar trims fitted to the XL and GT, the 1300E's were flared at the fronts to clear the car's wider wheelarches. Underneath, the sills were body-coloured. A flat metal oval in blue and silver was stuck to each inner doorstep, or sometimes just the nearside.

On the 1300E's rump was a satin black back panel with chrome strip along the boot lid and hockey sticks down the end of each rear wing. The only exceptions were black cars, which had body-coloured back panels.

Below, the rear bumper was fitted with overriders. Most 1300Es had the later-type Escort bumper with central cutout, although some December 1972-built cars had a completely straight part.

The boot lid was the same as every other Mk1, although the lock changed from having a flat to recessed barrel around November 1974. The boot lock and key matched the doors, but never the ignition barrel. Keys were metal until late 1974, when a Mk2-type ignition key with black plastic handle was used.

Ford didn't bother with special badges for the 1300E Series One. Instead, there was the usual FORD lettering on bonnet and boot lid, Escort script on the driver's side and front wing badges simply saying 1300. On each rear pillar was an "executive crest" motif taken from the Cortina 1600E.

For the Series Two, Ford splashed out on 1300E badges for the front wings, followed in April 1974 by a large E crest further up the rear pillars; four-door 1300Es always featured this style.

Every 1300E had a triple coachline, as found in the AVO Custom Pack. At the back it was trimmed a few millimetres before the chrome trim, while at the doors it was cut short of the trailing edges and did not wrap around.

It was fairly common for a 1300E to be fitted with an optional radio, along with stainless steel telescopic manual aerial, the base of which was stamped with a Ford logo. Usually this would be mounted on the offside front wing above a rubber water seal.

Lighting

Despite the presence of an Escort Sport underneath the 1300E's fancy clothes, the headlights were taken from the XL to keep Ford's marketing men happy. Their insistence on rectangular lamps for posh models meant the 1300E received the inferior Escort 9in wide Lucas 45/40-watt semi-sealed beams with replaceable tungsten bulbs. An ultra-rare headlamp wiper kit was available in the UK from August 1973.

Between the headlights was a pair of rectangular Lucas LR8 chrome-backed driving lamps. They were mounted on Z-shaped brackets beneath the grille which were bolted to the front panel through holes hand-drilled at the factory. Black plastic covers were a period accessory. The Escort GXL used square-edged Wipac oblong lamps on flat brackets mounted lower down.

The 1300E's front indicators were amber plastic with chrome rims, although towards the end of production some cars were equipped with plain orange lenses.

Export-spec side indicator repeaters were fitted to the front wings ahead of the wheelarches; hand-drilled and mounted with nuts and bolts or self-tapping screws, they were never in a specific place. Early 1300Es had Ford repeaters, but later

Lucas LR8 driving lamps made up for a shortfall in the rectangular headlamps' candlepower. They bolted to these black brackets on the front panel.

cars gained similar-shaped Lucas units instead.

Everything else was regular Escort kit. The back lights had plastic lenses, chrome surrounds and black plastic seals, a single-bulb number plate lamp was mounted on the rear panel and reversing lights were standard. Ford branded, they featured plastic lenses with stainless lens surrounds and black plastic backs.

A Ford-branded single rear fog lamp was a dealer option, dangled from the offside rear bumper bracket. Where fitted, a toggle switch with warning lamp would normally be added under the main headlamp switch.

Inside the car was the usual Escort courtesy light with override switch. The 1300E always came with later-type round, rubber-encased door pillar contacts.

Underbonnet

Contrary to modern opinion, the 1300E was never built with AVO inner wings or export-spec strengthening plates. In fact, most of the underbonnet area was pure Escort Sport.

The bulkhead was unchanged, with an oil pressure pipe running through a hole on the driver's side and the stock black plastic, twisted-shape bulkhead drain.

A late-model rounded windscreen washer reservoir was slid onto a spot-welded bracket on the nearside bulkhead. There were clear plastic washer pipes with a white T-connector. When specified, an optional Trico electric washer would be screwed to the flat spot on the bulkhead heater dome, and operated by a dashboard-mounted flick switch.

The 1300E's bonnet was painted in situ, so there were body-coloured hinges and retaining bolts. The bonnet prop could also be coloured, but on many cars it was plain metal. It had a clear/white plastic retaining clip attached to a welded-on loop under the bonnet. There was a black plastic-coated bonnet release cable running down the driver's side inner wing, with release handle under the dashboard. From November 1973, the slam panel cable retaining clip was deleted.

In addition to the usual Escort equipment, the 1300E was fitted with black Hardura sound dampening material on the bonnet's underside. But its proximity to the exhaust manifold resulted in worries over fire risk; subsequently it was dropped from production models and there was a low-key Ford recall to remove insulation from existing 1300Es.

Beneath the engine bay there was also a black cardboard undertray, held onto the front chassis legs with six screws plus clips to the engine crossmember and lower valance.

For its standard-equipment driving lamps, the 1300E was fitted with a suitable relay; until April 1974 a Lucas 6RA was sited on the bulkhead next to the fuse box. Later 1300Es had a Mixo or Hella Mk2 Escort-type driving lamp relay affixed to the passenger-side inner wing top. Alongside this change, the relevant light switch was removed from the dashboard and the driving lamp function was incorporated into the headlamp main beam circuit.

Later 1300Es featured a single white E-marked conformity sticker (E11/E2) adjacent to the relay on the inner wing (and sometimes an additional blue sticker near the fuse box), but cars with a bulkhead relay had none. Other underbonnet decals applied to the 1300E included a white/black negative earth sticker on the nearside inner wing or bulkhead heater dome, a silver engine setup sticker on the offside strut top (but not always) and a coolant decal on the slam panel.

On the subject of the slam panel, a 1300E's identity plates were pretty much regular Escort parts – the two-door 1300E had a chassis number beginning BBAT and the four-door's started BBAF.

Series One 1300Es wore a colour plate that said SPCL CAMPAIGN across the top. On the bottom line these cars' plates quoted the colour, followed by the word Sport rather than 1300E (for example, PURPLE A SPORT).

Series Two machines read 1300E at the top and Sport along the bottom. From around April 1974 this was swapped for the body colour followed by VINYL.

Relay for driving lamps was found on the nearside inner wing but until April 1974 it was screwed to the bulkhead. This is a Hella relay, but other brands were also used.

ESCORT 1300E

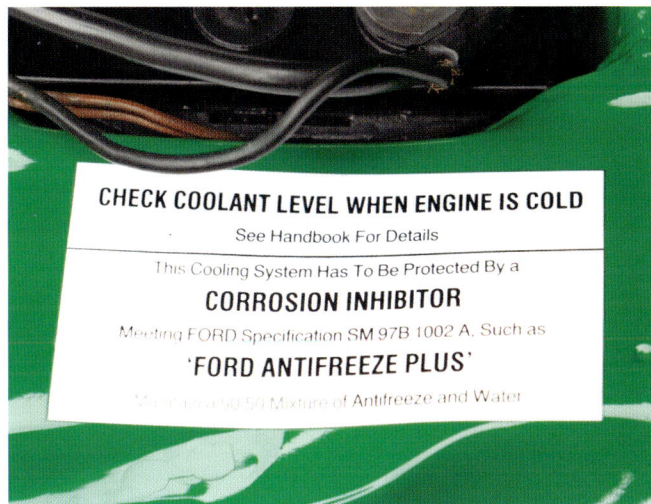

Coolant information sticker was the same across the Escort range, usually sited on the slam panel.

Regular Escort engine mounts, in black with black rubber. Paint splashes were applied at the factory in a random selection of bright colours to confirm bolt tightness.

Series Two colour tag clearly stated 1300E, but Series One said SPCL CAMPAIGN across the top.

Silver tuning information sticker gave details on metric Escort engines. Late-type Escort Macpherson strut tops had waisted middles, and were present on all 1300Es.

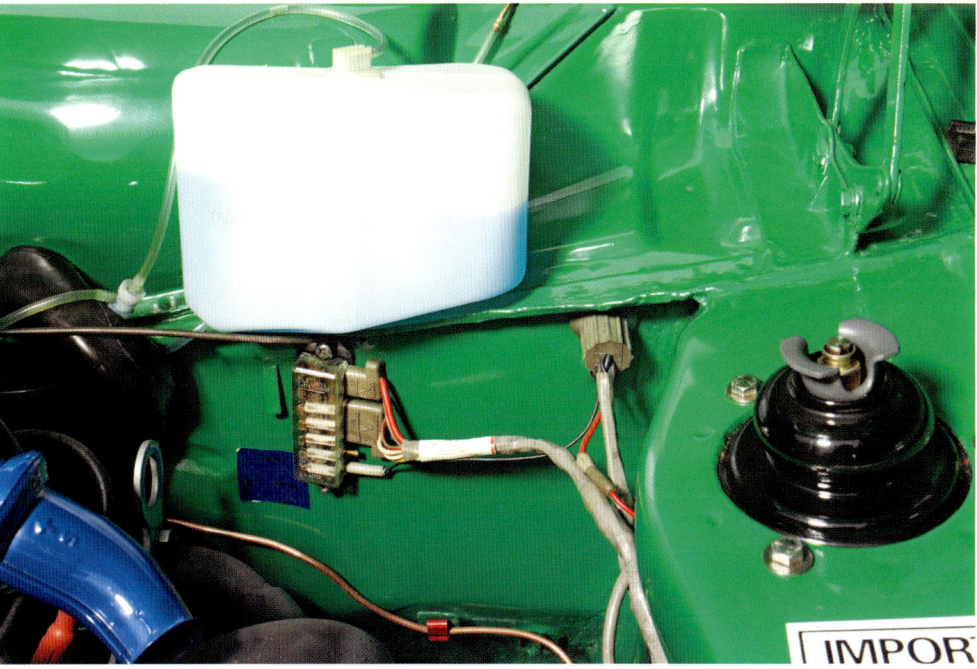

By the time of 1300E production, Ford had settled on this type of washer bottle, which slid onto a bracket welded to the bulkhead. Note the fuse box, with extra tag for accessories.

FACTORY ORIGINAL SPORTING MK1 ESCORTS

Interior

Luxury was the theme, and for the 1973 executive saloon buyer it certainly looked the part. The 1300E's cabin was kitted out with almost every extra from the Escort options list, with a few plush parts thrown on top.

Most obvious of all was the polished wooden trim, a throwback to traditional British sports cars and Ford's celebrated Cortina 1600E. Light American cherry veneer cappings were attached to the dashboard, door tops and rear quarters plus a glovebox front panel, which folded-down from within a wooden surround screwed to the passenger-side parcel shelf (the driver's was a normal black cardboard item).

The Series One's trim was secured to the instrument cluster with four external screws, while the wood around the Series Two's gauges had internal screws. In April 1974 the small bakelite glovebox knob was swapped for a large plastic knob with silver-painted edging.

All 1300Es had the post-1970-spec satin black metal six-dial dashboard pressing, with padded black vinyl top, adjustable round air vents and late-style heater controls with black Mazak diagram stuck onto an aluminium surround. On the main dashboard was a circular warning light for the hazard flashers; on early models it was solid orange within a chrome surround but from April 1974 the lens was swapped for transparent red plastic. Series One 1300Es had no cigar lighter but it was standard-fit for the Series Two – a normal Escort AC deep-reach lighter, positioned on the dashboard.

The 1300E featured the usual six-clock instruments in a black plastic binnacle, with the chrome-look bezels covered by its wooden capping. Underneath the wood, Sport-based Series Ones usually had a plain black surround, while the generally XL-based Series Two had a mock-wood sticker.

The 1300E's AC-manufactured instruments comprised large speedometer (incorporating main beam warning light) and rev counter, plus small fuel gauge, battery level gauge, oil pressure gauge and water temperature gauge mounted to the right. All had black faces and white needles, with chrome bosses on the speedometer and rev counter. Round warning lights for the alternator and direction indicators were mounted between the two main instruments.

Some 1300Es built during December 1972 had a 6,300rpm rev counter red line. There was no red line after this date. Until mid-1973 the oil pressure gauge had imperial lettering but empty blocks depicting bar were gradually phased in instead.

A black plastic five-slot fascia panel was screwed to the

An executive environment – Ford's luxury Escort was the comfiest of all.

ESCORT 1300E

Beneath the veneer was a set of Escort Sport or XL gauges. Until December 1972 the rev counter had a 6,300rpm red line. There was no red line after this date.

Light American Cherry veneer cappings gave the dashboard a traditional British luxury style. This car's driving lamp rocker switch was normally found only on the Series One. The push-button radio and surround were a Ford factory option.

Wooden glovebox lid gained this large plastic knob in April 1974. Heated rear window switch gained amber lens rather than red after December 1972.

Centre console was standard but originally found as an option on the GT. Handbrake lever knob swapped to black in November 1974.

Escort XL-type back seat was cloth trimmed for 1300E.

dashboard, housing a swivel ashtray with grained finish. It was flanked by narrow rocker switches with chromed plastic surrounds and a black plastic choke knob. Until April 1974, from right to left, the switches were: two-speed wiper switch, two-speed heater switch, heated rear window switch, driving lamp switch, hazard warning light switch. After April 1974 the order was: two-speed wiper switch, two-speed heater switch, heated rear window switch, blanking plate (the

Cloth-covered 1300E seats were taken from Escort XL options list. Series Two featured fixed bases and tipping backrests.

Round grille in rear parcel shelf contained the might of a single Ford 2.5W speaker.

ESCORT 1300E

driving lamps were now integrated into the main beam), and hazard warning light switch.

December 1972 models had a red warning light on the heated rear windscreen switch, after which it was amber. In May 1974 the bulb became longer, rising from 4mm to 8mm. The headlamp switch always lived under the instruments, while accessories like a rear fog lamp or electric screen washers gained supplementary dealer-fitted switches.

Immediately ahead of the driver was a stock black bakelite three-spoke steering wheel with grey Escort badge in the centre. The Series One used a GT version with brushed aluminium spokes and padded leather rim. Series Twos had black spokes and thin leather rim with no padding. Late 1974 steering wheels had stitching at the quarter-past-three position, rather than joined at the bottom like earlier models.

The column usually had a ribbed black metal effect, but on very late cars this was covered with a black plastic shroud similar to that on the Mk2 Escort.

There was a single column stalk to operate indicators, headlamp dipping/flashing and horn. It had a chrome horn push, but aftermarket Lucas stalks with a black button were often retrofitted.

Raiding the parts bin gave the 1300E's cabin the cloth-covered seats normally found fitted as an optional extra to the XL and GT. Featuring fixed backs (rather than recliners), the fronts had fabric facings with vinyl backs and sides. The rear seat was the same contoured two-bucket-effect bench.

Seat covers were eventually colour-coordinated to the car's paintwork but the first Series Ones (built from December

Sound insulation was stuffed into Ford's 'known reverberation points' – here helping to cut rattles from the steering column and bulkhead breezes.

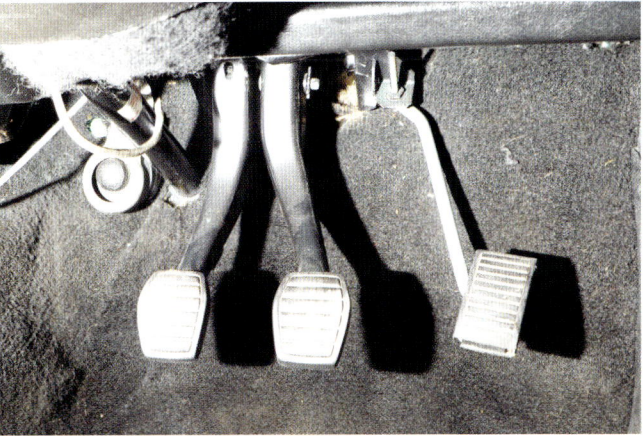

Accelerator pedal and lever swapped from black to angled silver part for 1300E Series Two.

Putty-coloured headlining and padded sun visors came with passenger vanity mirror on 1300E Series Two.

Standard Escort steering wheel had leather rim for 1300E. Very late cars had this Mk2 Escort-type plastic shroud.

Series One 1300E had numerous differences from later models. This press shot shows original Purple Velvet metallic paint, along with early badging. At this stage, Ford still hadn't opted to fit wheel trim rings.

1972 till January 1973) wore charcoal brushed nylon covers. January 1973 brought dark grey Beta cloth, with other shades following suit.

Series Two front seats were trimmed in black Beta cloth. They featured fixed bases and tipping backrests, with plastic seat runners screwed through the carpet.

Door cards were the XL/GT padded type. They were always vinyl-covered, not cloth, in a colour corresponding with the seats. The window winders and door release handles were chrome, while there were three types of door lock buttons. Until March 1973 they were slimline black pins, which were then swapped for black mushroom-headed versions. Series Twos had chrome buttons instead. The two-door 1300E's rear three-quarter trims were black fibreboard with plastic armrests and push-round black plastic ashtrays.

A cut-pile one-piece carpet and several layers of sound deadening aided the luxury feel – similar to the AVO Custom Pack's but with the gearstick hole further forward. For the 1300E it was always black unless the car's bodywork was Amber Gold, when the carpet was brown. Two- and four-door carpets weren't the same shape, but all had aluminium edging screwed to the inner sill. The rear seat crossmember was body-coloured on Series One cars but painted black on Series Twos; all but the very last cars had a black vinyl covering.

In the front footwells were black cardboard kick panels, the driver's side including a stitched-on vinyl map pocket. The very last 1300Es were fitted with black plastic Mk2-type kick panels instead.

A normal Escort cable-clutch pedal box was used, with black metal levers and black pedal rubbers with moulded horizontal lines. The Series One had a small accelerator pad and square pedal, while the Series Two gained a large silver accelerator pedal, angled inwards to the left in June 1974; a pad was added around November 1974. Beside the pedal box was a round floor-mounted windscreen washer button – again in satin black.

With the 1300E's GT gearbox came a chrome gearstick and standard Escort plastic four-speed gearknob. The black metal handbrake lever had a bare steel push button until November 1974, when the whole part was changed for a Mk2 lever with black button and a revised ratchet mechanism.

The gearstick and handbrake were enclosed by a black plastic centre console, as found in the AVO Custom Pack and optional on the GT and XL. It was held in place using screws at the front under the heater, one under the handbrake gaiter and two in the middle under the detachable ice scraper, along with a stiffening bracket. The GXL's console contained a round Kienzle clock with white hands (as found standard in the Cortina 1600E Series Two) mounted in a pod; this was optional on the 1300E.

Seat belt stalks sat on the transmission tunnel, with black plastic coating and silver push buttons until very late production, when Mk2-type gold push buttons were used instead. The Series One featured static three-point belts or optional inertia reels. On the Series Two inertia reels were always supplied; the reel in early models was rounded, but late cars had a squared-off shape. Rear seat belt kits were offered from October 1973.

A radio was also available at extra cost – sometimes a manual Plessey unit but usually a Ford P21 LW/MW with single Ford 2.5W speaker covered by a round black grille in the parcel shelf. The wiring ran under the rear seat and down the nearside inner sill; it was sometimes taped to the wiring loom but occasionally left loose.

The 1300E's rear parcel shelf was the normal black cardboard part, attached with two screw fixings covered by black plastic domed caps. Series Two models lost the metal strips at either side of the shelf.

Unlike other AVO-built Escorts, the 1300E featured the normal Escort putty-coloured headlining and padded sun

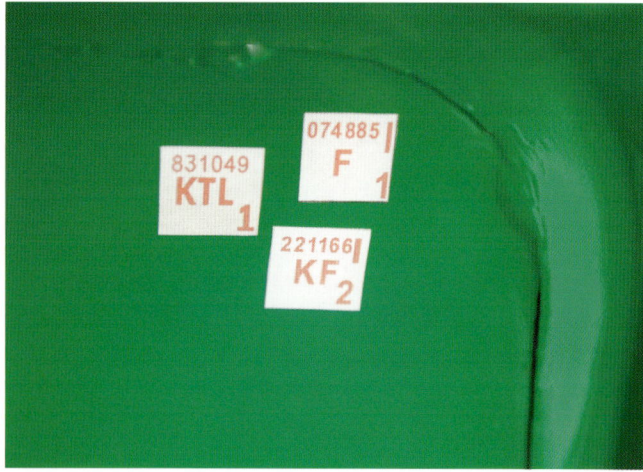

Quality control stickers were plastered under the boot lid, often in a haphazard fashion.

visors. A passenger-side vanity mirror was optional on the Series One and standard on Series Twos.

A grey plastic dipping rear-view mirror with tapered sides was found on the Series One, while the Series Two switched to a black plastic version with tapered sides. In October 1974 a black Mk2-type flat-sided mirror head was fitted onto the black Mk1 stalk.

Grab handles weren't usually fitted to the Series One (with the exception of press cars) but the Series Two included three black grab handles (one on the passenger side plus a pair in the back) with chrome end caps and black sliding hooks on the rear two. From December 1974 the caps were black rather than chrome.

Boot

Inside the 1300E's luggage compartment it was business as usual. A black Hardura rubberised boot mat was the same as fitted to other Mk1s, with a shorter version found on Series Twos to make room for the shock absorber crossmember.

All 1300Es had a spare wheel mounted vertically in the standard well but with an angled bracket fitted to the boot hinge panel for clearance when the lid was closed. The normal woven strap was extended by an inch and fastened onto a meal tag.

The tool kit came inside a fawn muslin bag found behind the spare wheel; it contained a mid-blue vertical jack and satin black wheel brace. From November 1973 the jack

Angled bracket allowed boot lid to shut with full-size spare wheel in space designed for tiny 12in tyres.

Sport 13in spare wheel was strapped into boot well, lacking the 1300E's trim ring and centre cap.

Late-model light protectors were clear plastic, rather than black of early cars.

Brush-painted A on boot floor meant car was painted in acrylic.

FACTORY ORIGINAL SPORTING MK1 ESCORTS

became darker blue and lost its winder knob, while in November 1974 the bag was changed for black.

A grey primer (not gloss grey) 41-litre fuel tank was fitted in the right-hand rear wing until October 1974, after which most cars had a satin black tank. Externally there was a heavy, body-coloured, flush-mounted petrol cap with slightly convex centre bar. A PJ chrome locking cap was an optional extra.

No boot lamp was fitted to the 1300E Series One, but it was standard on the Series Two. A black rubber boot latch cover was added from autumn 1974, when the light protectors swapped from black to clear plastic.

Sound deadening kit included felt pad under standard Escort Hardura boot mat.

Luggage compartment lamp wasn't fitted to the Series One, but was standard on the Series Two.

Series Two had upright rear shock absorbers, with top mountings protruding through boot floor. Petrol tanks were painted black after November 1974.

Colour schemes and interior trim

Colour	Colour code	Introduced	Discontinued	Interior colour	Pinstripe colour
Purple Velvet	F	December 1972	December 1974	Charcoal or black (depending on year built)	White
Amber Gold	7 or 4	February 1973	October 1973	Tan	Black or white (early always black)
Venetian Gold	CT	March 1973	October 1973	Charcoal	Black or white
Modena Green	M	October 1973	December 1974	Tan or black	Black or white
Diamond White	B	October 1973	December 1974	Saddle Brown or black	Black
Daytona Yellow	T	October 1973	December 1974	Saddle Brown or black	Black
Olympic Blue	E	October 1973	December 1974	Blue or black	Black or white
Sunset Red	J	October 1973	December 1974	Black or tan	White
Sebring Red	N	October 1973	December 1974	Saddle Brown or black	Black or white
Sahara Beige	C	October 1973	December 1974	Saddle Brown or black	Black
Vista Orange	V	October 1973	December 1974	Saddle Brown or black	Black
Silver Fox (very rare)	3	October 1973	January 1974	Blue or black	Black
Stardust Silver	3	October 1973	December 1974	Blue or black	Black, white or blue
Tawny Brown (rare)	S	October 1973	November 1973	Tan	White
Copper Brown	S	October 1973	December 1974	Tan or Saddle Brown	White
Flame Orange	4	October 1973	December 1974	Black, tan or Saddle Brown	Black or white
Miami Blue	1	October 1973	December 1974	Blue	White
Jade Green	5	October 1973	December 1974	Tan	Black
Arizona Gold	Q	October 1973	December 1974	Tan or black	Black or white
Black	Y (special order)	November 1973	December 1974	Blue	Blue
				Ruby	Red
				Saddle Brown	Red
				Tan	White
Royal Blue	G	November 1973	December 1974	Black or blue	White
Special order				Cloud	
Special order				Ruby	

Although we're not dealing with confirmed facts, combined wisdom adds the following about 1300E colours: ten were black (six four-door models and four two-doors); large numbers of Purple Velvet cars were built in January 1973; many Venetian Gold 1300Es came in March 1973; April and May 1973 saw the production of most Amber Gold; about 800 Sunset Red 1300Es were made during February 1974; Sebring was mostly in March 1974; Diamond White in December 1973 and April 1974; Silver Fox was for a batch of around 160 in November 1973; about 450 1300Es were finished in Stardust between November 1973 and November 1974, many of which were four-doors.

ESCORT RS2000

FACTORY ORIGINAL SPORTING MK1 ESCORTS

Built by AVO and restored at Aveley too, Stuart James's September 1974 RS2000 had been abandoned in a back garden for 15 years before he bought it in July 1997. It was pretty rotten, and had a con rod-shaped hole in the cylinder block. Stuart spent the next three years stripping and restoring his Escort, before sending the bodyshell back to the Aveley factory for a full repaint. The perks of being a Ford employee, eh? According to Stuart, his RS2000 was originally built for the Swedish market, which explains the export-spec features including opening front quarter windows, Sekurit (rather than Triplex) glass and twin rear number plate lamps. He's since added a pair of retrimmed Scheel seats and period German Group One steering wheel. Eventually he hopes to fit opening rear quarter windows and reinstate the heated front seats, for which wiring is still in situ.

Big engine: check. Brightly-coloured graphics: check. Motorsport ability: check. Executive luxury spec: check. Yes, the RS2000 was arguably the most complete Mk1 ever made.

The RS2000 was an entire purpose-built package that was all things to all Escort men. From the AVO-built exclusivity to the ease of maintenance, from the Mexico's off-the-shelf rallying potential to the 1300E's high-level trim, the RS2000 had it all. No wonder it kept on selling after mainstream Mk1 production ended.

Unlike previous Rallye Sport machines, the RS2000 was developed with an eye on the German market, which demanded a more civilised package than previous Advanced Vehicle Operations products. It also required RS1600 levels of performance, without any of the 16-valve engine's complexity or reliability worries.

The solution was simply to drop in a big, unstressed powerplant – the two-litre, single overhead cam Pinto. Found

ESCORT RS2000

RS2000's big-header radiator was subtly different from previous models, having a coolant temperature sensor for the electric fan.

Above the block sat a normal Pinto cast iron cylinder head in semi-gloss black, with four individual inlet ports on the left of the engine and four exhaust on the right. The part number and year of production were cast in big numbers under the camshaft, but visible only with the cam cover removed. Lifting the lid also revealed a run-of-the-mill 2.0 Pinto single camshaft, driven by a toothed rubber belt (although a WC30 cam was offered among the Group One options from April 1974). The valves were stock too, with 42mm inlet faces and 35.8-36.2mm exhaust.

The ribbed cam cover was finished in a mid-blue gloss paint, as was the timing belt cover. The latter featured a long 2000HC decal plus a production-line sticker – often a letter E (possibly meaning high-performance Pinto in Ford engine rating terms) but F, J and H have all been seen on original cars. An oil filler cap plugged the cam cover, in black plastic with a central Ford logo and 71HF part number in raised characters.

Underneath the engine was a unique aluminium alloy sump with anti-surge baffling and central pick-up pipe. It had a bare alloy finish and was cast with FORD lettering; there was a big wing protrusion on the rear left-hand side towards the gearbox.

The RS2000's dipstick was located at the back of the crankcase, accessed from the nearside inner wing. Typically the handle was bare alloy, but some very late engines may have been red..

The Pinto's oil pump was mounted internally on the crankcase base. A disposable oil filter cartridge screwed into the left-hand side of the cylinder block. An oil cooler was optional as part of the Group One upgrades.

Cooling System

Keeping the RS2000 cool was a 12.2-pint development of the RS1600 system, including a similar big-header radiator. In satin black with an overflow outlet on the left-hand side (standing at the front of the car), it featured angled brackets down the sides to allow clearance for the water pump – a semi-gloss black part in an alloy housing, bolted to the front of the engine.

Most importantly, the radiator had a temperature sensor in the top right-hand side of the header tank, used to run a Kenlowe thermostatically-controlled electric fan. With seven white plastic blades, it was mounted in front of the radiator on a three-legged support.

Everything else was pretty straightforward: there was a wax thermostat and standard 13psi AC radiator cap. The black rubber hoses were unique to the Mk1 RS2000, and were attached using normal Ford wire clips.

Kenlowe electric fan sat in front of the radiator to save under-bonnet space.

FACTORY ORIGINAL SPORTING MK1 ESCORTS

Downdraught Weber 32/36 DGAV carburettor with automatic choke mechanism was bolted to a cast alloy inlet manifold. Hoses had wire clips.

Fuel System

Lack of engine complexity was key to the RS2000's success, so the RS1600's twin carburettors were ousted in favour of a sole Weber 32/36 DGAV, complete with automatic choke mechanism.

A metal tag was attached to one of the float chamber screws, along with a code on the flange where it met the inlet manifold. This gave the carburettor type, followed by intended use and internal calibration. It was also stamped Made in Italy.

The Weber sat atop a cast alloy Ford inlet manifold and was fed by an AC diaphragm fuel pump, taken directly from the Cortina. It had a bare finish, with black rubber pipework, and sat underneath the distributor on the left-hand side of the cylinder block.

Above the carburettor was a round metal airbox in mid-blue gloss, with black support straps. The top cover said FORD OHC; it was held in place with four nuts and four screws. There was also a bolt connecting an intake pipe, which could be pivoted towards or away from the exhaust manifold to winter/summer air feed, and was marked accordingly. Inside was a paper element.

A dual carburettor kit with two downdraught twin-choke Solex 40/42mm (later switched for Weber 44IDF) carbs was an official AVO optional extra, as part of the Group One upgrades (homologated on 1 April 1974 but in use for several months beforehand). They sat on a special cast alloy Ford manifold, and were topped with an oval airbox featuring a pair of RS logos.

Exhaust System

Getting gases out of an RS2000's engine began with a plain, cast iron Cortina Mk3 exhaust manifold, with part number starting in 71HF. It was painted dark grey. Above the manifold was a separate heat shield to protect the rearmost three spark plugs, with a large clip on the back stud to hold the heater hose clear. A separate collar secured the manifold to the downpipe.

Unlike the later Mk2 RS2000, the Mk1 had a single downpipe, feeding into a large-bore exhaust system in mild steel, painted silver/grey. There was a round centre silencer and oval rear box, with double-loop rear silencer hanger welded onto the rearmost chassis rail. Until November 1973 a spot-welded bracket sat above the axle in place of the normal AVO twin hooks; later types were bolted on.

Clunky Mk3 Cortina cast iron exhaust manifold was used, along with heat shield to protect the plug leads.

ESCORT RS2000

A Group One setup was optional, including Mk2-style manifold with cast RS lettering (different from the Mk2, in that the logo was like the early steering wheel badge, rather than entwined), twin downpipes, big-bore system and double tailpipes.

Ignition and Electrical System

A variety of ignition and electrical components found their way onto the RS2000, mainly dependant on the origins and intended destination of the car.

Up front there was a Motorcraft 58Ah battery in the engine bay on a standard Escort battery tray (but with the triangular support piece moved to the outer end), mounted in line with the driver (whether LHD or RHD); Saarlouis-built RS2000s featured the typical European inner wing battery tray cutout, but left-hand drive cars built at AVO lacked this setup.

A pre-engaged starter motor was used, with ten teeth on the pinion. A Lucas item was usually fitted to British cars, but left-hookers had a Bosch. Similarly, UK and German cars used different alternators – a Lucas 17ACR 35-amp alternator or Bosch equivalent, upgraded to 55-amp from October 1974. Each was found on the right-hand front of the engine with a cast iron mount (unlike the Mk2 RS2000, which used alloy).

A regular Ford Cortina ballast resistor ignition coil was fitted (Motorcraft 711M part number for British cars; 71HM for German) in a bare alloy standard Escort bracket under the battery tray, while there were two different distributors: an Autolite (73BB 12100 AA) or Bosch (73HF 12100 JA) with mechanical and vacuum advance. There was always a black Motorcraft cap, black siliconised rubber Ford leads with printed white writing and black rubber caps. The spark plugs were Motorcraft BF32s.

The RS2000 had a late-type AVO wiring loom, wrapped in grey tape. There was a seven-fuse box with clear plastic cover and extra accessory spade terminal at the bottom. As always, it was screwed onto the passenger-side bulkhead, with internal connectors and the wiring fed in from behind.

Transmission

Like its Pinto powerplant, the RS2000's four-speed gearbox came from the Cortina. Well, kind of. In the Escort, the German-sourced Type E transmission was mated to a cast aluminium alloy bellhousing, which had provision for right- or left-handed starter motor mounting position; the non-used hole had a large blanking grommet. It also featured a modified Cortina rod change mechanism and modified stick with raised gear lever pivot point to act as a quick shifter.

Gear ratios in the Type E were first: 3.651:1, second: 1.968:1, third: 1.368:1, fourth: 1.000:1 and reverse: 3.660:1.

Visibly it was very different from standard Escort gearboxes – the RS2000's Type E had a much longer casing with pressed alloy top cover, bare alloy bellhousing, black middle

Lucas 6RA headlight relay was screwed onto the left-hand-side inner wing, fed from the AVO Escort wiring loom.

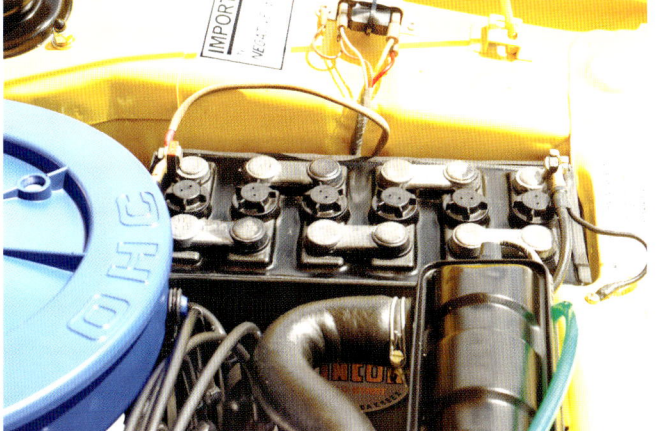

Despite cramming in the big Cortina engine, AVO managed to keep the RS2000's battery on a tray under the bonnet, in the normal Escort position but with repositioned support.

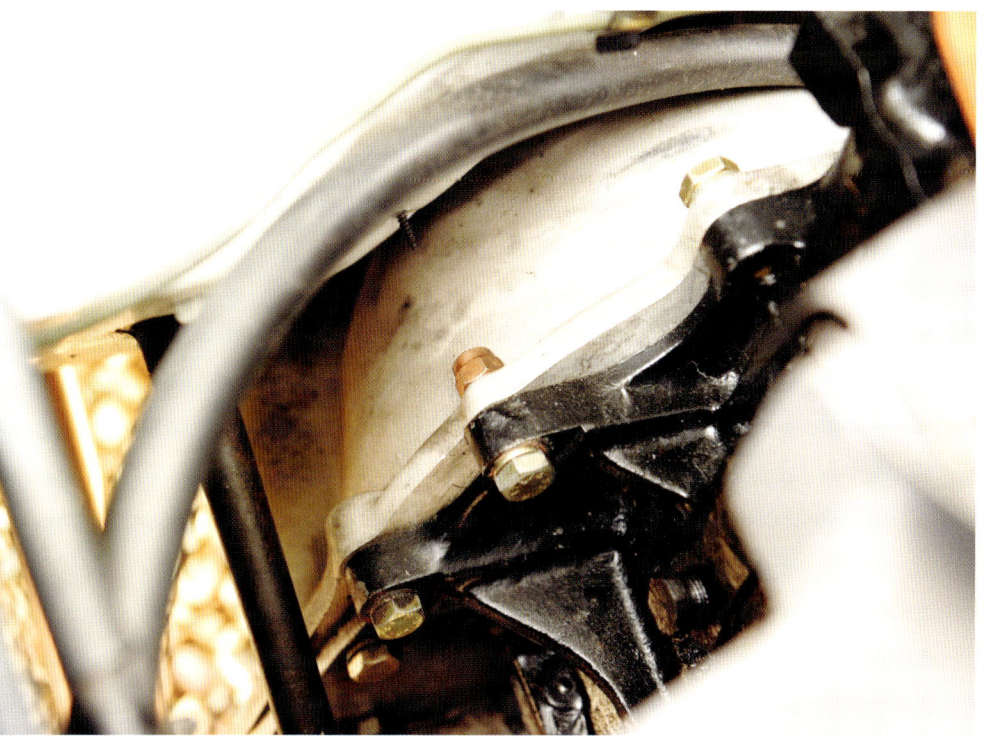

Alloy bellhousing was unique to the RS2000; it linked to a four-speed Type E gearbox.

and alloy tail. Unlike previous RS Escorts, reverse gear was left and forward towards the dash.

Naturally, it was a squeeze into the Escort's body, so the tunnel was tapped out with a lump hammer on both sides. The original Escort gearstick hole was plated up, and a new section (with aperture) welded in further back; the tunnel stiffener was chopped out by AVO.

The gearbox mounting was also modified – RS2000 mounts were the same as those of basic (non-AVO) Escorts but steel spacer blocks were used to lower the rear of the gearbox by half an inch.

Inside the bellhousing was a cable-operated 8.47in diaphragm-spring single dry plate clutch. The cable was unique to the Mk1 RS2000 but routed through the bulkhead in the normal Escort position through the brake reinforcing plate tube.

The RS2000 had a one-piece propshaft, linked to the Timken (English) hypoid bevel rear axle found in previous RS Escorts. Again, there was a pair of forward-facing brackets to pick up twin radius arms, so from November 1973 the axle was altered for later-type mounting points.

The standard differential ratio was 3.545:1 (pinion/crown wheel number of teeth: 11/39). A close-ratio Rocket gearbox and 4.44:1 final drive ratio were available as part of the Group One package. Meanwhile, a limited-slip differential was optional from the factory.

A ZF five-speed gearbox for the RS2000 was found in the Ford Motorsport accessories list, but was never fitted to production cars on the AVO line.

Suspension and Steering

Much was made of the RS2000's revised suspension, incorporating lots of minor alterations while the basics of the AVO Escort setup stayed the same.

Starting at the front, the normal Mexico and RS1600 crossmember was uprated for the RS2000 with extra strengthening fillets welded on around the engine mount uprights. The steering rack was a different part, with 17.5:1 ratio. Unlike the Mk2 RS2000, the Mk1's engine mounts were common cast items rather than alloy.

As usual there was a Twin Cam 20mm anti-roll bar with

Multi-leaf rear springs were decambered for the RS2000. Upright rear shocks were found on all but the very first right-hand drive examples.

Almost all RHD RS2000s had upright rear dampers poking through the boot floor. Parcel shelf-mounted speaker had protective cover underneath.

Bilstein gas suspension was a worthwhile factory upgrade, which came with roller bearing top mounts.

Clive Shaw restored this stunning RS2000 from wreck into show-stopping masterpiece. Today, it's better than factory finished inside, outside and underneath. First built in April 1974, the RS2000's Daytona Yellow paintwork was the car's standard shade. Its Webasto sunroof was a period (but non-original) modification but the wood pack was included from new. Its opening rear quarter windows have been lost along the way. Clive has added rare Ronal Group One RS four-spoke alloys, which suit the car admirably.

in the Cortina from 1970, this rough-and-ready inline four-cylinder unit squeezed reasonably neatly between the Escort's inner wings. Of course, this wasn't a new trick – tuners had been putting Pintos into Escort Mexicos and Sports for ages – and Ford engineers followed a familiar path of hacking about bits of bodywork to make the transplant easier.

The most obvious alteration was made at the front of the engine, where the Cortina's mechanical fan was dropped in favour of a thermostatically-controlled Kenlowe electric component slotted behind the grille. According to Ford, this also released 2bhp, conveniently taking the RS2000's power to a round ton. Meanwhile, the slam panel was chopped to bring the radiator forward, and the bulkhead trimmed back to accommodate the longer lump's cam cover.

AVO designed an aluminium sump to clear the Escort crossmember, along with an alloy bellhousing that coupled up to a new German-sourced Type E gearbox. Relaxed ratios meant motorway cruising speeds were less buzzy than previous AVO machines, while cable operation of the 8.5in clutch was a Rallye Sport Escort first. A Cortina change mechanism was modified to provide a quick-shift effect.

Aiding the user-friendly appeal was a revised suspension setup, tweaked on track by works racing driver Gerry Birrell. Softer rear springs and harder fronts tamed the car considerably, reducing the RS1600's rally-ready propensity for oversteer. Even the brakes were optimised for road use, gaining greater balance by retaining the RS front discs but reducing the rears to Escort van-sourced drums; officially this was for the European market's requirement for fitting snow chains.

The RS2000 came equipped with 5.5x13in steel wheels but many were specified with four-spoke alloys, proving the importance of dramatic looks to its target market of young professionals and thrusting executives. No wonder they fell in love with the new 12-piece decal kit, a delete option but usually seen in a contrasting colour to the car's paintwork.

Buyers were suitably impressed with the RS2000's refinement. Along with improved road manners, the cabin received luxury treatment as standard (rendering the Custom Pack redundant). That meant extra soundproofing, looped-pile carpet, flat three-spoke leather steering wheel and an options list offering wood trim and centre console. Reclining sports seats were fitted, although British machines lacked the expensive Scheel recliners found on left-hand-drive models and UK press cars.

Driven by German demand, AVO began development of the two-litre Escort in spring 1972. Briefly named Puma, the RS2000 tag was settled on during early 1973.

Twelve-piece sticker set helped to produce an extremely handsome machine. It was a delete option for fast drivers seeking a more discreet look.

Sitting lower than usual, the RS2000's suspension settings were revised for better road manners than its rallying predecessors.

The RS2000 was introduced to the public on 4 July 1973, only in left-hand drive, with the first examples marketed by German Ford Rallye Sport dealers; rumours of 2,000 cars set aside seem greatly exaggerated.

It wasn't until 11 October 1973 that UK enthusiasts could get their hands on a right-hand-drive RS2000, starting with chassis number BFATNC00066. Like previous AVO-built cars, basic Type 49 shells were shipped from Halewood to Essex, painted, trimmed and wired-up. A limited number of RS2000s (published figures suggest somewhere between 1,162 and 2,200) were also manufactured for Europe in Saarlouis using locally-sourced Escort bodies, complete with spot-welded anti-tramp bar brackets and inner wing battery tray cutout not seen on left-hand drive AVO-made machines.

Little changed during RS2000 production, but in November 1973 it received upright rear shock absorbers like the rest of the Escort range. Needless to say, very few UK RS2000s were built with inclined rear dampers.

Still, the car was immensely popular, quickly stealing sales from the Mexico and RS1600. As a marketing tool it was ideal, casting a halo effect over every Ford model. But despite being designed primarily as a damned good road car, Ford couldn't help but take the RS2000 into motorsport. It was raced in the British Saloon Car Championship and found moderate success as a Group 1 rally car, for which an engine upgrade kit was homologated – including German-devel-

There was no mistaking an RS2000 in your rear-view mirror. You'd need nothing less than an RS1600 not to move across.

RS2000 boot decals were similar to the Mexico's but extended beyond the boot lid, giving the car a wider appearance.

You can't argue with that colour scheme. Daytona Yellow and black coachlines are a classic Mk1 Escort combination.

It might look pretty low, but this RS2000's rear suspension is very similar to what came out of Aveley.

oped carburettors, performance camshaft, exhaust, Rocket gearbox, 4:1 differential ratio and uprated suspension. Clubmen were also offered a choice of Race Pack or Rallye Pack, plus many competition options.

A sole RS2000 estate was built (registered VEV 678L), converted by Ford in 1974 from one of the original batch of 1972 Mexico wagons. It kept the early inclined rear dampers and charcoal grey Mexico rear seat but gained black RS2000 front recliners, centre console, blue decals over white bodywork and black vinyl roof. The concept went no further than evaluation but the car survived.

The best-researched figures suggest 5,334 RS2000s were produced, with 3,759 sold to the British market. Twenty-five were officially exported to Australia and fitted with inertia-reel seat belts, a dashboard dimmer and carbon canister; all were standard RS2000 colours, with full-body decals or triple coachlines.

RS2000 production ceased in January 1975 after Mk1 bodyshells dried up when mainstream assembly switched to the Escort Mk2. The final chassis number was BFATRC00470, and the RS2000 remained officially on sale until 24 January 1975. And it stayed remarkably popular, mainly thanks to delays in introducing its beak-nosed successor.

With the last RS2000 Mk1 came the closure of AVO and the end of an era. The RS Mk1 was gone. But certainly not forgotten.

Without the decal kit, the RS2000 looked like a normal Escort from the back – until it quickly disappeared into the distance.

Front suspension negative camber is particularly obvious in this shot and was familiar to all AVO Escorts.

FACTORY ORIGINAL SPORTING MK1 ESCORTS

Strong and simple, the RS2000's Pinto powerplant provided performance just shy of the RS1600 with none of the complications.

Freshly restored engine bay gives us another look at the packed-in Pinto powerplant. Amazing that huge battery fits in place too.

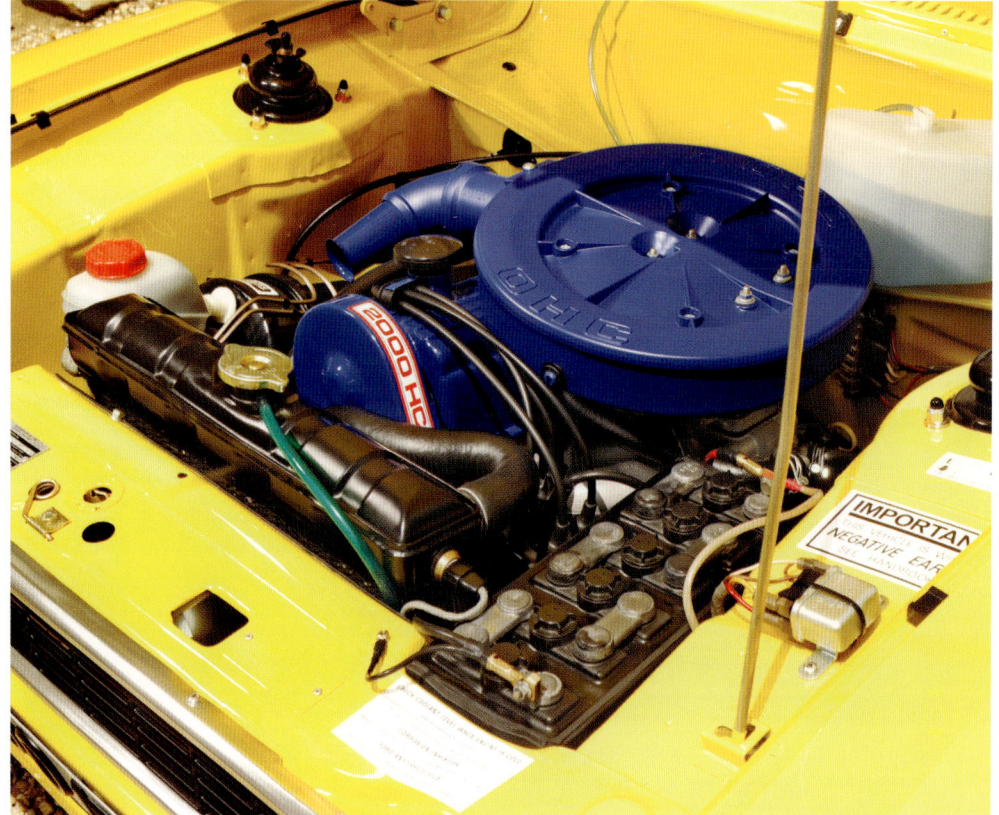

Engine – Block, Head and Sump

Cortina in origin, maybe, but the RS2000's simple two-litre powerplant certainly gave enough push from its 100bhp output. By and large it was the regular T88 Pinto, belt-driven, single overhead cam, 1993cc unit found in the aforementioned Cortina and Capris of the period, which also carried forward into the RS2000 Mk2.

The Pinto's thin-wall cast iron cylinder block was made in Cologne and painted semi-gloss black. It had a unique engine number stamped into a machined flat face under the exhaust manifold, just in front of the offside engine mount; the digits were the same as the last part of the car's chassis number. Underneath, the part number 70HM6015BA was cast onto the side of the block, along with the identification code 20 (for two-litre) in front of the exhaust-side engine mount (the mounts were steel, not aluminium).

Pinto blocks also had a code relating to the date of manufacture, cast in an oval behind the engine mount; the first numbers related to the day, the next a letter for the month (A meant January, B was for February and so on) and two numbers for the year (so, 73 equalled 1973).

Internally, the RS2000's engine was completely standard, featuring 9.2:1 compression ratio, flat-topped alloy pistons with two compression rings and one oil scraper, and a cast iron, fully counterweighted five-bearing crankshaft with copper-lead or aluminium-tin shell coatings, depending on supplier.

wider mounts and black rubber bushes at each front corner. The Macpherson struts were black with a green colour splash; they contained Armstrong oil-filled dampers with rubber bump stops and a shroud covering the piston rod.

Stock RS2000 springs were 130lb 5.3in coils in black, coated in black plastic at each coil end.

Gas Bilstein dampers were factory optional, along with uprated rally springs and roller bearing top mounts; as standard, the RS2000 received late-type waisted strut top mounts, in semi-gloss black with black collars.

The RS2000's rear end received less attention, although the semi-elliptic three-leaf springs were quite different from the RS1600 and Mexico. Decambered for lower ride height, they were rated at 85lb, with 51mm wide leaves with blue and red colour code. They were connected to the back axle using the usual U-bolt setup, featuring metal U-shaped saddles and moulded rubber sandwich pads. Single-leaf springs could be

supplied through RS dealers, and were also part of the Group One package.

Like other RS Escorts, a pair of radius rods located the RS2000's rear axle. Their shape changed from virtually straight to angled in November 1973, when the RS2000's rear shock absorbers were swapped from an inclined to upright position. Very few British RS2000's received the early-type layout (which connected to a black mounting beam underneath), and most had their rear dampers poking through the boot floor. Armstrong telescopic oil-filled shock absorbers were the norm (in black with yellow and white identification codes), but gas dampers were available as part of the aforementioned Bilstein rally suspension option.

Like other RS Escorts, the English rear axle was standard factory fitment. This car's lowering blocks are a recent addition in favour of decambered leaf springs, while the Bilstein dampers are in modern colours.

Front suspension featured Capri-sourced struts and 130lb coil springs. Factory black paintwork wasn't usually this good...

For the RS2000, the usual AVO crossmember was uprated with extra strengthening fillets. The Mk1 alloy sump featured FORD lettering in the casting.

FACTORY ORIGINAL SPORTING MK1 ESCORTS

The humble Escort van donated its Girling 8x1.5in rear drums, which aided the RS2000's brake balance.

Brakes

Maybe it was to improve brake balance, perhaps it was to save costs, or possibly the official line of needing to fit snow chains in Europe was correct. Either way, the most noteworthy alteration to an RS2000's anchors compared to other AVO cars was the use of Girling 8x1.5in drums taken from the Escort van. Smaller than normal, they were manually-adjustable, with external square-headed adjusters on their back plates (although early examples until November 1973 used pedal adjusters). The exceptions were RS2000s destined for Sweden, which gained regular RS 9in Lockheed rear drums from June 1974.

RS2000 front brakes were Girling 9.625in discs and pads, plus Girling 16PB calipers with imperial fittings. The calipers had a pale gold finish, while the front discs' stone guards were satin black.

A dual-circuit brake system was used, with a Girling Hydrovac direct vacuum servo mounted on an extended bracket bolted to the bulkhead (although ATE parts were generally fitted to German versions). A tandem brake master cylinder with integral reservoir was on the front of the servo; there was a red (Girling) cap but later replacements were clear.

Mild steel Bundy brake lines were clipped to the inner wing and bulkhead, while on the right-hand-side inner wing (underneath the servo unless the car was a left-hooker) in place of the normal Escort T-piece, was a black brake balancing valve. There were UNF fittings and flexible rubber ribbed hoses. A brake system warning lamp on the dashboard was linked to the balancer assembly.

Wheels and Tyres

Think of an RS2000 and, if you're like most people, you'll picture the traditional four-spoke RS alloys. But they were merely a popular optional extra – the standard car came with the 5.5x13in spoke-style sports steels found on the Mexico and RS1600. Similar in design to the wheels available on a multitude of lower-spec Escorts (always in 5x13in), Cortinas (with different offset) and Capris, they

RS four-spoke alloys were a popular factory option. The rims were polished, while the backs and spoke centres were painted dark grey.

RS four-spoke alloys were also available in this 6in width – although Ford didn't recommend fitting them under standard wheelarches.

156

ESCORT RS2000

weren't date-stamped, and had a flat inner rim – without the recess to take wheel trims.

On the RS2000 the steel wheels were always Silver Fox with metallic Pearl Grey centres. They were held on with 7/16 UNF chrome, domed, closed-ended wheel nuts, as used on other AVO machines and the Escort Sport.

As for the four-spoke alloys, each had a 70mm centre aperture, with a dark grey, RS-logo'd centre cap pushed through from behind. Lettering on the flat face of the spokes gave the 5.5Jx13 size (as 13x5½-H2) and part number (H71AB-1007-A-C). The wheel nuts and valves were chrome, while the wheel rims and spokes were polished alloy. Each spoke centre and the rear of all Mk1 RS alloys was painted dark grey – not Pearl Grey, which was a Ford colour that wasn't used by the wheels' manufacturer GKN Kent Alloys. That said, pre-production models possibly wore Pearl Grey-painted spokes, so there's a chance some consumer cars did too.

RS2000s were also offered with 6x13in RS four-spokes (again with grey centre caps) through the RS parts network and Special Build Programme (and came from the factory when extended wheelarches were specified). They had a different offset from equivalently-sized Mk2 wheels, also lacking the Mk2's H76 part numbers.

Wrapping the wheels was a job for 165SR13 Pirelli CN36 or Dunlop SP68 rubber, with the option of Dunlop SP Sports. Low-profile 175HR70x13s or 185HR70x13s were also offered, the latter when fitted with 6x13in rims.

Bodywork

It should go without saying that RS2000s were always built into Type 49 bodyshells, but Saarlouis-made machines weren't quite the same – they had the typical left-hand drive inner wing battery recess, and it's probable that the familiar strengthening parts were added while their shells were converted to RS-spec.

AVO RS2000s, of course, followed the regular theme of modified heavy-duty shell, with Sport/Mexico front wings and flared wheelarch lips. The vast majority left the factory without a starting handle hole in the round-headlamp front panel (including most LHD L-reg pre-launch RS2000s) but one or two early press cars did have them.

The usual Escort grille was in place, with satin black middle and polished surround; behind it the car's bodywork was sprayed satin black.

A pair of chrome Escort van back bumpers were on the RS2000's front quarters, mounted on special AVO brackets. It's not uncommon to see an RS2000 fitted with a flat-blade front chin spoiler, which was an optional Rallye Sport accessory for the 1974 model year. It was held onto brackets with two rivets either side, roughly in alignment with the bumper bolts.

A stock Escort bonnet was fitted by Halewood, but AVO

British-registered pre-launch left-hand-drive press car from March 1973. Specification included opening front quarter windows and door mirror. Note the low rear suspension and lack of starting handle hole.

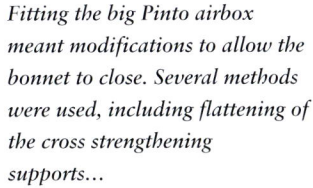

Fitting the big Pinto airbox meant modifications to allow the bonnet to close. Several methods were used, including flattening of the cross strengthening supports…

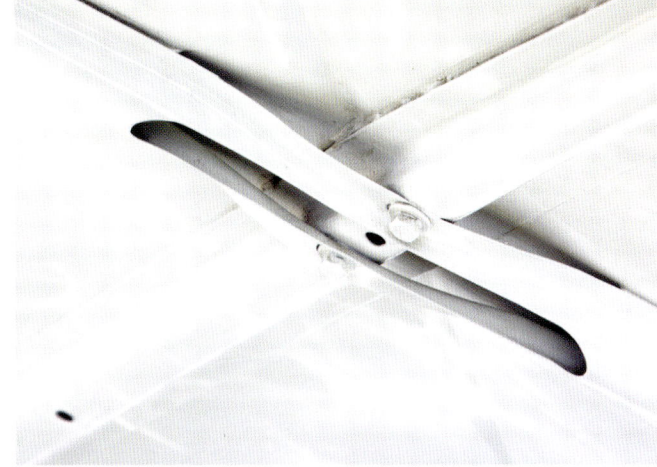

…or simply hacking them with whatever came to hand – usually an angle grinder.

FACTORY ORIGINAL SPORTING MK1 ESCORTS

RS2000 graphics were even bolder than the Mexico's, adding this proud three-section bonnet decal. FORD lettering was stock Escort.

Opening front quarter lights were offered on overseas-spec RS2000s. Note the Sekurit glass, rather than UK-type Triplex.

Like mainstream models, the RS2000's boot lock had a recessed slot from late 1974.

Period Wingard door mirror looked great but offered poor visibility; some export cars got upright 1300E-type mirror instead.

Although one or two press cars had a starting handle hole, it's unlikely any UK machines had anything other than a plain front panel.

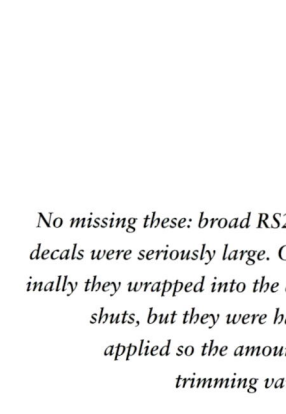

No missing these: broad RS2000 decals were seriously large. Originally they wrapped into the door shuts, but they were hand-applied so the amount of trimming varied.

ESCORT RS2000

Although this car's wasn't fitted at the factory, a Webasto sunroof could be ordered from dealers. Genuine conversions were accompanied by a badge under the bonnet.

The back lights and Escort script were what you'd find on any mainstream model. Triple coachlines tucked neatly under lamp gaskets.

Triple coachline led to bullet points on the leading edges of the front wings.

made an alteration to the underside – where the strengthening supports crossed over in the middle, the ribbed steelwork was cut and/or flattened to clear the Pinto's airbox. It's not known whether all RS2000s had these modifications, or the extent to which they were carried out, but original cars have been seen with jagged angle-grinder slashes, hammered-flat sections or complete slots cut out; usually the cross braces would be riveted (rather than bolted) back together.

The RS2000 always had a late-style Escort bonnet without a washer nozzle hole – instead, a pair of copper nozzles protruded through the scuttle vents, which were riveted and screwed onto the shell.

A self-parking Lucas two-speed windscreen wiper motor was used, with normal Escort stainless arms and twin-wire Trico Speedblade wiper blades. A wiper arm spoiler was fitted on the driver's side of British RS2000s.

The 'screen itself was a laminated Triplex but it's possible that some cars had toughened windscreens from the factory. Toughened 'screens wore a small blue or green sticker across the bottom, whereas laminated versions had a yellow

Normally (right) there'd be a single-bulb number plate light, but export-spec RS2000s had this twin-lamp setup (left).

FACTORY ORIGINAL SPORTING MK1 ESCORTS

RS2000 badges were fitted to each front wing. They were identical to the boot lid badge.

Just the normal Mk1 Escort door handle, but the big locks on this car are later versions from a Mk2 van or estate.

Rear lights and reversing lamps were standard Escort stuff. RS2000 badge sat on the boot lid's nearside.

and red sticker.

Meanwhile, a heated rear window was standard, some having a red Triplex Hotline sticker. The wiring was fed from the standard harness in the boot, while the earth cable was usually mounted on the right.

As for the side glass, it was plain Escort kit, although tints were a rare export option. Opening front quarter lights were available for foreign markets, as were hinged rear quarter windows, which were a regular factory option; they used stainless steel hinges.

Otherwise, RS2000 window rubbers were taken from the mainstream Escort, with ridged rear quarters and chrome inserts around the front and rear windscreens.

RS2000 doors were always late Mk1-style with small door locks (never the bigger Mk2 estate type). Their quarter window pillars were body-coloured until October 1973 (therefore unlikely to be found on a UK RS2000), after which they were satin black. Door handles were chrome, and from 1974 had Mk2 estate-type hollow backs. Exterior door or wing mirrors were available as accessories, although some export cars received an upright 1300E-type door mirror from the factory.

Like other Escorts, the RS2000's door and boot locks shared the same key, which never matched the ignition barrel; the latter's key got a black plastic handle from late 1974, while the former kept an all-metal finish.

Aluminium scuff plates were fitted within each door step, with a small metal Ford oval on the passenger side.

Above the side windows was a rain gutter trim in chrome-effect plastic. A black vinyl roof covering was offfered at extra cost. Where specified, the vinyl roof was fitted by hand with contact adhesive, stuck under front and rear windscreen rubbers and featured a seam roughly 5in from each side.

The vinyl roof was never available in conjunction with the RS2000's broad side stripes, which comprised a set of 12 stickers, including 8in high contrasting decals down each side. They came as standard from Ford but were a common delete option – in which case the car got Custom Pack-style triple coachlines. Remember, the Custom Pack wasn't offered on this already-well equipped model.

Regardless of the exterior specification, badges always read RS2000; they were fitted to both front wings and the boot lid's nearside.

The lid itself was a normal Escort part, without an aluminium edge trim or hockey sticks down the back panel. A flat boot lock was fitted at first, but from late 1974 was swapped for a recessed type. A rubber rear spoiler was an official Rallye Sport accessory in Germany, stamped underneath with the part number and RS logo.

The RS2000's chrome rear bumper was always the later Mk1 design, with centre cutout. Like every other Escort of the period, the car had a heavy, flush-mounted, body-

ESCORT RS2000

coloured petrol cap with convex centre bar; a chrome locking cap was a dealer accessory.

The only other alterations from regular Halewood Escort spec were the rear wheelarches, which were rolled under with a hammer by AVO staff. Rally wheelarch extensions were a readily-available factory Special Build option.

Lighting

By the time of RS2000 production, AVO was pretty happy with what lighting an Escort should wear.

Up front was a pair of Cibie 7in circular halogen headlamps with 55/55W bulbs and amber plastic indicator lenses with chrome rims. In late 1974, plain orange plastic was gradually introduced instead.

Oscar 6in driving lamps, available in pairs and mounted on brackets, were factory optional – although for the road-biased RS2000 they were perhaps less popular than on its clubman-rallied predecessors. Where fitted, the auxiliary lights would be accompanied in the cockpit by Ford rocker switches – mounted in centre console slots if fitted.

On the tail, the lights were the usual late-type Escort design with chrome surrounds and black plastic seals. Beneath them were flush-mounted reversing lights. Exactly the same as those on mainstream Escorts, they were Ford branded with plastic lenses, stainless lens surrounds and black plastic backs.

The RS2000 had a single-bulb number plate lamp in the UK, but export markets had twin lamps, again mounted on the rear panel.

A single Ford rear fog lamp was a dealer accessory, usually dangled from the driver's-side rear bumper bracket. It was operated by an official Ford rocker switch in the cabin.

Underbonnet

Lifting an RS2000's bonnet revealed the usual Type 49 inner wings with spot-welded suspension top plates.

Unlike the RS1600 and early Mexico, the RS2000's battery was always in the engine bay, clamped to a normal Escort tray on the passenger-side inner wing; the difference was the RS2000's triangular support bracket was moved a few inches to the outer end of the tray. Left-hand-drive RS2000s built at Aveley retained this layout, but Saarlouis-produced versions had a big recess for the battery in the right-hand inner wing.

The bulkhead top featured the usual body-coloured Escort bonnet hinges and retaining bolts, with a flat spot on the heater dome for an optional Trico electric washer pump. Normally the washers were foot-operated from within the car, fed from a reservoir on the left-hand side – it was always the later 70AG opaque plastic rounded bottle with central water outlet, on a bracket spot-welded onto the bulkhead. The washer pipes were clear plastic, with a white plastic T-piece.

Below the heater dome, the bulkhead was roughly cut out

RS2000 headlamps were 7in circular Cibie halogens.

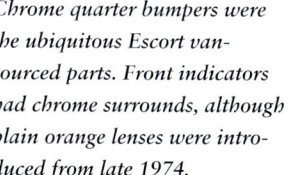

Chrome quarter bumpers were the ubiquitous Escort van-sourced parts. Front indicators had chrome surrounds, although plain orange lenses were introduced from late 1974.

161

FACTORY ORIGINAL SPORTING MK1 ESCORTS

Aveley-built left-hand-drive RS2000s never featured Euro-spec inner wings (with battery cutout). On this shot you can also see the brake balancing valve just in front of the bulkhead.

Single E11/E2 lighting sticker was generally found on the nearside strut top of later-model RS2000s.

The RS2000's dipstick was often bare alloy, but some were seen with painted handles.

ESCORT RS2000

A mid blue was picked off the shelves for the round airbox, which matched the ribbed cam cover. This car's intake pipe is in the summer running position.

Traces of the Mexico remained in the RS2000's bodyshell, with a hole remaining for the bulkhead-mounted clutch reservoir. The cable-clutch RS2000 had a bung here instead.

Pinto timing belt cover was painted mid-blue. The 2000HC sticker was always present, but the E was sometimes swapped for other letters.

Girling Hydrovac servo helped to power the RS2000's dual-circuit brake system, whereas German-spec cars featured ATE components.

Alternator swung from a cast iron mount – unlike the Mk2 Escort RS2000, which used an alloy part.

If the Pinto appeared to be a tight squeeze, that's because it was! AVO chopped back the bulkhead to make room for the OHC engine's cam cover.

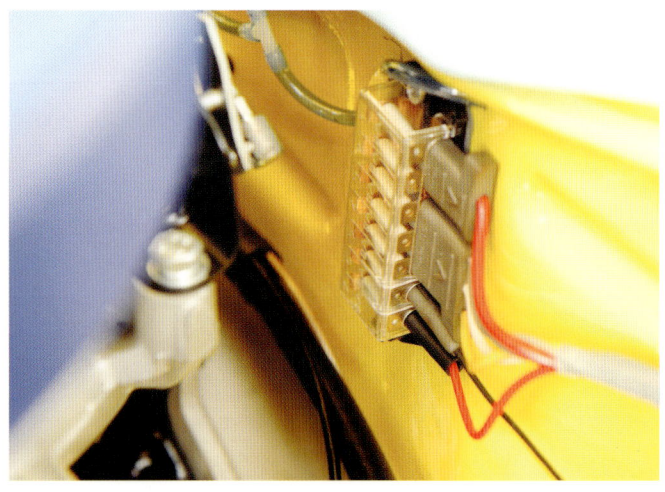

Girling tandem master cylinder complete with Girling red cap.

RS2000 had AVO wiring loom and seven-fuse box with clear plastic cover.

to take the big Pinto powerplant's cam cover, and no bulkhead drain tube was fitted into the hole. In front of the driver, the flat bulkhead top had an unused opening for the late-spec Mexico clutch reservoir, with a black grommet to seal it off. Like a normal Escort, the pedal box reinforcing plate had a tube through which the clutch cable passed.

As on regular Escorts, the RS2000 had a prop attached to the bonnet's underside, with a clear/white plastic retaining clip connected to a welded-on loop.

The bonnet cable ran down the driver's-side inner wing,

Sporty yet luxurious, the RS2000's cabin was still a sombre affair. This example is equipped with German-spec Scheel seats and Group One steering wheel.

ESCORT RS2000

wearing a black plastic coating. The slam panel was updated during November 1973, when the bonnet catch received a smaller hole with retaining lip; the striker plate was deleted but the bonnet gained a small strengthening tab beside the catch. To take the big-header radiator forward, all RS2000s had a couple of inches hacked way from the centre section of their slam panels, with the steel folded over and the central vertical support removed. The radiator panel gained extra hand-drilled holes for loom clips to feed the electric fan.

Typical of an AVO Escort, the RS2000 had a fused Lucas 6RA headlight relay on the left-hand-side inner wing, fed by wiring from the main loom plus a short brown earth cable

Scheel seats were fitted to German-market RS2000s. These have been retrimmed to original spec, in reproduction black Beta cloth.

When there was no wood pack, an RS2000's plain black dashboard had its cigarette lighter alongside the hazard warning light. The deep centre console was a popular RS accessory, which came with a blanking plug in place of a lighter. The push-button radio was pricey factory option.

Flat-faced instruments were always present, rather than dished dials of earlier AVO cars. Speedo read up to 130mph.

FACTORY ORIGINAL SPORTING MK1 ESCORTS

Polished wood pack covered the usual RS instrument cluster. It was screwed on from underneath, like the late-spec 1300E.

A familiar UK-spec RS2000 cockpit, featuring roll-top seats and optional wood pack – which lacked the door cappings found in the similarly-equipped 1300E.

connecting to one of the relay screws.

Late RS2000s had a single E11/E2 lighting sticker on the nearside strut top but the first cars featured separate white E2 and blue E11 decals. There was also a negative earth sticker (generally on the nearside inner wing) plus a white/black coolant sticker on the slam panel.

Interior

Fulfilling its role as an executive express, the RS2000's luxurious cabin contained a hand-picked concoction of the best bits from the Mk1 range, combining sporty RS appeal with 1300E-type comfort. So much so that the traditional AVO Custom Pack was never offered as an RS2000 option – because most of the kit came as standard.

Like its predecessors, the RS2000 could only be bought with a black interior, with just body-coloured metalwork around the doors and rear quarters to break up the gloom.

The dashboard was what we'd come to expect from a Rallye Sport Escort, featuring satin black six-clock metal pressing, padded black vinyl top, late-type adjustable black plastic air vents and heater controls with aluminium surround and black Mazak diagram. In front of the passenger was a standard cigarette lighter and warning lamp for the stock hazard flashers.

The RS2000's instruments always had flat black faces, rather than the dished dials of earlier models. Similar to the instruments in mainstream Escorts, they comprised a large speedometer (incorporating main beam warning light) and rev counter plus small gauges for fuel, battery charge, oil pressure and water temperature to the right.

There were white needles, with chrome bosses on the speedometer and rev counter; the speedo reached 130mph, while the 7,000rpm rev counter had no red line on all but the very first pre-production cars. The oil pressure gauge featured no writing.

On the dashboard underneath and to the right of the instruments was the RS2000's headlamp switch. Other switches were in the black plastic multi-hole fascia panel, which also served as a cover for the two-speed heater. All were black plastic rocker switches with chromed plastic surrounds.

From left to right, the switch panel was laid out as follows: hazard warning lights, brake failure warning, heated rear window (with orange lens), two-speed heater, two-speed wiper. In the middle was the regular grained-finish plastic ashtray, while the far right had a black plastic blanking cover in place of the normal Escort's choke knob.

Each side of the cabin had black cardboard parcel shelves under the dashboard, attached with plastic-headed brass clips into black metal brackets.

A flip-down glovebox panel was included as part of the RS2000's optional wooden trim, which comprised polished Light American cherry veneer cappings to the dashboard and instruments. Similar to those of the Escort 1300E, the RS2000's wood pack came without cappings on the doors or rear quarters, and there were no holes on the fascia panels for a choke knob or cigarette lighter.

Wooden trim was not available as a stand-alone option unless the car was a special order – it was either a dealer-fit accessory or came in a factory option package complete with a full-height centre console. The console contained a radio aperture, Kienzle clock (with black bezel and orange hands), slots for auxiliary lamp switches and hole for the cigarette lighter – which was automatically moved down from the dashboard when factory fitted.

Like the wood pack, the centre console was a popular aftermarket accessory for the RS2000. It is likely that a car which has had a console retro-fitted will still have the dashboard-mounted cigarette lighter plus a blanking plug in the console.

A Ford-branded five-push-button radio was optional from launch, attached to the heater panel cover in a plastic mount or the aforementioned centre console. It was accompanied by a single Ford 2.5W speaker in the rear parcel shelf, which was topped with a round black speaker grille and had a protective cover underneath (seen from the boot compartment).

RS recliners were nicknamed "roll tops" thanks to their optional rounded head rests. Black Beta cloth was standard.

Wood pack meant the cigarette lighter was moved from the dashboard to the centre console. Map reading light came as part of the Rallye Pack.

FACTORY ORIGINAL SPORTING MK1 ESCORTS

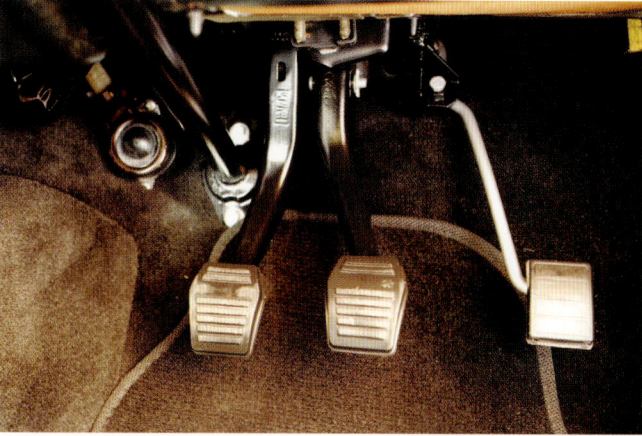

The RS2000's steering wheel was the flat three-spoke 14in type with padded, stitched leather-effect rim, black spokes and RS silver-on-black logo in the centre. The column had a black plastic shroud and single stalk for indicators, headlamp dipping/flashing and horn with chrome push button (RS2000s were equipped with dual-torn horns behind the front grille).

German RS2000s, left-hand-drive cars and early UK press demonstrators contained black Beta cloth Scheel front seats with built-up sides and padding under the knees (very distinctive, they featured curved roll top-type head rests, chrome

The RS2000's back seat was black Beta cloth, as found in Custom Pack AVO cars and 1300Es.

RS2000 pedal box was what you'd find on a mainstream model, complete with cable-operated clutch.

Rocker switches for brake circuit, heater and windscreen wipers. Note the blanking plug where other Escorts had a choke cable.

RS reclining seats had these chrome levers on the base, along with plastic levers on the back rests to provide the tipping motion.

adjuster handles and RS buttons on the upper sections). For the British market they were replaced with Ford RS recliners, as found in late-spec AVO Custom Pack cars. They looked similar to normal black Beta cloth Escort XL seats but had chunkier bolsters and chrome backrest reclining levers. Of course, they also boasted a small circular RS badge on the forward-facing back of each front seat. These seats became known as "roll tops" thanks to the frequently-specified front head rests, which were optional at extra cost. Like the seats, they were black Beta cloth with the pattern running vertically.

There was a matching rear seat – the padded XL-type bench – again trimmed in black Beta cloth.

Despite its standard fabric trim, the RS2000's door cards were the usual black vinyl XL items, with flat, textured internal handles and black mushroom-headed door lock buttons. The rear quarter panels were black cardboard, with plastic rear armrest extensions and push-round plastic ashtrays.

The RS2000 was equipped with a plush, black, one-piece looped-pile carpet, mildly revised in November 1973 for a change in the seat runners and floorpan. Like the AVO Custom Pack, the car also included a sound insulation kit of absorbent panels at known reverberation points, especially around the bulkhead.

In each footwell was a black cardboard kick panel, with a vinyl map pocket stitched onto the driver's side. The very last cars probably received black plastic kick panels instead, minus the map pocket.

A normal Escort pedal box (the same as was found on late

Spare wheel was stuffed into the regular Escort well, with angled bracket to allow clearance for the boot hinges.

Alloy wheels came in sets of five, including the spare. Strap attached to bracket was spot-welded to boot floor.

Boot compartment was the same as late-spec Mexico. Fuel tank was primer grey.

FACTORY ORIGINAL SPORTING MK1 ESCORTS

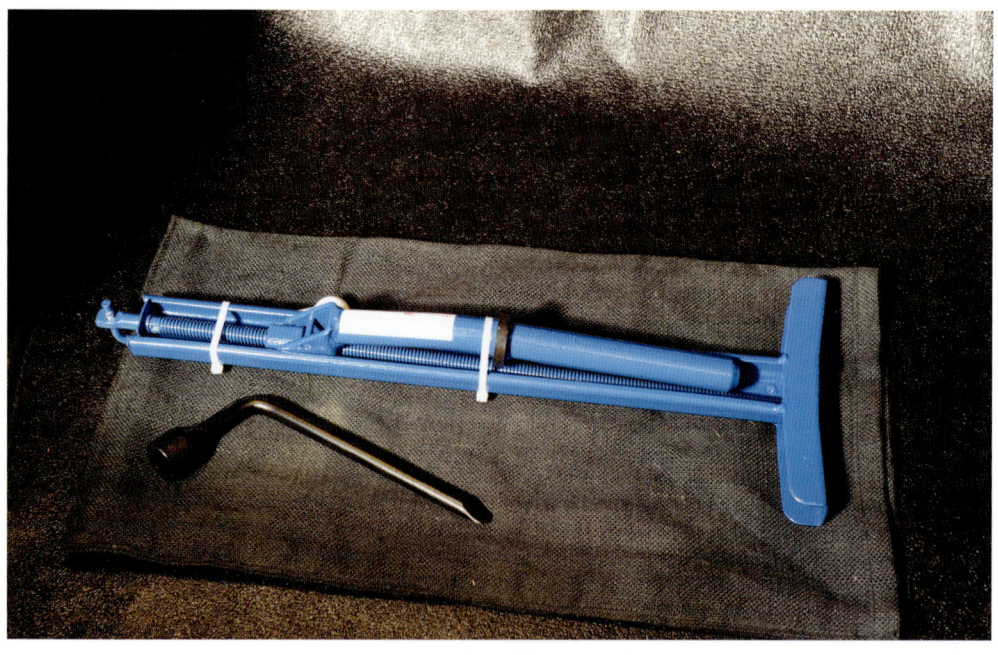

Blue jack and black wheelbrace came in a bag, usually found behind the spare wheel. Prior to November 1974 the bag was fawn in colour.

RS2000 retained the regular AVO Escort boot floor, complete with studs for an underbody stone deflector (not fitted).

Mexicos) was fitted to the RS2000, complete with clutch cable routed through the bulkhead tube. Brake and clutch levers were black with rubber pads, but the long accelerator pedal was silver, with a pad probably added in June 1974. To the left of the pedal box was the satin black floor-mounted wash/wipe button.

The RS2000 had a chrome gearstick and black plastic gearknob, which looked very similar to the normal Escort's. The usual black metal handbrake lever with bare steel push button sat behind it, while fixed seat belt stalks with black plastic coating and silver push buttons were bolted to the tunnel; Mk2-type gold-coloured buttons were found on late 1974 cars. Inertia-reel seat belts were standard.

Like its AVO predecessors, the RS2000 wore a black vinyl headlining, along with black sun visors; the passenger's included a vanity mirror. Early cars had three black grab handles, with black sliding coat hooks on the rears. It's possible that some very late cars lost the passenger-side front handle for just the two in the back.

The dipping rear-view mirror changed several times during the RS2000's short lifespan. The first cars had grey plastic, which was swapped for black plastic with tapered sides from around October 1973. The last cars (probably from October 1974) had a black Mk2-type flat-sided mirror head with black Mk1 stalk.

There was a standard Escort interior light with override switch, plus a pair of round, rubber-encased switches on the A-pillars.

Behind the back seat was a black cardboard rear parcel shelf. From around November 1973 it was a complete piece without metal strips along each side.

Boot latches: a rubber boot latch protector was fitted to many cars from autumn 1974.

Inside Boot

Making the RS2000 into a proper grand tourer, the size of its luggage compartment was boosted by fitting the spare 13in wheel (steel or alloy, depending on what was fitted to the car) into the nearside well. An angled bracket was mounted to the boot hinge panel to allow the spare to clear the boot lid when shut, and its woven strap extended by an inch; a bracket for the strap was welded to the boot floor.

There was a standard Escort Mk1 tool kit – including mid-blue vertical jack (with red-on-white sticker) and satin black wheelbrace – in a fawn muslin bag behind the spare wheel. From November 1974 the bag was a black Mk2-type.

A black Hardura rubberized mat sat on the boot floor, just like other Mk1s. From November 1973 there was a shorter mat to fit around the later shock absorber mountings. Beneath it were the eight bolt fittings for an AVO stone deflector, which was not fitted as standard.

A zinc grey primer nine-gallon fuel tank was bolted into the right-hand rear wing, which possibly changed for black from very late 1974.

The RS2000 was equipped with an Escort XL-type boot lamp as standard, a black rubber boot latch cover from autumn 1974 and black plastic rear light protectors until late 1974, after which they were clear.

RS2000 colour schemes

Code	Colour	Introduced	Discontinued	Decal colour (where fitted)	Coachline colour (where fitted)
B	Diamond White	July 1973	January 1975	Blue	Red
T	Daytona Yellow	July 1973	January 1975	Yellow ochre or blue	Black
N	Sebring Red	July 1973	January 1975	Orange	Black
M	Modena Green	October 1973	January 1975	Green (metallic)	Black
E	Olympic Blue	October 1973	January 1975	Blue	Black
3	Stardust Silver	October 1973	January 1975	Blue	Black
A	Black	October 1973	January 1975	–	Gold
V	Vista Orange	August 1974	January 1975	–	Black
Y	Special order				

Race Pack
Full roll cage
Fireproof rear bulkhead
Oil catch tank
Two battery isolator switches for electrical system (one interior, one exterior)
Bilstein dampers (race settings) all round
Four-point safety harness

Rallye Pack
Full roll cage
Fireproof rear bulkhead
Two battery isolator switches for electrical system (one interior, one exterior)
Four-point safety harness
Map reading light
Sump shield
Bilstein suspension
Oil cooler

ACCESSORIES AND SPECIAL BUILDS

Most of AVO's Special Build production was centred around Mexicos and RS1600s – mainly for motorsport use. The big-winged Escort seen here is one of the handful of Special Build RS2000s – presumably ordered for its tough looks rather than rallying ability. Brent Mould is the car's third owner, having found it nearly five years ago. Still unrestored, the RS2000 has covered 49,000 miles. It was ordered by the original buyer in unusual Marine Blue, with wheelarch extensions over the 6in RS four-spoke alloy wheels. Other extras included opening front and rear quarter windows (the rears have since been swapped for fixed versions), black vinyl roof and interior wood pack with centre console. It was preserved with Ziebart rust-proofing. The door mirrors and mud flaps are non-standard, as are the Janspeed exhaust system and manifold.

What constitutes an original sporting Escort? Perhaps you believe it needs to carry the exact parts it wore on the day it left Ford's assembly line. Maybe you think what matters is its specification when first registered by the supplying dealer. You might even concede that period modifications are acceptable for a car of this kind.

Whatever your opinion, it's clear to see how easily and comprehensively the lines were blurred by the huge volume of options and accessories offered throughout production.

And it wasn't a simple case of ordering metallic paint or a roof rack, tow bar and mud flaps (yes, all those glamorous goodies were available). More importantly, with the launch of the Twin Cam, Boreham's competitions department made masses of motorsport spares available to the man in the street.

By 1972, there were more than 800 performance parts on offer through Rallye Sport dealers – and that's on top of the usual, mundane stuff. Plus, of course, there were several well-known option packs and the Special Build Programme. As the saying goes, there's no such thing as a standard Mexico. Or RS1600. Or RS2000...

Listing all the Ford accessories would take up a book in its own right. To save paper (and sanity), here's a taster of the kit officially available for Escorts from new.

ACCESSORIES AND SPECIAL BUILDS

Clubman Pack
(optional on Mexico and RS1600 from July 1971)
- Two quartz iodine fog lamps and long range auxiliaries on brackets
- Roll-over bar (hoop)
- Competition seats (wrap-around buckets)
- Map reading lamp
- Bilstein gas dampers
- Stiffer front coil springs

Optional on top of the Clubman Pack was a package of off-road equipment including open-tread tyres, magnesium sump shield and oil cooler (not RS1600).

Rally Lighting Pack
(optional on Mexico, RS1600 and RS2000)
Twin quartz halogen 7in driving lamps and quartz halogen 7in fog lamps on brackets; not available when Clubman Pack specified. Early Lighting Pack provided Cibie Oscar fog and spot lights plus stone guards, mounting brackets, ancillary lamp and map-reading light.

Race Pack
(optional on Mexico, RS1600 and RS2000)
- Full roll cage
- Fire-proofed rear bulkhead
- Oil-catch tank
- Battery isolator switches
- Front seat safety harness
- Bilstein gas shock absorbers

Custom Pack
(optional on Mexico and RS1600 from 16 October 1971)
- Sound insulation kit at known reverberation points
- Deep pile black carpet (carpet made standard from October 1972, so dropped from Custom Pack)
- Cloth bucket seats with rear trimmed to match
- Small key tray centre console (until November 1973)
- RS2000-style centre console with clock (from November 1973)
- Wooden dashboard trim, four pieces (from November 1973)
- Map reading light (until November 1973)
- Triple coachline
- Heated rear windscreen
- Vinyl roof (from November 1973)

Rallye Pack
(optional on Mexico, RS1600 and RS2000 from 1973)
- Four Cibie lamps
- Roll cage
- Sports seats
- Stiffer springs
- Map reading light
- Fireproofed rear bulkhead
- Battery isolator switches
- Front seat safety harness
- Bilstein gas shock absorbers
- Sump shield
- Oil cooler (not RS1600)

More than 800 performance parts were available from Ford Rallye Sport dealers – all of which could be fitted to an Escort before registration.

A brochure page showing some AVO Escort options and accessories.

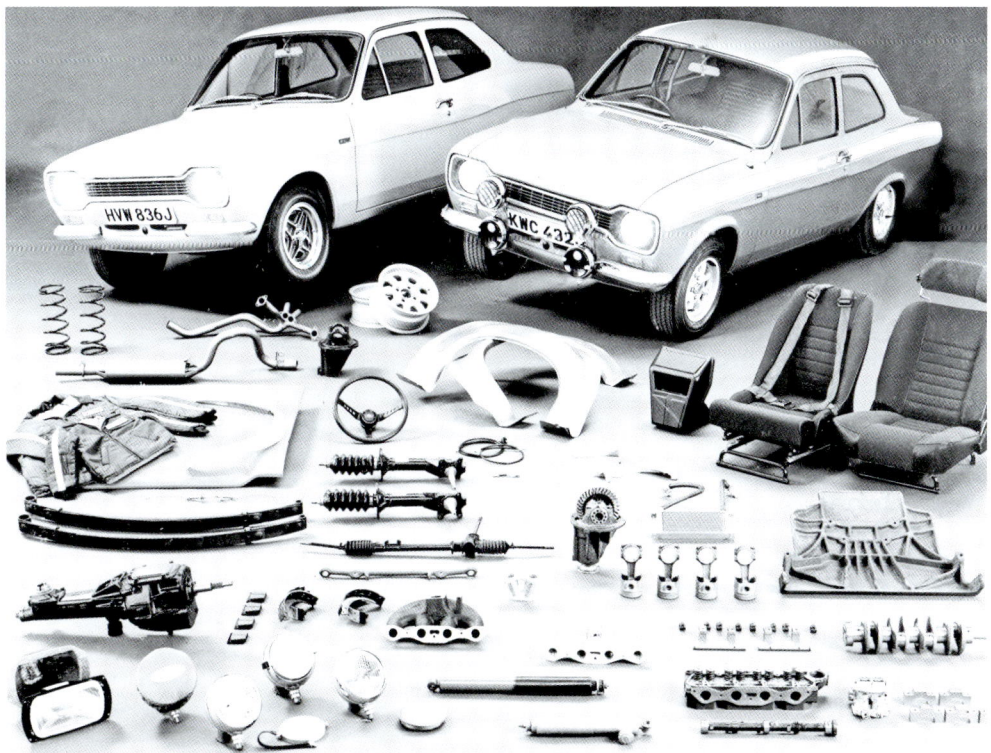

FACTORY ORIGINAL SPORTING MK1 ESCORTS

What happens when your Type 49 shell rots away, leaving only the Clubman Pack intact. No wonder he looks so fed up.

Rallye Sport dealer accessories

Engine

No matter which Escort you'd ordered, Ford was happy to supply you with bags of go-faster accessories. Even the 1100cc Crossflow was catered for, being offered the GT exhaust manifold and system as an official dealer upgrade.

Owners of 1300GT and 1600GT powerplants were able to buy a fast road camshaft (inlet 0.374in, exhaust 0.373in), used with standard valve springs for more power above 4,000rpm. A Rallye cam was the next step up, with 0.376in inlet and 0.374in exhaust; this was recommended for use with a raised compression ratio, big-bore exhaust and twin carburettors.

Of course, Ford was itching to sell you the uprated parts – including double valve springs, a tuftrided crankshaft, steel main bearing caps, forged pistons and steel con rods (for 1300cc engines), high-pressure oil pump, oil cooler kit, extra-high capacity sump (plus pickup) and a selection of exhausts. For 1300cc Escorts was a Rallye manifold and system but the Mexico had a choice of Group One manifold (for use with the standard system) or World Cup Rallye manifold and full system.

The Escort Twin Cam was offered a thick-walled cylinder block, tuftrided crankshaft, steel main bearing caps, forged pistons, big sump, and a choice of exhaust manifolds and systems. Boreham's competitions department also offered buyers a motorsport-ready engine with cams, valves and even fuel injection, but that's somewhat outside the realms of "factory original".

Likewise the RS1600, for which a multitude of high-

This wasn't your average Escort, make no mistake. Special Build usually signified substantial under-the-skin modifications.

Styled-in reversing lights were an optional extra on early Escorts but standard by the time of RS2000 production. The mounting holes remained hand-drilled.

ACCESSORIES AND SPECIAL BUILDS

performance parts were available off-the-shelf from new. These included alloy cylinder blocks (in standard 1601cc bore or 2000cc), steel crankshafts, steel main bearing caps, steel connecting rods, steel pistons (for 1601cc, 1790cc or 2000cc applications), Rallye cams, special head gaskets, large-bore exhaust systems and so on.

The RS2000 had fewer upgrades at first, but by 1974 grew to be offered with a Group One parts package; not fitted on the production line, the goodies were nevertheless available on a new car direct from Rallye Sport dealers. The full engine assembly was fitted with a big-valve cylinder head, race-spec camshaft (inlet 0.165in and exhaust 0.125in), oil cooler kit (different from other models'), two down-draught twin-choke Solex 40/42mm (or later Weber 44IDF) carburettors and inlet manifold, special oval air box and twin-downpipe exhaust system.

All cars could be equipped with a heavy-duty oil pump and dry sump setup. There was also the option of hard rubber heavy-duty engine mounts (the Mexico, RS1600 and RS2000 used the same parts but the Twin Cam's were different) and World Cup crossmember, along with aluminium spacer plate for pre-Crossflow-based engine blocks.

Transmission

Escort buyers had a complex choice of transmission options – not necessarily fitted on the production line but all available from Rallye Sport dealers.

A so-called Rocket gearbox was a popular upgrade, based on the RS2000 Type E four-speed but with closer-ratio gears (first: 2.54:1, second: 1.66:1, third: 1.255:1, fourth: 1.000:1). Rated up to 170bhp, the Rocket 'box was recommended for

Tough stance looked like a thoroughbred rally car on the road – which in many cases was what the Special Build Programme was all about.

Wide wheelarches were fitted at Aveley's Special Build facility alongside the general RS production line before paint refinishing and final assembly.

Wide wheelarches were required to cover the 6in four-spokes, which were an almost identical design to the contemporary 5.5in RS alloys. Spoke recesses still wear the original dark grey paint. Mk1 6in rims were quite dissimilar from later Mk2 versions, having different offset, valve hole through a circle in the spoke (rather than the rim), rear-fitting centre caps and lacking the Mk2's cast-on H76 part numbers.

FACTORY ORIGINAL SPORTING MK1 ESCORTS

AVO carousel carried a colourful display, including plenty of ready-modified Escorts.

AVO's Special Build facility meant wide wheelarches could be ordered as a factory option from new.

Heavy-duty clutches were offered for all models (including the 1300GT engine); the Twin Cam, RS1600 and Mexico could have a magnesium gearbox casing or tail housing; a steel flywheel was offered for the Twin Cam and RS1600 (for standard clutch or sintered clutches), and there was a heavy-duty gearbox crossmember – Twin Cams, RS1600s and Mexicos used the same version but for the Type E it was a different part.

The standard rear axle was generally retained, but there was always a massive choice of ratios plus lightweight differential casing, factory-optional limited-slip diff and heavy-duty propshafts to suit 2000E or Rocket gearboxes. Even a ZF five-speed gearbox could be supplied and fitted by a Rallye Sport dealer, although not from the factory production line.

Ford was also happy to supply a heavy-duty Atlas axle for any Escort, plus fitting kit. Based on the Capri 3.0 part, the Atlas increased rear track by an inch (thus requiring wheel-arch extensions) and came with repositioned spring locations, heat-treated halfshafts and limited-slip differential. Again, a suitable heavy-duty propshaft was offered.

use in the Twin Cam, RS1600 and Mexico when combined with the appropriate fitting kit – this included a magnesium or alloy bellhousing, heavy-duty clutch, release bearing and so on. Official Ford literature admitted the Rocket gearbox required relieving of the transmission tunnel and relocation of the gearstick hole further back.

Suspension

So many suspension options were offered for sporting Escorts – from the factory or through Rallye Sport dealers – that it's probably impossible to tell exactly what was fitted from new.

Suspension upgrades were frequently specified as part of a factory option pack, while a multitude of parts was available separately – including Bilstein gas-filled shock absorbers, heavy-duty front springs, roller bearing strut top mounts, fully-adjustable front struts, uprated rear springs (labelled CD, which stood for competitions department), rear one-inch lowering blocks, locating spacers to replace the rubber sandwich plates, Bilstein gas-filled rear shock absorbers (rally or race settings) and even a turret kit for mounting fully upright rear dampers – available as a special order or even from Rallye Sport dealers.

At the front, popular items included hard rubber heavy-duty anti-roll bar bushes, double-width mounting kit (for Twin Cam, Mexico, RS1600 and RS2000) and high-ratio steering rack giving 2.5 turns lock-to-lock; the 1300GT and

Front springs

Car	Spring	Spring rate	Ride height
Twin Cam, Mexico, RS1600, RS2000	Road	130lb	-2in
Twin Cam, Mexico, RS1600, RS2000	Rally	115lb	standard
Twin Cam, Mexico, RS1600, RS2000	World Cup	100lb	+1in
Twin Cam, Mexico, RS1600, RS2000	Safari	115lb	+1in
Twin Cam, Mexico, RS1600, RS2000	Group Two	145lb	+1in
1100, 1300, GT, Sport	Road	130lb	-1in

ACCESSORIES AND SPECIAL BUILDS

Rear springs

Spring	Spring rate	Ride height
CD5	75lb	+1/2in
CD6	85lb	standard
CD7	85lb	-1in
CD8	115lb	+1in

Sport used a different part from the Twin Cam, Mexico, RS1600 and RS2000.

It's worth noting that the Group One RS2000 package comprised Bilstein dampers, roller bearing top mounts, 145lb front coil springs and 112lb rear leafs. It also added the World Cup crossmember and engine mounts, quick steering rack, anti-dive kit with double-width mounts and heavy-duty bushes.

Brakes

Although the RS2000 Group One kit and the competitions department offered ventilated front discs, Ford's attitude was that the standard brakes on the Twin Cam and AVO models were "totally adequate for road use, and for rallying it is only necessary to fit heavy-duty brake pads and shoes."

So uprated front pads were offered, in different patterns for cars built before and after January 1972 (when the Girling 16PB calipers replaced the 16Ps); there was also a heavy-duty pad available for 1300GT front calipers.

Likewise, heavy-duty rear shoes could be ordered for the GT, Twin Cam/Mexico/RS1600 and Atlas axles.

Wheels

Predictably, Ford's main options when it came to wheels were RS four-spokes or Minilites.

Both types were available from the factory or as Rallye Sport dealer accessories; the four-spokes (in 5.5x13in size) were generally found on road cars, although a 6x13in RS four-spoke was optional when steel "bubble" wheelarch extensions were specified.

Minilite magnesium wheels cost twice the price of four-spokes, so were usually destined for competition cars. Sizes of 5.5x13in to 9.25x13in were available throughout the Escort's life, but usually only 6x13in and 7x13in from Rallye Sport dealers.

Body

Most Escort bodywork modifications revolved around shell strengthening and the fitting of steel wheelarch extensions – a service always offered from new at Aveley; arches were spot-welded into position, sealed and filled with lead before painting in body colour.

For owners of Escort GTs and similar, Ford offered fibreglass

Magnesium Magard sump shield.

Opening front quarter windows were an Escort option from launch and fitted in many export markets.

Surprisingly standard for such a custom-built car, this RS2000's engine bay sports only an aftermarket high-performance manifold and exhaust to boost power output.

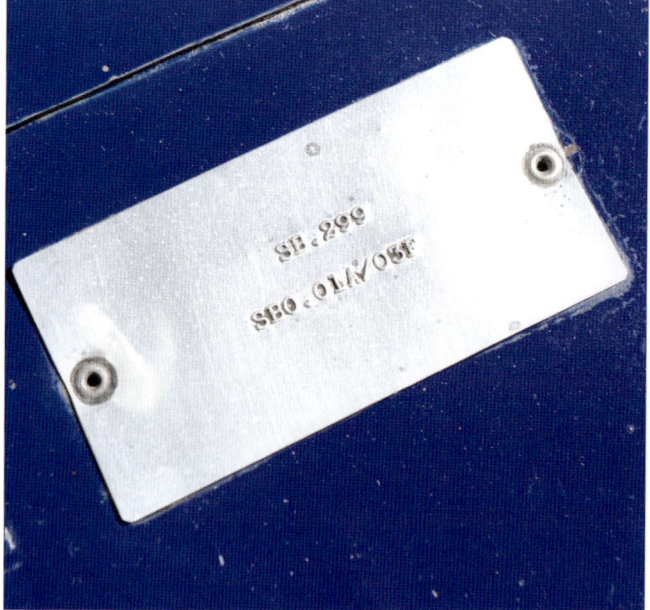

The Special Build plate confirms this car's exclusive identity. The 01A and 03F characters refer to wide wheelarches and 6x13in alloys. Surprisingly, the car's special paintwork isn't mentioned – although its VIN tag includes a Y in the paint code box.

front wheelarch spats to flare the wings out to Mexico size. From 1974 there was also a fibreglass front air dam. Much rarer was the rubber Rallye Sport rear spoiler for the German market, which looked like a narrower version of the Mk2 part.

Incidentally, the familiar windscreen wiper arm spoiler was only a dealer accessory, fitted on the driver's side from November 1973.

One of the most popular options was a pair or a set of four Cibie lamps on heavy-duty brackets. Available as part of an option pack or on their own, they sometimes came with plastic covers. Metal stone guards were offered for the auxiliary lighting, plus plastic shields for the headlamps.

Rally drivers would often choose from motorsport-related items like a magnesium sump shield, bonnet pins, long-range auxiliary fuel tank and broad front strut brace.

For competition use, there was a lightweight glassfibre bonnet and boot lid, plus plastic window kit. You could even order a full bodyshell from your Rallye Sport dealer, complete with export-spec strengthening, wide wheelarch extensions and turreted rear end.

ACCESSORIES AND SPECIAL BUILDS

Typically plush RS2000 interior was equipped with optional front head rests, wood pack and console – what more could a Special Build require?

Not strictly speaking a factory Escort, this Boreham-prepared Le Mans Green Mexico was kitted out with the stuff weekend rally drivers would order.

Interior

A range of optional front seats was offered throughout Escort production. Often (but not always), they would come in a mismatched pair of a fixed-back bucket (with high side bolsters) for the driver (with optional head rest) and a full recliner on the passenger side, usually with head rest.

AVO Custom Pack/RS2000 recliners were also a dealer accessory for the Escort from November 1973, again with optional head rests.

Full Britax harnesses were offered for competition cars, alongside a navigator's foot rest, Butlers flexible map reading lamp, FIA-approved fire extinguisher and firewall kits for the rear bulkhead and parcel shelf (these comprised aluminium sheeting that was pop-riveted into place and sealed with fibreglass matting).

A full FIA-approved roll cage could also be fitted by Ford, in matt black epoxy resin with optional front section; early Escorts and the Clubman Pack had a simple silver roll hoop instead.

Special Build Programme

If a plain old RS1600 wasn't exclusive enough, or you fancied a competitive clubman rally car direct from the factory, AVO offered a complete custom manufacturing facility.

Called the Special Build Programme, it offered a huge range of extras and a choice of non-standard body colours for cars plucked from the production line, all added at Aveley in a separate area. The end result was a unique, custom built machine that was still an official Ford product.

From AVO's inception, the plan was for 10 per cent of the facility's output to be special builds for individual customers, up to and including full race or rally specification. Plus, as Ford literature put it, "Although these parts have been developed primarily for competition many of them have either special visual or comfort qualities which make them suitable for use in luxury road cars."

In the end, the Special Build Programme didn't start offering customer cars until April 1972, all of which were sold through Rallye Sport dealers. Special Build Escorts were generally fitted with quite a few accessories above and beyond the regular extras, option packs and special order paint schemes – which were all available on the main production line. Some even ditched the typical AVO all-black interior in favour of red, green or blue.

It's unknown how many cars were produced in this manner, but it was only a small fraction of total Aveley output. The AVO Owners' Club estimated a figure of 350 cars, the majority of which were Mexicos. Each wore a Special Build chassis plate in its engine bay (on the inner wing or slam panel), as well as the two normal Escort tags.

Special Build options*
*1972 options – more were added later

Code	Description
SB001	Wheelarch extensions (bubble arches). No stripes when fitted
SB002J	Uprated road suspension with turrets (included gas-filled front struts, special front springs, rear turret kit, gas-filled rear shock absorbers, ride height lowered by 0.5in)
SB002K	Rally suspension with turrets (included gas-filled front struts, uprated front springs, rear turret kit, gas-filled rear shock absorbers, uprated rear springs, ride height raised by 1in)
SB002C	Safari suspension with turrets (included gas-filled front struts, heavy-duty uprated front springs, rear turret kit, gas-filled rear shock absorbers, heavy-duty uprated rear springs, front ride height raised by 1in, rear raised by 0.5in)
SB002G	Clubman suspension (included gas-filled front struts, uprated front springs, gas-filled rear shock absorbers, front ride height raised by 1in).
SB003A	7in wide magnesium wheels with 195HR70x13 rally tyres. Required wheelarch extensions
SB003B	6in wide magnesium wheels with 195HR70x13 rally tyres. Required wheelarch extensions
SB003C	6in wide magnesium wheels with 175/70x13 Ultragrip rally tyres. Required wheelarch extensions
SB003D	6in wide magnesium wheels with 175x13 SP44 tyres. Required wheelarch extensions
SB003E	5.5in wide RS alloy wheels with 165x13 SP44 tyres
SB003F	6in wide RS alloy wheels with 185/70x13 tyres. Required wheelarch extensions
SB004A	High ratio steering rack (RHD), required heavy-duty stabiliser bar brackets
SB004B	High ratio steering rack (LHD), required heavy-duty stabiliser bar brackets
SB005A	Heavy-duty anti-roll bar brackets
SB006	Front crossmember and engine mounts (World Cup crossmember)
SB007A	Sump shield for use with standard crossmember (Mexico also requires oil cooler kit)
SB007C	Sump shield for use with heavy-duty crossmember and engine mounts (Mexico also requires oil cooler kit)
SB008A	Modified bodyshell. Additional welding for body strengthening
SB009	Tuned engine
SB010	Catch tank
SB011A	Bullet gearbox. Included bellhousing
SB011B	Rocket gearbox for use with Atlas axle. Included bellhousing, clutch, propshaft, revised floor covering. Required Atlas axle
SB011C	Rocket gearbox for use with standard axle. Included bellhousing, clutch, propshaft, revised floor covering
SB012A	Heavy-duty clutch (RS1600)
SB012B	Heavy-duty clutch (Mexico). Included flywheel and ring gear

ACCESSORIES AND SPECIAL BUILDS

SB013A	Limited-slip differential for standard axle. Speedo drive 3.54:1
SB013B	Limited-slip differential for standard axle. Speedo drive 3.7:1
SB013C	Limited-slip differential for standard axle. Speedo drive 3.9:1
SB013E	Limited-slip differential for standard axle. Speedo drive 4.4:1
SB013F	Limited-slip differential for standard axle. Speedo drive 4.7:1
SB013G	Limited-slip differential for standard axle. Speedo drive 4.9:1
SB013H	Limited-slip differential for standard axle. Speedo drive 5.1:1
SB013J	Atlas axle. Included limited-slip differential and 4.11:1 speedo drive. Required Rocket gearbox, wheelarch extensions and uprated suspension
SB013K	Atlas axle. Included limited-slip differential and 4.37:1 speedo drive. Required Rocket gearbox, wheelarch extensions and uprated suspension
SB013L	Atlas axle. Included limited-slip differential and 4.63:1 speedo drive. Required Rocket gearbox, wheelarch extensions and uprated suspension
SB013M	Atlas axle. Included limited-slip differential and 5.14:1 speedo drive. Required Rocket gearbox, wheelarch extensions and uprated suspension
SB014A	Competition brake lining material front and rear (standard rear axle)
SB014B	Competition brake lining material front and rear (Atlas rear axle).
SB015A	Rally exhaust system (Mexico)
SB016E	Contour competition front seats, black. Included driver's bucket seat and reclining passenger seat, with rear seat trimmed in fabric to match
SB017B	Roll bar (Clubman type). Included static seat belts
SB017C	Roll bar (Clubman type). Included full safety harness
SB017D	Roll bar (FIA rally). Included full safety harness
SB018	Dress-up items
SB019A	Cibie Super Rally lighting pack including two Oscar fog lamps, two Super Oscar driving lamps, associated wiring, relays, fuses and brackets. Required heavy-duty battery
SB020A	Uprated marathon alternator kit with remote diode pack.
SB021	Master switch
SB022	Screen washer
SB023	Fuel tank
SB024	Lightweight body panels (bonnet, doors and boot lid)
SB025A	Bracing strut (across strut tops)
SB026	Centre console
SB027	Special paint finishes
SB028A	Full safety harness
SB029	Fire extinguisher
SB030A	Heavy-duty battery (57A/h)
SB031A	Heated rear window
SB032	Bonnet pins and boot catches
SB033A	Fireproof rear bulkhead for car without wheelarch extensions
SB033B	Fireproof rear bulkhead for car with wheelarch extensions
SB034	Map reading light
SB035A	Thick loop-pile carpet, black
SB036	Sound deadening
SB037A	Oil cooler and uprated oil pump (Mexico)
SB038	Ammeter
SB039	Brake and fuel lines
SB040	Halda Twinmaster trip meter
SB041	Gearbox installation
SB042	Turret kit

BODYSHELLS

Dozens of different bodyshells were produced for the Mk1 Escort – two-door, four-door, estate and van, with countless variations of each.

Early bodies were quite unlike those built from September 1970, which in turn were substantially altered in November 1973. There were radical dissimilarities between right- and left-hand-drive cars. And that's not to mention all the changes to make heavy-duty, GT (Type 48) or Type 49 shells.

Type 49 is the term applied to extra-strengthened shells used for the Twin Cam, RS1600, Mexico and RS2000. No other models were built with Type 49 shells. Many alterations were done by hand, so were often quite amateurish and unique in appearance.

The Type 49 designation stemmed simply from the standard early (November 1967 until September 1970) Escort line-up, which included body type codes (seen on the chassis plate) as follows:

40: standard two-door
41: Super estate
42: De Luxe two-door
43: De Luxe estate
44: Super two-door
48: GT two-door
49: Twin Cam and RS1600
50: standard van (6cwt)
51: De Luxe van (8cwt)
5A: standard van (8cwt)
5D: De Luxe four-door
5G: GT four-door
5P: Super four-door
5S: standard four-door

Left-hand drive (LHD) and strengthened heavy-duty versions of each type (except the 49) were available. LHD shells had a large battery cutout in the offside inner wing. Heavy-duty shells gained strut top reinforcing plates and strengthening underneath the strut tops plus rear leaf spring reinforcements; some cars had stone deflectors beneath the boot floor. Many – but not all - export markets (whether LHD or RHD) received heavy-duty bodies. Likewise, not all heavy-duty bodies went abroad – for example, they were specified for the British MoD and some police forces.

Differences between most domestic two-door shells were fairly minimal, such as the Type 44 having more drillings for the Super's extra trim than the standard Type 40. Beyond that, the Type 48 GT shell added a six-dial dashboard pressing and different-shaped forward-most rear spring hangers (not skidded). Although the very first Twin Cams used this shell, production cars had their own Type 49 bodies – basically, modified heavy-duty Type 48s plus front wings with flared arches and even more strengthening.

From September 1970 the different shell designations were put to one side, with only the Type 49 having any real meaning.

In this chapter we've tried to highlight the major distinguishing features between bodyshells and how they were finished from the factory. Most sporting Escorts, of course, were built around two-door bodies, but all shells were cut from the same steel and rolled out down the same assembly lines – before alterations to create some rather special models, naturally.

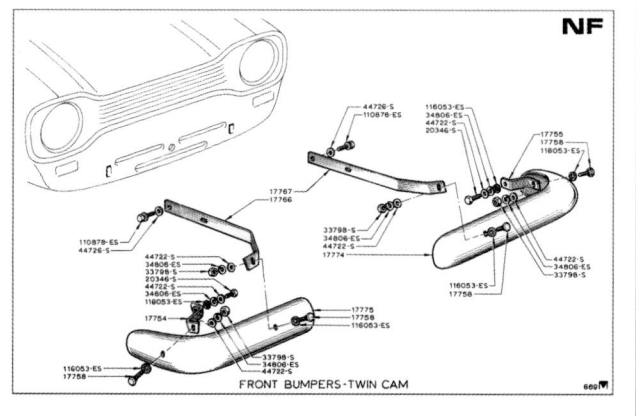

Chrome front quarter bumpers were straight from the back of an Escort van, fitted on different brackets.

BODYSHELLS

The factory-stamped chassis number was never a precisely-measured creation – it was done by hand after the car was painted, before having wax or clear lacquer brushed over for preservation. It was in a similar size and position on every Mk1 – curved or straight in front of the strut top hole on later cars (as these examples demonstrate), but generally straight across on pre-August 1970 Escorts.

Early Escorts (until August 1970) had this type of chassis plate riveted to the offside inner wing.

From March 1973 all Escorts' chassis plates were moved to the bonnet slam panel, to the left of the bonnet release spring (looking from the front of the car).

After August 1970 Escorts wore this later-type chassis plate, again found on the offside inner wing.

Service bodies were available to replace damaged shells for any model. They were sold primed or painted, with bonnet and boot lid, with or without doors. Type 49 bodies were offered with or without wide wheelarches. This tag belongs to a Copper Brown Mexico that was reshelled in 1973.

FACTORY ORIGINAL SPORTING MK1 ESCORTS

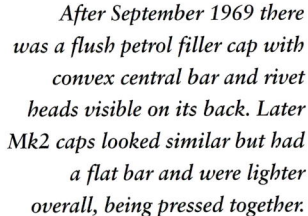

All early Escorts had a protruding petrol cap.

After September 1969 there was a flush petrol filler cap with convex central bar and rivet heads visible on its back. Later Mk2 caps looked similar but had a flat bar and were lighter overall, being pressed together.

Early Escort bonnets had external release mechanism, with button found in the middle of the grille.

Twin Cams, RS1600s, Mexicos, RS2000s and heavy-duty shells all featured these double-skinned spot-welded front suspension top plates. It's worth noting that replacement inner wings for heavy-duty bodyshells had the same part number as the Type 49 Twin Cam.

Pre-September 1970 dashboard had wider rocker switches than later version, including fan switch next to the heater controls.

Early Maize Mexico on the AVO production line. This shot shows the front panel, sprayed satin black behind the grille, covering more of the aperture than the Daytona Yellow Mexico in the top right photo on the page opposite. All Escorts after September 1968 received the black-behind-grille treatment.

BODYSHELLS

Shells were body-colour in the wheelarches and the floorpans, up to and including the under sill areas and underneath of the chassis rails. This shot shows a Sunset Red Mexico at Aveley in late 1970.

Escort floorpans had one coat of phosphate and electrocoat (here a greeny-grey primer from a dipping process, although early cars were red oxide), followed by bitumen-based underseal protection to the wheel-arches and underbody areas. The topcoat was applied with oscillating spray guns on a conveyor, with manual painting of the door shuts and interior afterwards. The body colour didn't reach the section of floorpan between the chassis rails, which remained primer coloured (plus a little overspray wafted on).

Type 49 Escort bodies were shipped from Halewood to Aveley by transporter with glass, lights, electrics and back bumpers already in place.

Aveley production line, probably around late 1973. Note the grey fuel tank, black door quarter light pillars, cutout back bumper and short rain gutters. Their plastic-chrome trims and the car's badges were still to be fitted. Early cars had their spare wheel wells painted black underneath but this practice eventually stopped.

185

Solid rear bulkhead was seen on Escorts until September 1970, after which it was pressed with these cutouts. Early shells also had extra drain holes with metal caps in the rear footwells.

Early shells (built before September 1969) wore rubber buffers at the top of each B-pillar and the far corner of each inner door skin.

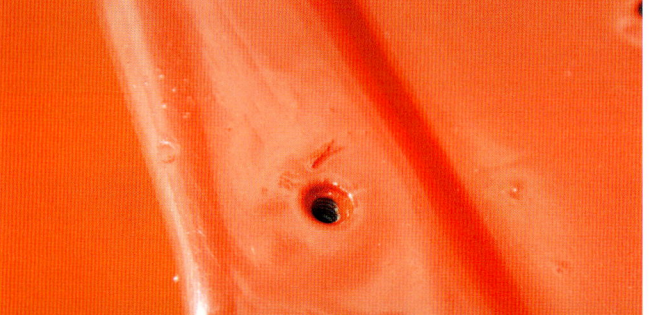

Genuine Ford slam panels always had threaded earth connections at both sides of the radiator.

Seam sealer wasn't exactly used neatly – this original AVO machine had the stuff splashed carelessly around the strut tops. On other cars, barely enough was used to cover the gaps.

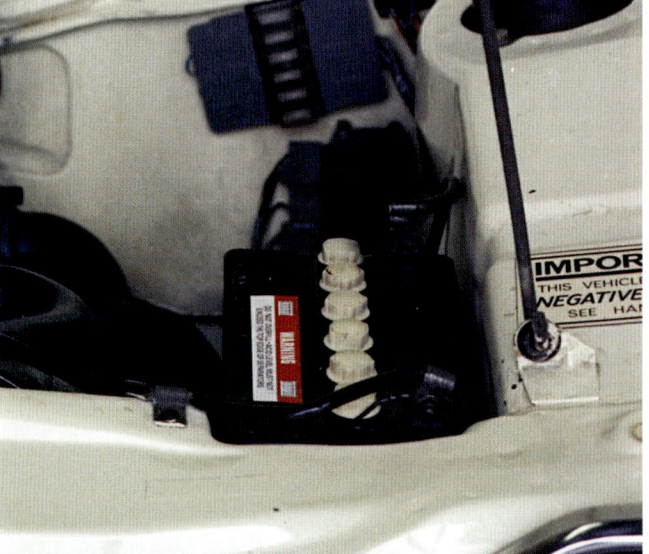

Until September 1969 the nearside inner wing had a bracket for the bonnet prop, which lay across the slam panel when not in use, retained in a clear/white plastic clip.

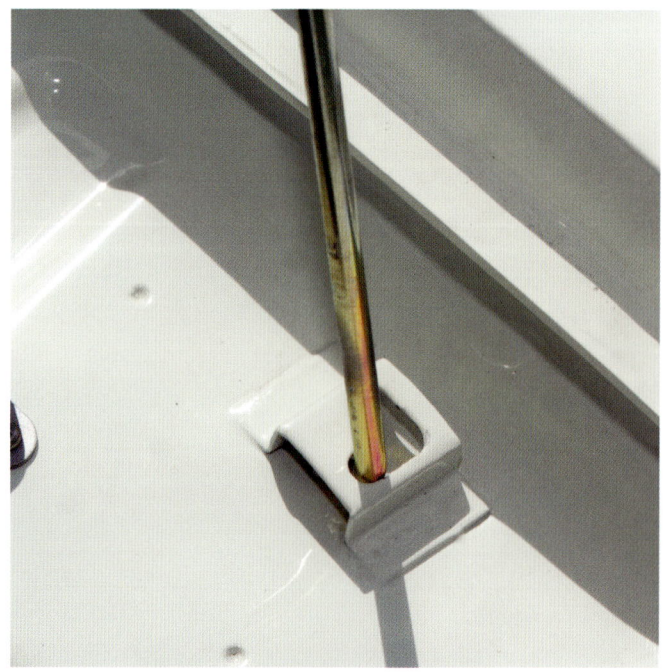

Bonnet prop from September 1969 onwards dangled from beneath the bonnet's underside, often in bare metal but sometimes painted on the car. Inner wings now featured this retainer for when the prop was in use.

BODYSHELLS

In September 1969, Escorts received updated doors, hinges and pillars, with different handles and small, separate locks.

Until September 1969 Escort doors had this handle, lock and latch arrangement, with regulator mechanism instead of rod, and no lock holes in the door skin or locking pins on the inside.

Pre-September 1969 B-pillars featured this early-type latch.

After September 1969, the doors were fitted with these locks and B-pillar latches.

From winter 1973 the B-pillar strikers were revised, with two upper rubbers.

FACTORY ORIGINAL SPORTING MK1 ESCORTS

Until around April 1970, there was a single windscreen washer nozzle mounted in a central bonnet cutout.

After April 1970 a pair of windscreen washer nozzles were positioned between slats in the scuttle panel.

Pre-September 1969 bulkhead differed from later Escorts, lacking the subsequent heater dome's flat spot and notched ends. All such cars had the three-pin "cheese wedge" washer bottle. Early bulkheads had shorter bases on their bonnet hinges.

Rear seat crossmember was body-coloured on early Escorts, changing to satin black in late 1973. Many models (of L-specification and above) also had a black vinyl trim covering the crossmember.

Most Mk1s had their front grilles screwed into the slam panel at each hole.

From November 1973 the slam panel was a different shape, leaving the grille's outer screw holes with nowhere to fasten. Horn swapped from nearside to offside too.

BODYSHELLS

Regular Escort boot floor had this normal ribbed and dimpled pattern.

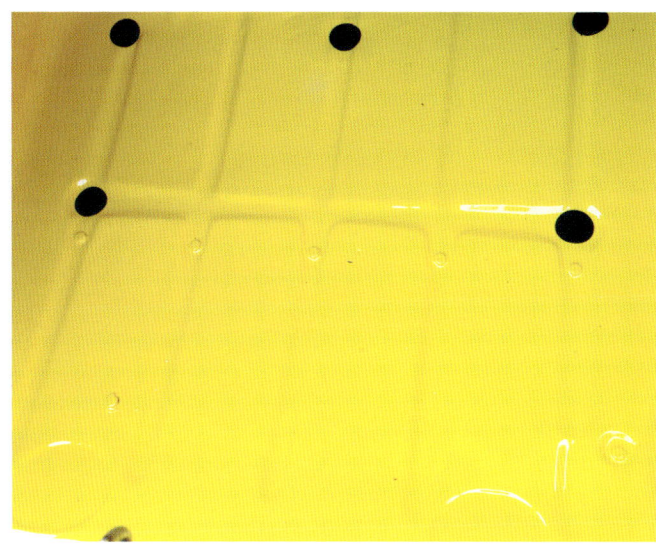

AVO Escort boot floor (plus a number of early Sports) featured eight bolts welded and brazed into the boot floor, poking down underneath to accommodate a stone deflector, whether or not it was fitted. Battery-in-boot models used one hole to attach the spare wheel retaining bolt.

The Type 49 stone deflector mounted to the boot floor on six bolts. The deflector was omitted on RS2000s, late Mexicos and some RS1600s (it became an option) but the floor studs remained. Some export heavy-duty shells also wore stone deflectors, which were one rib wider and fasted on with only seven brazed-in bolts. The Type 49's extra fixing was second in from the nearside, through a flat part of floor rather than a pressing recess, welded (not brazed) into place. The two nearside bolts were used on the export shells but not Type 49s.

Escort rain gutters generally looked the same, but towards the end of production they became a little longer. Early examples finished about an inch before the rear windscreen, but on later cars the seam was much closer. There were two main of drip rail trims – stainless steel, then chromed plastic from 1973.

Type 49 and heavy-duty shells were fitted with these large fillet pieces welded to the tops of the strut towers and wing rails.

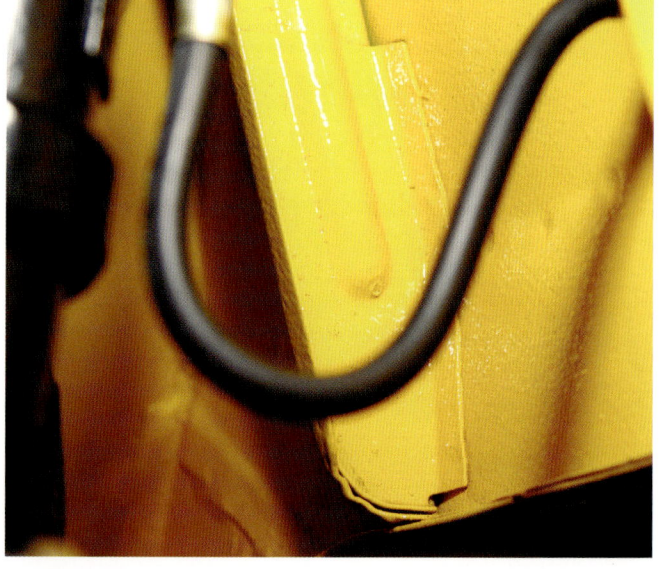

Under the front wheelarches, the lower ends of each Type 49 or heavy-duty suspension turret had reinforced flitch plates - two small strengthening pieces at each side.

Exhaust systems on hotter Escorts were a different shape from standard models, so the Type 49 shell used unique centre and rear exhaust hangers.

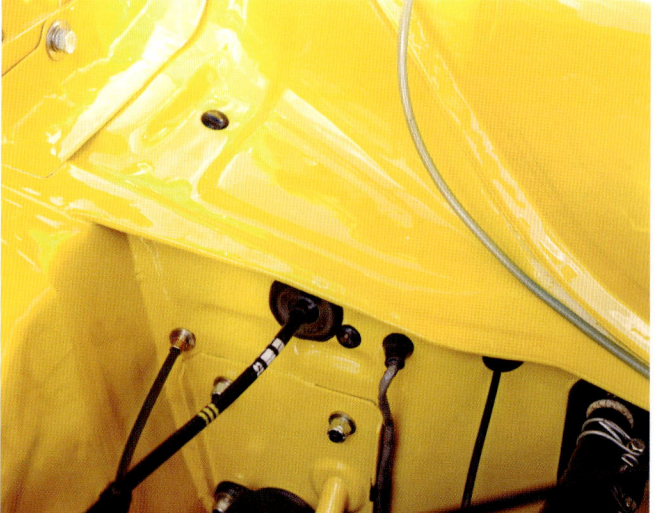

Tops of upright rear shock absorbers from November 1973 protruded through boot floor in large box section. Front seat mountings changed then too.

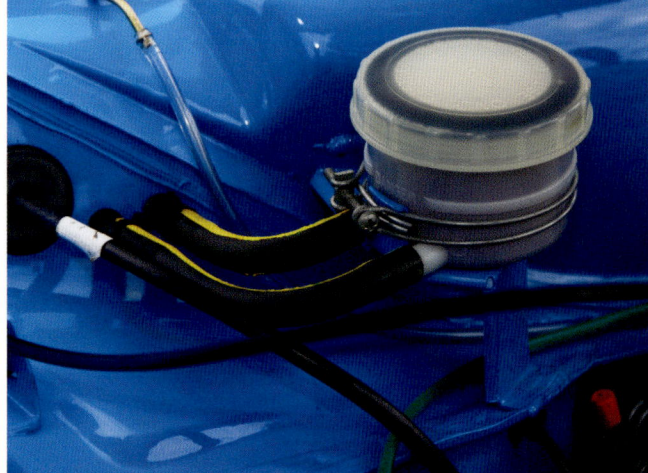

The combined brake/clutch reservoir found on Twin Cams, RS1600s and pre-October 1972 Mexicos was seated on a crudely welded bracket attached to the upper bulkhead.

Type 49 bulkheads had a variety of extra holes and additions, depending on individual model. The RS2000 shared the upper bulkhead with the late-spec Mexico (thus the grommet in its redundant clutch cylinder hole) but had a standard Escort brake reinforcement plate (the late Mexico had no clutch cable tube).

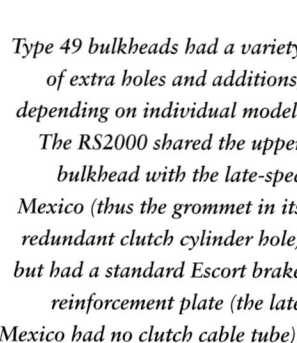

BODYSHELLS

Type 49 transmission tunnels were all subtly different, because each was modified by hand – usually involving mild hammer therapy to help the gearbox to fit. The standard Escort gearstick opening was chopped out and plated over, with a new hole made further back. Most Type 49 tunnels had the front edges of their stiffening braces cut back with an oxy acetylene torch but on RS2000vs they were hacked away almost completely.

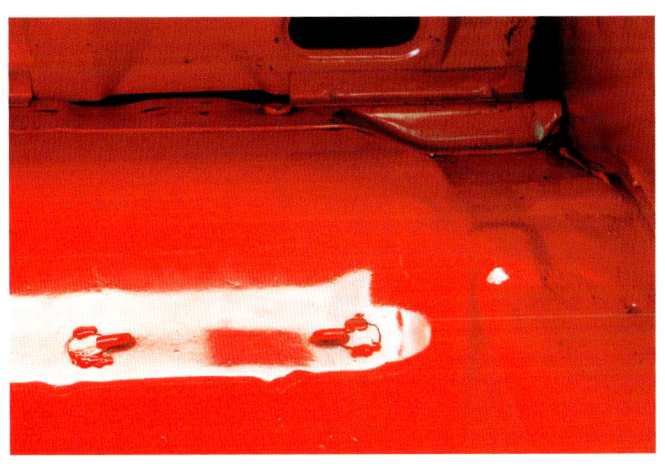

Hooks were welded to AVO cars' boot floors. Shot of this RS1600 also shows the pre-October 1973 layout, with inclined rear shock absorbers on a locating bracket beneath the floor.

Paint runs and overspray were common, direct from the factory. AVO's rectification process was more about inspecting and respraying thin areas than polishing to a perfect finish. Panel gaps were often even worse!

Most obvious of all, the Sport, 1300E, Mexico, RS2000, Twin Cam and RS1600 always wore flared front wings, unless fitted with wide rally wheelarch extensions.

Late shells (left) had a flat bulkhead next to the fuse box, whereas earlier cars (right) had a horizontal swage line in the pressing.

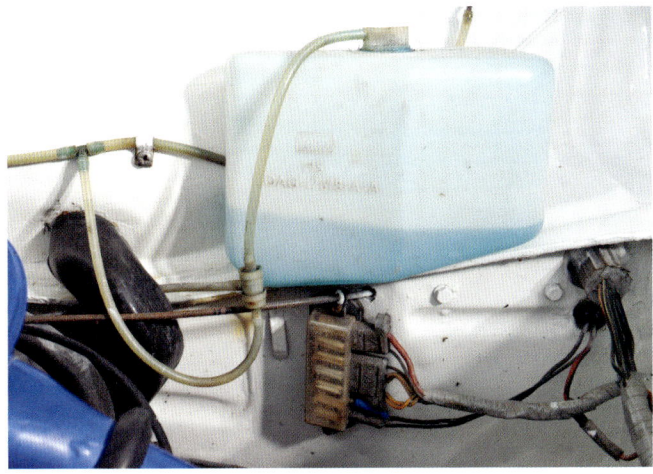

FACTORY ORIGINAL SPORTING MK1 ESCORTS

Chassis rails curved up just before the rear spring hangers on a normal Escort.

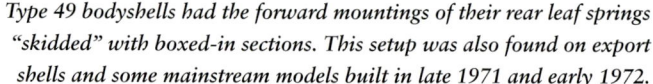

Type 49 bodyshells had the forward mountings of their rear leaf springs "skidded" with boxed-in sections. This setup was also found on export shells and some mainstream models built in late 1971 and early 1972.

The Type 49 shell boasted rear radius rods, which had mounting points on the back axle plus brackets welded to the chassis rails.

The Twin Cam, RS1600 and pre-October 1972 Mexico had a boot-mounted battery, which lived on a tray welded into the spare wheel well.

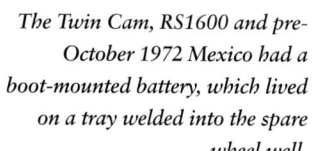

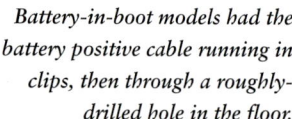

Battery-in-boot models had the battery positive cable running in clips, then through a roughly-drilled hole in the floor.

Front panels changed throughout production; round-headlamp bodies had lost the starting handle hole by October 1973 but it was a gradual process begun earlier in the year. For cars with rectangular headlamps it was a real lottery – some still had the hole in late 1974.

BODYSHELLS

Most sporting Escorts (well, all except the pre-August 1972 Sport) housed a six-dial dashboard pressing. There were no exceptions. From September 1970, the pressing had a headlamp switch cutout underneath.

No matter what colour the parcel shelf (most were black, although GTs were allowed a choice), the bodywork directly beneath the slats was dusted with satin black (not very neatly) over body colour.

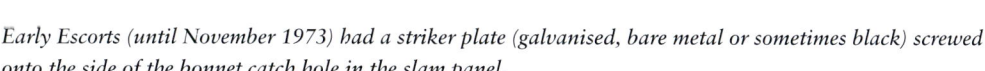

AVO rear wheelarch lips were tucked under from the factory to clear chunky 13in tyres. It was rarely a neat process, involving a hammer rather than a complicated rolling device.

Early Escorts (until November 1973) had a striker plate (galvanised, bare metal or sometimes black) screwed onto the side of the bonnet catch hole in the slam panel.

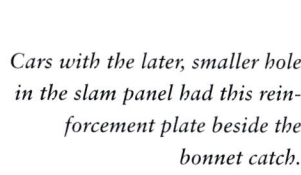

From November 1973, the slam panel had a smaller hole (with small lip underneath) for the bonnet catch, and the striker plate was deleted.

Cars with the later, smaller hole in the slam panel had this reinforcement plate beside the bonnet catch.

BUILD PLATES

An Escort's main identification plate was its stamped bare alloy chassis plate located under the bonnet.

Two types of chassis plates were fitted to Mk1 Escorts – the first on bodyshells built prior to August 1970 and the second fitted thereafter.

Of course, chassis plates could easily be swapped from car to car by undoing the rivets, and aftermarket reproduction tags are available, printed to look like the real thing. So unless the shell still bears its original chassis number stamped into the offside strut top (by now, most have rusted away and/or been replaced) it's impossible to know for sure whether the car and chassis plate match up.

Up to August 1970
Until August 1970, Escorts featured the first style of chassis plate. It was always situated on the offside inner wing, riveted through the bodywork and readable from the offside front wing. The style of chassis plate changed on cars built after August 1970.

Drive
1 – right-hand drive, 2 – left-hand drive

Eng.
C – 1098cc LC (low compression), B – 1098cc HC (high compression), T – 1298cc LC (low compression), S – 1298cc HC (high compression), R – 1298cc G, Z – 1558cc (Twin Cam), V – 1601cc (RS1600)

Trans.
1 or 5 – manual, 7 – automatic

Axle
9 – 3.777:1, A – 3.777:1 heavy duty, 2 – 3.900:1, J – 3.89:1, P – 3.89:1 heavy duty, D – 3.900:1 heavy duty, 4 – 4.125:1, B – 4.125:1 heavy duty, 5 – 4.444:1, C – 4.444:1 heavy duty

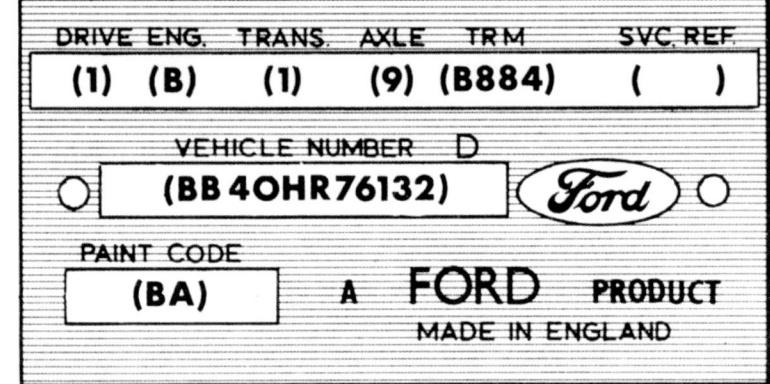

Trim
B884 Ravenna Red (vinyl), B885 Aqua, medium (vinyl), B886 Saddle (vinyl), B887 Black (vinyl), B888 Ravenna Red (cloth), B889 Aqua, medium (cloth), B890 Saddle (cloth), B891 Black (cloth), D401 Black (vinyl), D402 Parchment (vinyl), D403 Cherry (vinyl), D404 Beechnut (vinyl), D405 Aqua (vinyl), D406 Blue (vinyl), D407 Black (cloth), D408 Cherry (cloth), D409 Beechnut (cloth), D410 Aqua (cloth), D411 Blue (cloth)

SVC ref.
Usually blank – denoted date of manufacture for cars supplied as knock-down kits for assembly in a different factory.

Vehicle number
An 11-character unique vehicle identity number, which all being well should be the same as the car's chassis number.

The first letter denoted the car's country of origin.
B – Ford Great Britain, C – Ford Great Britain (affiliated company assembly), E – Ford Germany (affiliated company assembly), G – Ford Germany

The second letter related to the assembly plant.
B – Halewood (or Genk, on 1968/69 cars with G as first letter), C – Saarlouis, F – Aveley, J – Boreham, K – Sydney

The third and fourth characters were the car's body type.
40 – Standard two-door saloon, 41 – Super estate, 42 – De Luxe two-door saloon, 43 – De Luxe estate, 44 – Super two-door saloon, 48 – GT two-door saloon, 49 – Twin Cam or RS1600 two-door saloon, 50 – Standard van (6cwt), 51 – De Luxe van (8cwt), 5A – Standard van (8cwt), 5D – De Luxe four-door saloon, 5G – GT four-door saloon, 5P – Super four-door saloon, 5S – Standard four-door saloon, AT – Export saloon, AF – Export four-door, AD – Export estate, AV – Export van

The fifth letter was the year of manufacture, and the sixth was the month of build.

Letter	Year	Jan	Feb	Mar	Apr	May	June	July	Aug	Sep	Oct	Nov	Dec
G	1967	C	K	D	E	L	Y	S	T	J	U	M	P
H	1968	B	R	A	G	C	K	D	E	L	Y	S	T
J	1969	J	U	M	P	B	R	A	G	C	K	D	E
K	1970	L	Y	S	T	J	U	M	P	B	R	A	G

The remaining characters were the car's own individual serial number, in order of vehicles produced during the month. Numbering was started at 00001 for all types, with domestic cars receiving serials up to 69999 and exports from 70000 to 99999.

Paint code
ABP or BA – Ermine White, A or Y – Black or Ebony, BNP – Red 11 65, BS – Monaco Red, BVP – Beige 67, BZ – Spruce Green, BY – Glacier, C – Maroon, CGP – Light Blue, CH – Purbeck Grey, CJ – Lagoon Blue, CL – Burgundy Red/Black Cherry, CM – Alpina Green, CR or A3P – Blue Mink, CRP – Light Green, CS/A6P – Saluki Bronze, CT – Venetian Gold, CU – Dragoon Red, CV or A2P – Silver Fox, CW or BJP – Anchor Blue, CGP – Light Blue, CRP – Light Green, D – Light Grey, A5P – Aquatic Jade, P – Garnet, Y – Non-standard, 9 – Pacific Blue

August 1970 onwards

Escorts built before March 1973 had a chassis plate riveted to the offside inner wing, readable from the offside front wing. Bodyshells built after March 1973 had their chassis plates moved to the bonnet slam panel, to the left of the bonnet release spring (looking from the front of the car).

Typ/Type
The first letter (where used) denoted the car's country of origin.
B – Ford Great Britain, C – Ford Great Britain (affiliated company assembly), E – Ford Germany (affiliated company assembly), G – Ford Germany

The second letter related to the model.
A – Escort

The third character referred to the body type.
T – two-door saloon, F – four-door saloon, D – estate

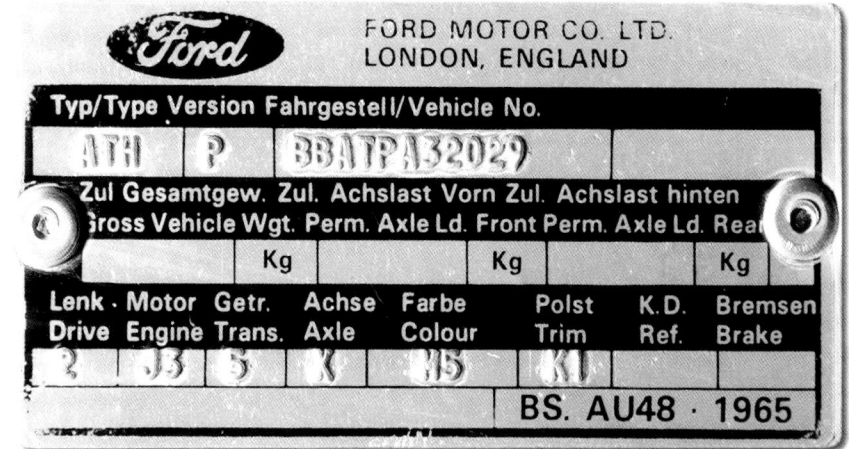

The fourth letter was the model year (this could precede the year of build).
K – 1970, L – 1971, M – 1972, N – 1973, P – 1974, R – 1975
The fifth and six characters (where used) denote engine capacity and type.
G1 – 1098cc LC (low compression), G2 – 1098cc HC (high compression), J1 – 1298cc LC (low compression), J2 – 1298cc HC (high compression), J3 – 1298cc GT, L7 – 1598cc GT (Mexico), K6 – 1558cc Twin Cam, K5 – 1601cc RS1600, L5 – 1601cc RS1600, NE – 1998cc RS2000

Version
S – standard, D – base, M – L, P – XL, Q – Sport, W – 1300E, G – GT or Mexico, L – Twin Cam/RS1600/RS2000, Z – GXL

Fahrgestell/Vehicle No.
The first letter denoted the car's country of origin.
B – Ford Great Britain, C – Ford Great Britain (affiliate assembly), E – Ford Germany (affiliate assembly), G – Ford Germany

The second letter related to the assembly plant.
B – Halewood, C – Saarlouis, F – Aveley, J – Boreham, K – Sydney

The third character denoted the model.
A – Escort

The fourth letter referred to the body type.
T – two-door saloon, F – four-door saloon, D – estate

The fifth and six letters were the year and month of production.

Letter	Year	Jan	Feb	Mar	Apr	May	June	July	Aug	Sep	Oct	Nov	Dec
K	1970	L	Y	S	T	J	U	M	P	B	R	A	G
L	1971	C	K	D	E	L	Y	S	T	J	U	M	P
M	1972	B	R	A	G	C	K	D	E	L	Y	S	T
N	1973	J	U	M	P	B	R	A	G	C	K	D	E
P	1974	L	Y	S	T	J	U	M	P	B	R	A	G
R	1975	C	K	D	E	L	Y	S	T	J	U	M	P

The remaining characters were the car's own individual serial number, in order of vehicles produced during that month. Numbering was started at 00001 for all types, with domestic cars receiving serials up to 69999 and exports from 70000 to 99999.
After April 1972 AVO-built machines were numbered between 00001 to 00500 or 70001 to 70500. It's worth noting, though, that not all Escorts built at Aveley received AVO identities – some genuine shells were stamped with Halewood BB codes.

Lenk/Drive
1 – left-hand drive , 2 – right-hand drive

FACTORY ORIGINAL SPORTING MK1 ESCORTS

Motor/Engine
G1 – 1098cc LC (low compression), G2 – 1098cc HC (high compression), J1 – 1298cc LC (low compression), J2 – 1298cc HC (high compression), J3 – 1298cc GT, L7 – 1598cc GT (Mexico), K6 – 1558cc (Twin Cam), K5 – 1601cc (RS1600), L5 – 1601cc (RS1600), NE – 1998cc (RS2000)

Getr./Trans.
1 or 5 – manual, 7 – automatic

Achse/Axle
A – 3.545:1, Z – 3.545:1 heavy duty, B – 3.777:1, W – 3.777:1 heavy duty, C – 3.89:1, D – 4.125:1, X – 4.125:1 heavy duty

Farbe/Colour
This was usually just one character, but a second digit will refer to the paint colour's model year (a 4 or 5, representing 1974 or 1975).
A – Black, B – Ermine White or Diamond White, C – Sahara Beige, CH – Purbeck Grey, CL – Burgundy Red/Black Cherry, CT – Venetian Gold, D – Carnival Red or Light Grey, E – Diamond Blue or Olympic Blue, F – Purple Velvet, G – Anchor Blue or Marine Blue or Royal Blue, H – Astral Silver, J – Sunset Red, M – Le Mans Green or Modena Green, N – Sebring Red, P – Garnet, Q – Arizona Spring Gold, S – Tawny Brown or Copper Brown, T – Maize Yellow or Daytona Yellow, U – Electric/Monza Blue, V – Vista Orange, Y – non-standard, 1 – Sapphire or Miami Blue 2 – Pearl Grey or Gunmetal , 3 – Silver Fox or Stardust/Aerosilver (non-UK), 4 – Amber Gold, Flame Orange or Glacier, 5 – Fern Green or Jade Green, 6 – Evergreen, 7 – Copper Brown or Amber Gold, 9 – Pacific Blue

Polst/Trim
This was a two-character combination. The first letter is for interior trim colour, the second character denotes trim material. Numbers in trim descriptions related to the model year in which the colour was first used by Ford.

Colours
A – Black, C – Cloud, E – Medium Blue, F – Marquis, H – Ruby, J – Tan, K – Parchment, L – Saddle Brown, M – Deep Aqua, N – Olive, Y – Non-standard

Materials
A – vinyl, G – vinyl, H – vinyl, K – vinyl, L – vinyl, 1 – cloth, 7 – cloth, 8 – cloth, 9 – cloth

Build date	Trim code	Trim colour	Trim material
Aug 1970 onwards	AA	Black	Vinyl
Aug 1970 onwards	A1	Black	Cloth
Aug 1973 to Dec 1974	C1	Cloud 74	Cloth
Aug 1973 onwards	EA	Medium Blue 74	Vinyl
Aug 1973 onwards	E1	Medium Blue 74	Cloth
Aug 1970 to Aug 1973	FA	Marquis / blue	Vinyl
Aug 1970 to Aug 1973	F1	Marquis / blue Beta cloth	Cloth
Aug 1970 to Aug 1973	HA	Ruby 71	Vinyl
Aug 1970 to Aug 1972	H1	Ruby 71	Cloth
Aug 1970 to Aug 1972	JA	Tan 70	Vinyl
Aug 1970 to Aug 1972	J1	Tan 70	Cloth
Aug 1970 to Aug 1972	KA	Parchment	Vinyl
Aug 1970 to Aug 1972	K1	Parchment	Cloth
Aug 1972 onwards	KA	Light Tan 73	Vinyl
Aug 1972 onwards	K1	Light Tan 73	Cloth
Aug 1973 to Dec 1974	LA	Saddle Brown 74	Vinyl
Aug 1973 to Dec 1974	L1	Saddle Brown 74	Cloth
Aug 1970 to Aug 1972	NA	Olive 70	Vinyl
Aug 1970 to Aug 1972	N1	Olive 70	Cloth
Aug 1970 onwards	YA	Special order	Vinyl
Aug 1970 onwards	Y1	Special order	Cloth

K.D. Ref.
Usually blank – denoted date of manufacture for cars supplied as knock-down kits for assembly in a different factory.

Bremsen/Brakes
For export markets. Usually blank.

Special Build Order chassis plate

From April 1972 until the end of Mk1 production AVO offered a Special Build Order programme. Special Build Escorts received an extra identifying plate in addition to their chassis and colour plates.

Roughly the same size as a normal chassis plate, a Special Build plate was a simple bare alloy rectangle, riveted to the driver's-side inner wing or the bonnet slam panel. It was stamped with a series of unique numbers and letters, denoting order number and which Special Build options had been specified from the factory. It's worth noting that a genuine Special Build car should also have a matching body plate, bearing the letter U under its section for extra information; if a non-standard body colour it may also have a Y in the Farbe/Colour section of its chassis plate.

BUILD PLATES

A (top row)
The letters SBO (Special Build Order) followed by a number. Special Build cars were numbered sequentially in order of production, so SB.299 was the 299th Special Build car.

B (second row)
An SBO code of SBO (Special Build Order) followed by a series of numbers and letters. Each number referred to a Special Build option, and each letter denoted a variation of the option.

Special Build codes
SBO.01 – Wheelarch extensions, SBO.02 – Suspension, SBO.03 – Wheels and tyres, SBO.04 – Steering rack, SBO.05 – Anti-roll bar brackets, SBO.06 – Front crossmember and engine mounts, SBO.07 – Sump shield, SBO.08 – Modified bodyshell, SBO.09 – Tuned engine, SBO.10 – Catch tank, SBO.11 – Gearbox, SBO.12 – Clutch, SBO.13 – Limited-slip differential, SBO.14 – Braking system, SBO.15 – Exhaust system, SBO.16 – Seats, SBO.17 – Rollover bar, SBO.18 – Dress-up items, SBO.19 – Lamps and brackets, SBO.20 – Alternator, SBO.21 – Master switch, SBO.22 – Screen washer, SBO.23 – Fuel tank, SBO.24 – Lightweight panels, SBO.25 – Bracing strut, SBO.26 – Centre console, SBO.27 – Special paint finish, SBO.28 – Seat belts, SBO.29 – Fire extinguisher, SBO.30 – Heavy-duty battery, SBO.31 – Heated rear window, SBO.32 – Bonnet pins and catches, SBO.33 – Fireproof bulkhead, SBO.34 – Map reading light, SBO.35 – Carpet, SBO.36 – Sound deadening, SBO.37 – Oil cooler unit, SBO.38 – Ammeter, SBO.39 – Brake and fuel lines, SBO.40 – Halda Twinmaster, SBO.41 – Rocket gearbox, SBO.42 – Turret kit

Escort Mk1 body plate

In addition to the standard Ford chassis plate, Mk1 Escorts featured a body plate (often referred to as colour plate or AVO plate, depending on who you're chatting with) riveted onto the bonnet slam panel, on the right of the bonnet release spring (looking from the front of the car).

Two main types of body plate were used (with several variations of each), one of which was common to all Halewood-built Escorts and AVO cars from November 1971. A rectangular plate, this bore the car's vehicle identification number. It was painted the same colour as the car's bodywork. Often the edges were shaped at the corners.

The other style was used only on Aveley-manufactured cars between October 1970 and November 1971. Again painted in body colour, these plates had an AVO unit number instead of the regular chassis number. The format of these early AVO plates varied throughout production, with no rigidity of layout or information provided. That said, a little detective work based on the codes below will generally reveal the facts.

Body plates were used on the production lines for specifying each car, so could (note the word could, not should) contain information relating to trim, colour, paint type, optional extras and so on.

Attached underneath the body plate would be a body plate tag - a thin metal strip affixed under the left or right-hand rivet. Used in quality control, the tag carried a single punched number or letter to confirm the shell had been inspected. Most of these tags are long gone from surviving Escorts but unrestored cars sometimes have the remains of such a tag poking out from beneath the body plate.

In our diagrams we've tried to create examples of typical Escort body plates, but a multitude of different layouts were used.

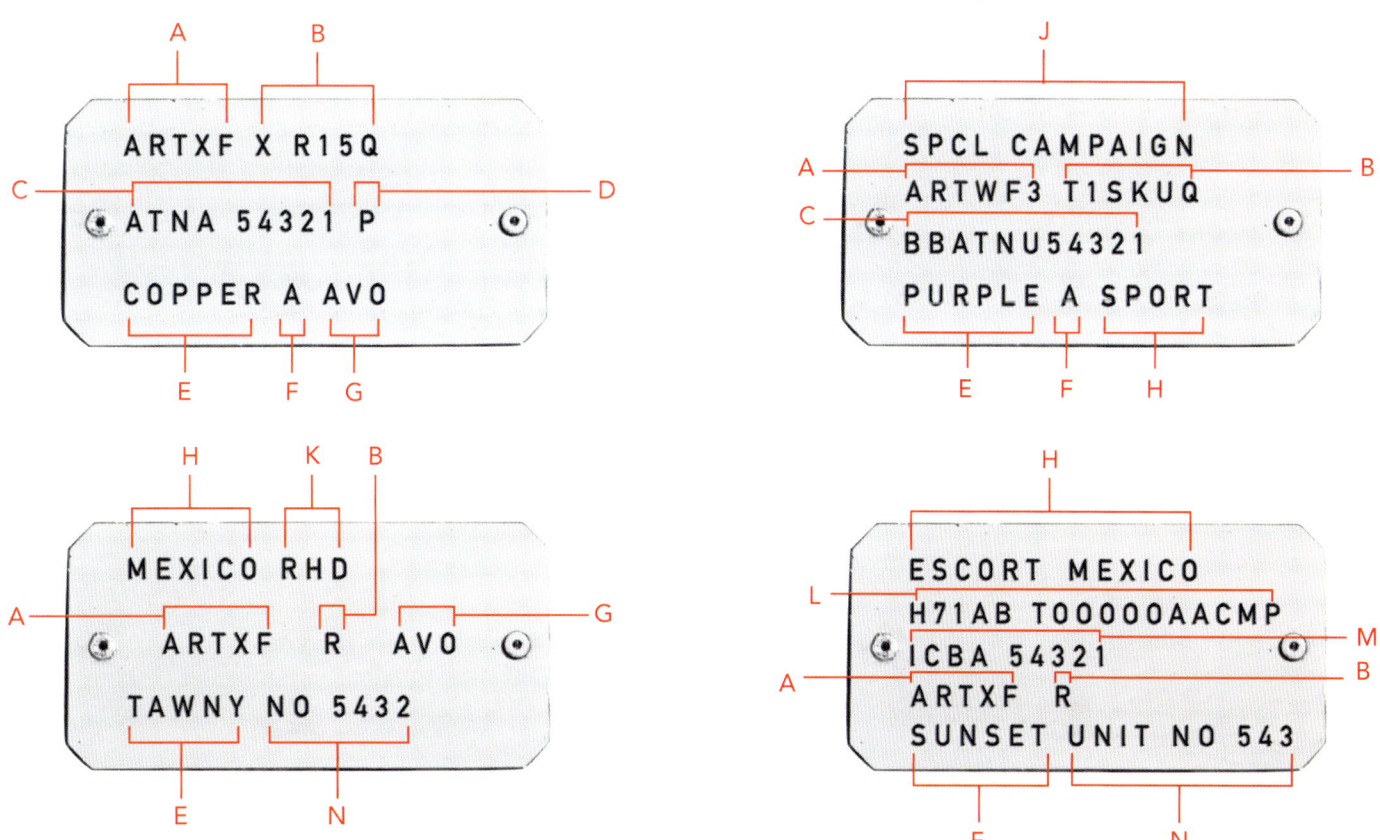

FACTORY ORIGINAL SPORTING MK1 ESCORTS

A
Vehicle description
i) Model
A – Escort
ii) Drive
R – RHD, L – LHD
iii) Body
T – two-door saloon, F – four-door saloon, D – estate
iv) Version
S – standard, D – base, M – L, P – XL, Q – Sport , W – 1300E, G – GT or Mexico, L – Twin Cam, C – RS1600, X – Mexico, Y – RS2000, Z – GXL
Note: some 1972 Mexicos had version L on their body plates; these shells also featured an RS1600 engine bay bulkhead cutout and washer bottle. What's more, 1300Es could say G, Q, P, W or Z.
v) Transmission
F – manual. B – automatic
vi) Engine
2 – 1100cc, 3 – 1300cc
(Not used on Twin Cam or AVO)

B
Extra information (where used)
Specification changes and factory (not dealer) options were listed here but it's worth noting that early Escorts, especially mainstream models for the UK domestic market, were rarely stamped with option codes. Plus, of course, individual items generally weren't listed if the item was part of the model's standard specification or included in a Custom Pack.
A – Austria, B – Opening rear quarter windows, C – Sweden, D – Heavy-duty bodyshell, E – Driver's mirror, fixed, F – Pair of mirrors, fixed, G – Radio, H – Vinyl roof, I – Heated rear window and alternator, J – Pair of mirrors, sprung, K – Side repeaters, L – France, M – Belgium, N – Germany, P – Opening front and rear quarter windows, Q – Hazard warning flashers, R – Reversing Lights, S – Brake servo, T – Temperature gauge, U – Special order*, V – Van roof vent, W – Driver's mirror, sprung, X – Cigarette lighter, Y – Italy, Z – Opening front quarter windows, 1 – Underbody rust-proofing, 2 – FM radio, 3 – Norway, 4 – Pre-engaged starter motor, 5 – Brake warning light, 6 – Custom Pack (RS1600/Mexico), 7 – Custom Pack (van), 8 – Clock, 9 – Comfort Pack (van)
*Special vehicle order was not the same as Special Build. Special vehicle orders would be for customer-requested options like non-standard paintwork, whereas Special Build cars were one-off machines crafted by AVO; these cars wore individual build plates as well as a body plate with the U (special order) code.

C
Vehicle identification number
This should be identical to the VIN on the car's chassis plate (see previous section). On AVO cars the first two characters of the VIN were often omitted.

D
Chassis number suffix
Not all build plates had this additional letter, but it almost certainly related to a specific build date.

E
Body colour
The car's original colour should be stamped here. In 1972 Ford's flowery names for shades were sometimes listed as simple descriptives – Daytona Yellow became Light Yellow, and Le Mans Green was stamped as Lime Green.
Service bodyshells could be supplied in primer or pre-painted – if a reshell, this would generally be the same colour as the original car or its equivalent replacement shade if the original colour was no longer in production.

F
Trim colour
Often blank. If the letter A was listed after the colour, it meant the paint was acrylic; where no A was present, the paint was cellulose. An acrylic car also had the letter A airbrushed beside its spare wheel well in red or black paint

G
AVO
Referring, of course, to Advanced Vehicle Operations.

H
Version
Model name, where used. Often found on AVO cars but less common on mainstream models.

J
Trim
Here was often the place for special trim options or variations relating to a particular model. This could be on the top or bottom row of the plate after the model name or body colour. VINYL (usually on the bottom row) referred to a vinyl roof, guiding the production line to fit one after painting the shell. SPCL CAMPAIGN was a pre-determined set of options for Series One 1300Es (based on Sport models).

BUILD PLATES

K
Drive (where used)
D – right-hand drive, LHD – left-hand drive

L
Part number
This was the part number of the bodyshell, as supplied from Halewood to Aveley. It was only used on very early shells.
H71AB TOOOOOBADLP – RS1600
H71AB TOOOOOAACMP – Mexico
H – AVO, 71 – model year for the part, A – Escort, B – British manufacture, TOOOOO – drawing design number. Bear in mind a 1971 part number could be found on a 1970 car, because the part was designed for the 1971 model year.

M
ICBA number
The Inter Company Buying Authority number was part of Ford bean counting, and won't reveal much about your Escort. Only found on very early bodyshells.

N
Unit number
UNIT NO was often shortened to UNIT, NO, or even just the number itself. The number referred to the bodyshell supplied to Aveley from Halewood and not the completed car.
The AVO Owners' Club has collated detailed figures for models and colours, should you wish to dig deeper about your own car. Generally, it's fair to say low unit numbers related to early shells.

Australian Twin Cam / GT1600 chassis numbers

Australian-produced Twin Cams' and GT1600s' chassis numbers were found stamped into the driver's-side strut top and on an aluminium identification plate riveted to the bulkhead heater dome. A unique system was used to number Australian cars, using the codes below.

The first letter (after an asterisk) related to the car's origin.
C – UK, J – Australia

The second was for the Assembly plant.
K – Sydney, G – Broadmeadows, H – Brisbane

The next two numbers referred to the model number (and bodyshell).
48 – XL or GT1300, 49 – GT1600 (Twin Cam)

The fifth and sixth digits related to the year and month of assembly.

	1970	1971	1972
January	KL	LC	MB
February	KY	LK	MR
March	KS	LD	MA
April	KT	LE	MG
May	KJ	LL	MC
June	KU	LY	MK
July	KM	LS	MD
August	KP	LT	ME
September	KB	LJ	ML
October	KR	LU	MY
November	KA	LM	MS
December	KG	LP	MT

The subsequent five digits were the car's individual serial number, given in series with other Escorts on the production line.

Finally, 1971 Twin Cams and all GT1600s had a letter A and an asterisk at the end of the chassis number.

Engine number
An Australian Twin Cam or 1600GT's engine number (of five digits and one letter) was stamped on the engine block, underneath the oil pressure pickup. In 1970 it was also found on the bulkhead chassis plate and offside strut top. Engine blocks were hand-stamped with the car's chassis number.

FACTORY ORIGINAL SPORTING MK1 ESCORTS

Model code

Code	Product line	Model year	Body	Series
11018	Escort	1970	Two-door	GT1300
11019	Escort	1970	Two-door	Twin Cam
11118	Escort	1971	Two-door	GT1300
11119	Escort	1971	Two-door	Twin Cam
11218	Escort	1972	Two-door	GT1300
11219	Escort	1972	Two-door	GT1600
11399	Escort	1975	Two-door	RS2000

Paint code

1970
A – Polar White, C – Imperial Burgundy, E – Quick Silver, F – Vintage Burgundy, G – Candy Apple Red, H – Track Red, J – Hot Orange, O – Yellow Ochre, P – Blue Ice, R – Diamond White, T – True Blue, U – Ultra White, V – Go-Green , Y – Grecian Gold , 2 – Bronze Wine , 3 – Peppermint , 4 – Harmony Grey, 6 – Vermillion Fire, 7 – Yukon Yellow, 8 – Silver Fox , 9 – Autumn Leaf Gold

1971
C – Bold Blue, D – Raw Orange, E – Quick Silver, H – Track Red, I – Jewel Green , K – Frosted Pewter , O – Yellow Ochre, P – Blue Ice, Q – Yellow Glow, U – Ultra White, Z – Wild Violet , 2 – Bronze Wine , 3 – Peppermint , 6 – Vermillion Fire

1972
A – Summer Gold, E – Wild Plum, F – Cool Violet, G – Lime Glaze, I – Jewel Green , M – Blaze Blue, P – Blue Ice, O/S – Yellow Glow , Q – Yellow Fire, R – Copper Bronze , U – Ultra White, V – Shadow Grey, X – Red Pepper, 5 – Teal Glow , SVO – Special Vehicle Order

Trim codes

B	Black	1970 to 1972
F	Dark Red	1970 to 1971
K	Dark Saddle	1970
P	Parchment	1972
S	Saddle	1971 to 1972
W	White	1971 to 1972

Triplex glass dating

Triplex glass was fitted to UK Mk1 Escorts, which came with its own manufacturing date. So there's an easy way to see if the glass matches the car's age – just join the dots. If the windows were made up to a few months before the car was built, there's a fair chance they're original.
Triplex's code was a simple system using dots printed onto the glass above and below the words Triplex and Toughened or Laminated.

Pre-January 1969
Until January 1969, Triplex glass was dated by the quarter-year of manufacture. The year was indicated by a dot under letters in the word Toughened or Laminated, with only the last digit rather than decade represented – if the dot's position was under the first letter it would mean a 1 and so on. The quarter-year was demonstrated by a dot placed above the letters T, R, E or X in the word Triplex.

Year — Quarter

LAMINATED
. . . .
1 2 3 4 5 6 7 8 9 0

TOUGHENED
. . . .
1 2 3 4 5 6 7 8 9 0

TRIPLEX – first quarter (Jan to Mar)
TRIPLEX – second quarter (Apr to Jun)
TRIPLEX – third quarter (Jul to Sep)
TRIPLEX – fourth quarter (Oct to Dec)

Post-January 1969
After January 1969, the year of manufacture was represented by a dot under letters in the words Toughened or Laminated, with just the last digit indicated.

Year — Month

LAMINATED
. . . .
1 2 3 4 5 6 7 8 9 0

TOUGHENED
. . . .
1 2 3 4 5 6 7 8 9 0

TRIPLEX – January
TRIPLEX – February
TRIPLEX – March
TRIPLEX – April
TRIPLEX – May
TRIPLEX – June
TRIPLEX – July
TRIPLEX – August
TRIPLEX – September
TRIPLEX – October
TRIPLEX – November
TRIPLEX – December